How to Change the World

Also by David Bornstein

The Price of a Dream: The Story of the Grameen Bank

How to Change the World

Social Entrepreneurs and the Power of New Ideas

David Bornstein

OXFORD
UNIVERSITY PRESS
2004

OXFORD

UNIVERSITY PRESS

Oxford   New York
Auckland   Bangkok   Buenos Aires   Cape Town   Chennai
Dar es Salaam   Delhi   Hong Kong   Istanbul   Karachi   Kolkata
Kuala Lumpur   Madrid   Melbourne   Mexico City   Mumbai   Nairobı
São Paulo   Shanghai   Taipei   Tokyo   Toronto

Copyright © 2004 by David Bornstein

Published by Oxford University Press, Inc.
198 Madison Avenue, New York, New York 10016

www.oup.com

Oxford is a registered trademark of Oxford University Press

Library of Congress Cataloging-in-Publication Data
Bornstein, David.
How to change the world :
social entrepreneurs and the power of new ideas /
David Bornstein.
p.   cm.
ISBN-13 978-0-19-513805-4
ISBN 0-19-513805-8
1. Social action—Case studies. 2. Social service—Case studies.
3. Social reformers—Case studies. I. Title.
HN18 .B6363 2003 361.2—dc21 2003011008

The photos on pages 23, 84, 127, 202 and 204 were taken by David
Bornstein. The author wishes to thank the following organizations and
individuals for permission to use the photographs and images appearing on
the following pages: Childline (Credit: Ruhani Kaur) (69, 78); College
Summit (167, 176); Bill Drayton (16, 17, 55); Doonesbury © 1982 G. B.
Trudeau. Reprinted with permission of UNIVERSAL PRESS SYNDICATE. All
rights reserved (59); Thys Dullaart (184, 198); Janet Jarman (www.janet
jarman.com) (100, 101, 105, 113, 153); NCPEDP (215, 220, 228); Skye
Raiser (www.skyephotography.com) (168); Renascer (130, 134); Fábio Rosa
(32); J. B. Schramm (160); UNICEF (UNICEF/HQ 93–1144/John Isaac (243);
UNICEF/BAWG 90–281/Ellan Young (250); UNICEF/HQ 85–0005/Balazar
(252); Verve Magazine (Credit: Deepa Parekh) (74).
The Polar-area diagram appearing on page 44 comes from Florence
Nightingale's book *Notes on Matters Affecting the Health, Efficiency and
Hospital Administration of the British Army* (1858).
The jacket photos are courtesy of (from left to right): UNICEF (Rwanda/
Press), NCPEDP, Bill Drayton and *Verve Magazine* (Deepa Parekh). The
background image of hills was created by Diana Todd.

12   14   16   18   19   17   15   13   11
Printed in the United States of America
on acid-free paper

For Abigail
who thrills me

Contents

Acknowledgments

I wish to express my gratitude to Peter Kellner and the Kellner Foundation, Lloyd Timberlake and the Avina Foundation, and James Jensen and The Jenesis Group, whose support made the researching and writing of this book possible. I am also grateful to C. Michael Curtis of *The Atlantic Monthly,* who accepted and edited the magazine article that grew into this book.

I am fortunate to have worked with an exceptionally conscientious and talented editor, Peter Ginna, and his associate Furaha Norton. It remains a pleasure and a privilege to work with Milly Marmur, my agent and friend.

From conception to completion, this book took five years. And I am indebted to platoons of people for their assistance. Karen Andrade, Selma Arnold, Susan Davis, Jed Emerson, Moses Gampel, Susan Gibson, Johanna Hamilton, Jane Jacobs, Jack Levinson, Rebecca Mead, Kevin O'Keefe, Mark Segal, Michael Shimkin, Lisa Silver, and Robert Tolmach read drafts or chapters and offered ideas that improved the book.

Martina Arruda, Zoltan Pogatsa, and Ania Samborska were wonderful translators and cultural guides. Barbara Eros, Manisha Gupta, Jody Jensen, Kalpana Kaul, Njogu Morgan, Anu Pillay, Ryszard Praskier, Monica de Roure, Anamaria Schindler, and Shannon Walbran helped arrange interviews and extended hospitality in foreign lands. I am grateful to many Ashoka staffers who gave their time for interviews. Thanks to Malie Russell and Meredith Lobel from Ashoka who responded to numerous requests for information. Carter Bales, William Baumol, David Bonbright, Derek Brown, Andre Dua, Dean Furbush, Sushmita Ghosh, Peter Goldmark, Pamela Hartigan, Sue Lehmann, Bill Matassoni, Gilbert

Acknowledgments

Mendoza, Julien Phillips, Laurie Stone, and Muhammad Yunus offered valuable insights that contributed to the book. The mistakes, of course, are my own.

Ellen Coon and Ted Riccardi and Barbara Fiorito and Michael Shimkin provided writing retreats in New York and New Mexico. Celia Cruz and Mark Lutes, Barbara Eros, Muzammel Huq and Maheen Sultan, Matthew Klam and Lara Cox, Jadwiga Łopata, Charles Maisel, Hudson McComb, Maria McElroy, Daniel Raviolo, Amarjit and Romolo Sahay, and Ania Samborska opened their homes to me in Budapest, Cape Town, Delhi, Dhaka, Fortaleza, Krakow, São Paulo, Warsaw, and Washington, D.C. Thys Dullaart, Janet Jarman and Skye Raiser provided photographs. Joseph Shapiro allowed me to quote from No Pity. Special thanks to Linda Rottenberg, who encouraged me to write a magazine article on Ashoka in 1997.

Social entrepreneurs are usually happy to have their work publicized, so it was not difficult to arrange the initial interviews for this book. However, I am grateful to Javed Abidi, Jeroo Billimoria, Vera Cordeiro, Bill Drayton, Veronica Khosa, Fábio Rosa, J. B. Schramm and Erzsébet Szekeres for responding to countless requests, over a four-year period, for interviews, documents, follow-up information, fact checks, and updates. Bill Drayton was particularly generous with his time. I'm sure they had no idea, going in, that there would be quite so many questions. I am grateful to Peter Adamson, Bob Berg, Lincoln Chen, William Foege, Kul Gautam, Richard Jolly, Richard Reid, Jon Rohde, Ted Thomas, and others who shared recollections about James Grant.

When I began researching this book, I thought it should include examples of thirty social entrepreneurs. So I visited sixty and interviewed another forty. As I got deeper into the writing, I realized that it was impossible to convey the essence of entrepreneurship without going into considerable detail. I therefore decided to concentrate on nine stories. I am grateful to the following people who took time to share their thoughts with me (I hope to have other opportunities to write about their work): Ravi Agarwal, Dora Andrade, Flick Asvat, Normando Batista Santos, Maria Aparecida Silva Bento, Dagmara Bienkowska, Gillian Caldwell, Suely Carneiro, Edison Carvalho, Silvia Carvalho, David Fortune, Leslie Ann Foster, Imre Furmann, Ágnes Geréb, David Green, Sara Horowitz, Jacek Jakubowski, João Jorge Rodrigues, Péter Lázár, Marilena Lazzarini, Bongani Linda, Paulo Longo, Maria de Lourdes Braz, Adrienne MacFarlane, Charles Maisel, Liane Marcondes, José Marmo da Silva, Hudson McComb, Harley Henriques do Nacimento, Nalini Nayak,

Wellington Nogueira Santos, Ana Teles de Noroes, Luke O'Neill, Piotr Pawlowski, Leonardo Pessina, Daniel Raviolo, Ratnaboli Ray, Padre Ricardo Rezende, João Roberto Ripper, Kailash Satyarthi, Thara Srinivasan, Elzbieta Skrzypczak, Bohdan Skrzypczak, Ildikó Szigeti, Grzegorz Tabasz, Bernadett Takacs, Beulah Thumbadoo, Levente Viszló, and Michal Wroniszewski. I extend my thoughts and appreciation to the family of Ryszard Golec, a pioneer in bringing alcohol treatment to rural Poland, who passed away in 2001.

Last, a personal thank you to my family: my parents, Barbara and Robert, the best advance book marketers in Montreal; Lisa and Steve, who both offered valuable advice on the manuscript; Garner, who still hasn't called the interest-free loan; Selma, who read the book four times; Susan and Emory, for their grace and strength; Joey, for tugging me away from the computer to play ball; and Abigail and Elijah, for every day.

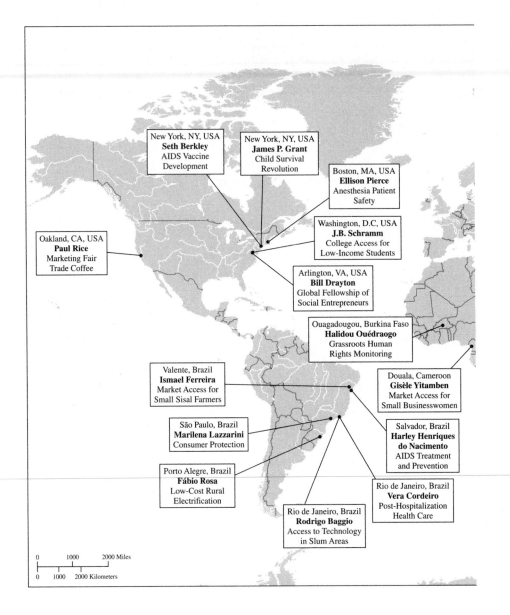

New York, NY, USA
Seth Berkley
AIDS Vaccine
Development

New York, NY, USA
James P. Grant
Child Survival
Revolution

Boston, MA, USA
Ellison Pierce
Anesthesia Patient
Safety

Washington, D.C, USA
J.B. Schramm
College Access for
Low-Income Students

Oakland, CA, USA
Paul Rice
Marketing Fair
Trade Coffee

Arlington, VA, USA
Bill Drayton
Global Fellowship of
Social Entrepreneurs

Ouagadougou, Burkina Faso
Halidou Ouédraogo
Grassroots Human
Rights Monitoring

Valente, Brazil
Ismael Ferreira
Market Access for
Small Sisal Farmers

Douala, Cameroon
Gisèle Yitamben
Market Access for
Small Businesswomen

São Paulo, Brazil
Marilena Lazzarini
Consumer Protection

Salvador, Brazil
**Harley Henriques
do Nacimento**
AIDS Treatment
and Prevention

Porto Alegre, Brazil
Fábio Rosa
Low-Cost Rural
Electrification

Rio de Janeiro, Brazil
Vera Cordeiro
Post-Hospitalization
Health Care

Rio de Janeiro, Brazil
Rodrigo Baggio
Access to Technology
in Slum Areas

0   1000   2000 Miles

0   1000   2000 Kilometers

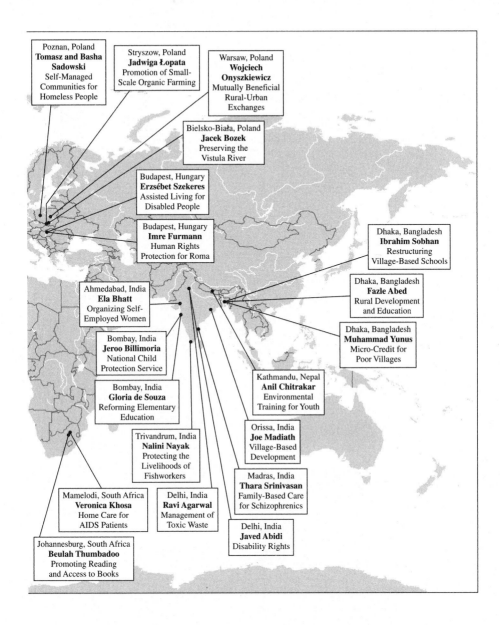

Poznan, Poland
Tomasz and Basha Sadowski
Self-Managed Communities for Homeless People

Stryszow, Poland
Jadwiga Łopata
Promotion of Small-Scale Organic Farming

Warsaw, Poland
Wojciech Onyszkiewicz
Mutually Beneficial Rural-Urban Exchanges

Bielsko-Biała, Poland
Jacek Bozek
Preserving the Vistula River

Budapest, Hungary
Erzsébet Szekeres
Assisted Living for Disabled People

Budapest, Hungary
Imre Furmann
Human Rights Protection for Roma

Dhaka, Bangladesh
Ibrahim Sobhan
Restructuring Village-Based Schools

Ahmedabad, India
Ela Bhatt
Organizing Self-Employed Women

Dhaka, Bangladesh
Fazle Abed
Rural Development and Education

Bombay, India
Jeroo Billimoria
National Child Protection Service

Dhaka, Bangladesh
Muhammad Yunus
Micro-Credit for Poor Villages

Bombay, India
Gloria de Souza
Reforming Elementary Education

Kathmandu, Nepal
Anil Chitrakar
Environmental Training for Youth

Trivandrum, India
Nalini Nayak
Protecting the Livelihoods of Fishworkers

Orissa, India
Joe Madiath
Village-Based Development

Mamelodi, South Africa
Veronica Khosa
Home Care for AIDS Patients

Delhi, India
Ravi Agarwal
Management of Toxic Waste

Madras, India
Thara Srinivasan
Family-Based Care for Schizophrenics

Johannesburg, South Africa
Beulah Thumbadoo
Promoting Reading and Access to Books

Delhi, India
Javed Abidi
Disability Rights

True compassion is more than flinging a coin to a beggar; it comes to see that an edifice which produces beggars needs restructuring.
—Martin Luther King Jr.

If we all did the things we are capable of doing, we would literally astound ourselves.
—Thomas Edison

Restless People

This is a book about people who solve social problems on a large scale. Most of its characters are not famous. They are not politicians or industrialists. Some are doctors, lawyers, and engineers. Others are management consultants, social workers, teachers, and journalists. Others began as parents. They are scattered far and wide—in Bangladesh, Brazil, Hungary, India, Poland, South Africa, and the United States. What unites them is their role as social innovators, or *social entrepreneurs*. They have powerful ideas to improve people's lives and they have implemented them across cities, countries, and, in some cases, the world.

The purpose of this book is not to exalt a few men or women, but to call attention to the role of a particular type of actor who propels social change. Social entrepreneurs have a profound effect on society, yet their corrective function remains poorly understood and underappreciated. Although they have always existed, for a variety of reasons their presence is on the rise today.

The designation "social entrepreneur" has gained popularity in recent years.[1] America's leading universities offer courses in social entrepreneurship. Journalists, philanthropists, and development workers frequently invoke the term. However, most of the attention focuses on how business and management skills can be applied to achieve social ends—for example, how nonprofits can operate for-profit ventures to generate revenues. While this is an important trend, this book looks at social entrepreneurs differently: It sees them as *transformative forces*: people with new ideas to address major problems who are relentless in the pursuit of their visions, people who simply will not take "no" for an answer, who will not give up until they have spread their ideas as far as they possibly can.

According to the management expert Peter F. Drucker, the term "entrepreneur" (from the French, meaning "one who takes into hand") was introduced two centuries ago by the French economist Jean-Baptiste Say to characterize a special economic actor—not someone who simply opens a business, but someone who "shifts economic resources out of an area of lower and into an area of higher productivity and greater yield."[2] The twentieth-century growth economist Joseph A. Schumpeter characterized the entrepreneur as the source of the "creative destruction" necessary for major economic advances.[3]

Consider two famous examples: Henry Ford and Steven Jobs. It is well known that Ford and Jobs, by reimagining cars and computers as mass-market goods, "destroyed" the patterns in their industries, paving the way for leaps in productivity and triggering waves of change. This book shows that social entrepreneurs play analogous roles in education, healthcare, environmental protection, disability, and many other fields. "The social entrepreneur changes the performance capacity of society," notes Drucker.[4]

Drawing on examples from a number of countries, this book illustrates how social entrepreneurs advance *systemic* change: how they shift behavior patterns and perceptions. All the characters in this book possess powerful ideas for attacking problems, and they are unwilling, or unable, to rest until they have spread their ideas society-wide. Along the way, the book examines how they actually make change happen—analyzing the strategies, the organizational characteristics, and the personal qualities that explain the social entrepreneurs' success.

I have chosen to take a global focus because social entrepreneurship is a global phenomenon and the world's most creative problem solvers are not concentrated in the United States and Canada. Around the world, people are encountering similar problems: inadequate education and health systems, environmental threats, declining trust in political institutions, entrenched poverty, high crime rates, and so forth. But in poorer countries, social entrepreneurs have to reach far more people with far less money, so they have to be especially innovative to advance solutions at scale. Their insights will be useful to all who seek to make a positive mark on the world, whether in the United States and Canada or in other countries.

The stories and analysis are intended for a broad range of readers. Anyone who has ever dreamt of solving a problem or making a positive change in his or her environment will find encouraging and instructive stories here. Additionally, business people and nonprofit managers will see how social entrepreneurs serve large "markets" with limited resources. Foundation donors and philanthropists will find ideas to inform their grant-making. Policymakers will discover problem-solving models with scope for national expansion. Journalists will find a vast landscape of human activity that is underreported. College students and professionals will discover new career paths or opportunities for second careers. College professors will find that the examples serve as useful case studies for a range of courses. And parents and school teachers will discover stories that can inspire young people.

Although this book looks at broad changes across the world, it offers detailed accounts of how those changes actually happen. It is emphatically a book about real people doing real things well. Above all, this book shows that it takes creative individuals with fixed determination and indomitable will to propel the innovation that society needs to tackle its toughest problems. It shows that an important social change frequently begins with a single entrepreneurial author: one obsessive individual who sees a problem and envisions a new solution, who takes the initiative to act on that vision, who gathers resources and builds organizations to protect and market that vision, who provides the energy and sustained focus to overcome the inevitable resistance, and who—decade after decade—keeps improving, strengthening, and broadening that vision until what was once a marginal idea has become a new norm.

Many implications follow from this observation, but they boil down to a fairly simple point. One of the most important things that can be done to improve the state of the world is to build a framework of social and economic supports to multiply the number and the effectiveness of the world's social entrepreneurs.

The Emergence of the Global Citizen Sector

Social entrepreneurs have existed throughout the ages. St. Francis of Assisi, founder of the Franciscan Order would qualify as a social entrepreneur, having built multiple organizations that advanced pattern changes in his field.[5] What is different today is that social entrepreneurship is becoming established as a vocation and a mainstream area of inquiry, not only in the United States, Canada, and Europe, but increasingly in Asia, Africa, and Latin America. The rise of social entrepreneurship can be seen as the leading edge of a remarkable development that has occurred across the world over the past three decades: the emergence of millions of new citizen organizations.

"It's got to strike you that a quarter of a century ago outside the United States there were very few NGOs [nongovernmental organizations involved in development and social work] and now there are millions of them all over the globe," Peter Goldmark, who was the president of the Rockefeller Foundation from 1988 to 1997, commented to me. "Nobody could make that happen at the same time. Why did they grow? They grew because the seed was there and the soil was right. You have restless people seeking to deal with problems that were not being successfully coped with by existing institutions. They escaped the old formats and were driven to invent new forms of organizations. They found more freedom, more effectiveness and more productive engagement. That is a key terrain."

Twenty years ago, for example, Indonesia had only one independent environmental organization. Today it has more than 2,000.[6] In Bangladesh, most of the country's development work is handled by 20,000 NGOs; almost all them were established in the past twenty-five years. India has well over a million citizen organizations. Slovakia, a tiny country, has more than 12,000. Between 1988 and 1995, 100,000 citizen groups opened shop in the former communist countries of Central Europe. In France, during the 1990s, an average of 70,000 new citizen groups were established each year, quadruple the figure for the 1960s. In Canada, the number of registered citizen groups has grown by more than 50 percent since 1987, reaching close to 200,000. In Brazil, in the 1990s, the number of registered citizen organizations jumped from 250,000 to 400,000, a 60 percent increase. In the United States, between 1989 and 1998, the number of public service groups registered with the Internal Revenue Service jumped from 464,000 to 734,000, also a 60 percent increase.[7] Some estimates hold that there are 1 million citizen groups in Brazil and 2 million in the United States.[8] Given the long history of citizen activity in the United States, it comes as a surprise that 70 percent of registered groups are less than thirty years old.[9] Finally, during the 1990s, the number of registered *international* citizen organizations increased from 6,000 to 26,000.[10]

Historically, these organizations have been defined in the negative—as *non*profit or *non*governmental organizations. Today they are understood to comprise a new "sector," variously dubbed the "independent sector," "nonprofit sector," "third sector," or, the term favored in this book, the "citizen sector." Hundreds of universities in the United States, including Harvard, Stanford, Yale, Duke and Johns Hopkins, have established college courses and centers to study this sector. In New York City, during the 1990s, while overall employment grew by only 4 percent, employment in the citizen sector grew by 25 percent.[11] Similarly, a Johns Hopkins study of eight developed countries found that, between 1990 and 1995, employment in this sector grew two and a half times faster than for the overall economy.[12] Peter Drucker has called this sector America's leading growth industry.

Although public service organizations are far from new, this worldwide mobilization of citizens is new in several respects:[13]

1. It is occurring on a scale never before seen.
2. The organizations are more globally dispersed and diverse than in the past.
3. Increasingly, we find organizations moving beyond stop-gap solutions to more systemic approaches to problems—offering better recipes, not just more cooking.
4. Citizen organizations are less encumbered by church and state and, in fact, exert considerable pressure on governments (as witnessed in the International Campaign to Ban Landmines and the creation of the International Criminal Court).
5. They are forging partnerships with businesses, academic institutions, and governments—and, in many cases, refining the government's representational function.[14]
6. Because of the natural jostling for position that occurs when a formerly restricted sector suddenly enjoys "open entry" and new players crowd onto the field, the citizen sector is experiencing the beneficial effects of entrepreneurialism, increased competition and collaboration, and a heightened attention to performance.[15]

There are, of course, many inefficient, wasteful, and corrupt organizations in the citizen sector. However, because of the new surge of activity, citizen organizations increasingly are being pressed to *demonstrate* their efficacy. Faced with a wave of energetic social entrepreneurs who are building organizations that are strategic and fast moving, people managing sluggish, outdated institutions no longer find "business as usual" to be a safe stance. In fact, it is getting riskier by the day to remain static or to coast on reputation. The arrival of entrepreneurialism and competition represents an early, but fundamental, change in the dynamics of the citizen sector, one that history has shown is highly conducive to innovation.[16] This development is explored in the book's conclusion.

Despite their magnitude, these changes have been underreported. In the United States and Canada, for example, almost everyone knows about the explosion of the dot-coms—a much smaller phenomenon—but millions have still not heard the big story: the worldwide explosion of dot-orgs. It is a story with far-reaching implications: By sharpening the role of government, shifting practices and attitudes in business and opening up waves of opportunity for people to apply their talents in new, positive ways, the emerging citizen sector is reorganizing the way the work of society gets done.

What Is Driving These Changes?

The simplest explanation for these changes is that the barriers that once impeded them have, with stunning speed, disappeared. The generals in southern Europe, Latin America, and Africa had little tolerance for citizens engaged in serious social reform. Nor did the communists in Central Europe and Russia, the apartheid regime in South Africa or the viceroys in colonial India. In most of these places, authoritarian governments have been succeeded by real or, at least, nominal democracies.

Citizens who seek to build organizations need more than freedom; they also need money. There must be surplus wealth in the economy to finance their efforts. During the twentieth century, the per-capita incomes in free market economies increased by at least 700 percent.[17] The economic expansion was particularly strong during the 1960s and 1970s, when the global economy grew at the rate of 5 percent a year and all regions experienced economic gains.[18] Although the prosperity was far from evenly distributed, the wealth gains—taxed by government or channeled through philanthropy—made it possible for significant numbers of people around the world to earn their livelihoods in the citizen sector. (Today, many citizen organizations are exploring ways to generate their own wealth through earned-income ventures.)[19]

The prosperity of the second half of the twentieth century was both a cause and an effect of social and scientific breakthroughs that have redefined human life. The biggest change is simply that people live longer and have far more freedom to think about things other than staying alive. Since 1900, average life spans have increased by thirty years in the industrialized world and by almost forty years in poor countries, an increase in longevity that has no precedent in history.[20] During the 1970s, basic education systems were extended to hundreds of millions of people in the developing world. Between 1970 and 1985, adult literacy rates in the developing world increased from 43 to 60 percent.[21] The growth of a middle class in many countries along with increased access to higher education—during the 1970s alone, the number of universities in the world more than doubled—has swelled the ranks of people who possess both the knowledge and the financial means to tackle social problems effectively.[22]

In addition, over the past three decades, the women's movement has gained a foothold across much of the world, weakening social constraints that have historically limited women's scope of action and expression.[23] The decline of racial barriers has opened up opportunities for many groups, such as for blacks in the United States, Brazil, and South Africa and for untouchables in India. In Asia, Africa, and Latin America, the postcolonial and postdictatorship generations have become more self-assured asserting their democratic rights. Technology, of course, permits people, money, and information to move quickly and cheaply around the globe.

To sum up, more people today have the freedom, time, wealth, health, exposure, social mobility, and confidence to address social problems in bold new ways.

Supply is up; so is demand.

An equally compelling explanation for the emergence of the citizen sector is that people recognize that change is urgently needed. The communications revolution has given millions of people both a wider and a more detailed understanding of the world. Because of technology, ordinary citizens enjoy access to information that formerly was available only to elites and nation-states. One consequence of this change is that citizens have become acutely conscious of environmental destruction, entrenched poverty, health catastrophes, human rights abuses, failing education systems, and escalating violence.[24] Another consequence is that people possess powerful communication tools to coordinate efforts to attack those problems.

One particularly strong impetus to action has been the environmental threat. In 1990, there were 100,000 independent environmental protection organizations in the world, and most of them had been established during the 1980s.[25] "In the past half century, the world has lost a fourth of its topsoil and a third of its forest cover," write Paul Hawken, Amory Lovins, and L. Hunter Lovins in their book *Natural Capitalism*. "At present rates of destruction, we will lose 70 percent of the world's coral reefs in our lifetime, host to 25 percent of marine life. In the past three decades, one-third of the planet's resources, its 'natural wealth,' has been consumed."[26]

According to a report released by the U.S. National Intelligence Council, over the next twelve years the world will witness significant degradation of arable land, substantially increased greenhouse gas emissions, and a depletion of tropical forests and other species-rich habitats, which will exacerbate the "historically large losses of biological species now occurring." More than 3 billion people will live in countries that are "water-stressed." Additionally, by 2010, 50 to 75 million people will be infected with HIV/AIDS in five countries alone: Nigeria, Ethiopia, Russia, India, and China.[27]

Another major change is that communications technologies have made global inequities far more visible and palpable than ever before. It is one thing to ponder the fact that the poorest half of the people in the world receive only 5 percent of its total income.[28] But what happens when those people are watching the economic winners on television every day? The bottom 50 percent no longer languish in incapacity and isolation. Increasingly, they are becoming urbanized, they are organizing, and they are discovering the power of technology.

While concerns have mounted about global problems, so has the conviction that governments are failing to solve them. Over the past two decades democracy has emerged triumphant around the globe, but voter turnout has declined almost everywhere, including in the United States, where it has hit near-historic lows.[29] Decades of failed development policies and discouraging wars on poverty, drugs, and crime have led many to conclude that, while governments must be held responsible for translating the will of the citizenry into public policy, they are not necessarily the most effective vehicles, and certainly are not the sole legitimate vehicles, for the actual delivery of many social goods, and they are often less inventive than entrepreneurial citizen organizations.

Additionally, governments appear increasingly impotent in the face of concentrated corporate power. (Three hundred multinational corporations control 25 percent of the world's assets.)[30] Too often, governments have failed to take serious measures to safeguard the environment, guarantee decent labor conditions, and, more recently, ensure the integrity of financial institutions.[31] "In the twenty-first century world of global capitalism . . . nations compete for investment flows and the jobs and growth that corporations can provide, and politicians need ever greater funds to compete with their rivals to win over the electorate," observes Noreena Hertz, associate director of the Centre for International Business at the University of Cambridge, in her book *The Silent Takeover.* As a result, adds Hertz: "Corporations have, in effect, begun to lay down with force what is and what is not permissible for politicians all over the world to do."[32]

When the short-term interests of the decision-making elite are bad for the long-term interests of society, there is a problem. It is easy to feel daunted when contemplating this problem. Today, however, the sector providing the leadership, energy, and creativity to help correct it is the citizen sector. "At a time of accelerating change, NGOs are quicker than governments to respond to new demands and opportunities," Jessica T. Mathews, president of the Carnegie Endowment for International Peace, has written in *Foreign Affairs*. "And they are better than governments at dealing with problems that grow slowly and affect society through their cumulative effect on individuals."[33]

Across the world, social entrepreneurs are demonstrating new approaches to many social ills and new models to create wealth, promote social well-being, *and* restore the environment. The citizen sector is conspicuously leading the push to reform the free market and political systems. The misnamed "antiglobalization" movement is not, in fact, a movement against globalization, but a strategy crafted by citizens to take back some of the power their governments have ceded to corporations.

For the time being, citizens, uninspired by political leaders, may be voting less, but they are fulfilling many needs in direct ways. Today individuals seeking meaningful work frequently opt to build, join, advocate for, or support organizations that are more innovative, more responsive, and operationally superior to the traditional social structures.

There is a personal side to this story. These people share the desires of people everywhere: to apply their talents in ways that bring security, recognition, and meaning—and to have some fun. What has changed in recent years is that the citizen sector now offers a broad avenue to satisfy those needs: to align what you care about, what you are good at, and what you enjoy doing—every day—and have real impact.

Of course, not everyone is, or wants to be, a social entrepreneur, just as not everyone wants to start a business. But almost everyone now has the option to participate in this new sector. Because it is growing so fast and in so many directions, the opportunities are wide open for people with diverse interests and skills. Citizen organizations desperately need good managers, marketers, finance experts, public relations agents, computer programmers, writers, salespeople, artists, accountants, filmmakers, and so forth. Depending on the mission, they also need journalists, agronomists, chemists, teachers, doctors, lawyers, biologists, architects, songwriters, engineers, mechanics, publishers, urban planners, psychologists, and the like. And, increasingly, businesses need employees and managers who appreciate the social and environmental dimensions of their work and who can spot opportunities to collaborate with this "other" entrepreneurial sector.

It is important to keep in mind how new these changes are. As recently as twenty years ago, the citizen sector was tightly restricted in most of the world. Social entrepreneurs encountered extraordinary political constraints and they had few identifiable structural supports or networks to turn to for financing, information, or encouragement. In many cases, they faced formidable opposition even within their own families. Even in countries with long histories of citizen organization, such as the United States, until recently relatively few people imagined that they could pursue a career in this sector. Now it is common for graduates of top U.S. universities to do so. Indeed, for anyone who has ever said, "This isn't working" or "We can do better!"—for anyone who gets a kick out of challenging the status quo, shaking up the system, or practicing a little entrepreneurial "creative destruction"—these are propitious times.

2.

From Little Acorns
Do Great Trees Grow

Every change begins with a vision and a decision to take action. In 1978, an American named Bill Drayton, the assistant administrator of the U.S. Environmental Protection Agency, decided to establish an organization to support leading social entrepreneurs around the world. The idea had been brewing in the back of his mind for fifteen years.

Drayton's idea was to search the world for individuals with fresh ideas for social change who combined entrepreneurial ability and strong ethical fiber.

Drayton, then thirty-five, was looking for people with compelling visions who possessed the creativity, savvy, and determination to realize their ideas on a large scale: people who would, in his words, leave their "scratch on history." As he conceived of it, building an organization that could find these wildflowers and help them grow would be the most "highly leveraged" approach to social change possible. It would be the single most powerful thing he could do to speed up development and democratization around the globe. To this end, Drayton set out like a modern-day explorer to map the world's social terrain in search of its most talented changemakers.

Today, the organization that he established—*Ashoka: Innovators for the Public*—operates in forty-six countries across Asia, Africa, the Americas, and Central Europe and has assisted 1,400 social entrepreneurs, providing them with close to $40 million in direct funding, analyzing their strategies, offering "professional" services, and—by virtue of Ashoka's reputation for selectivity—lending credibility to their efforts.

Ashoka works a little like a venture capital firm. It seeks high yields from modest, well-targeted investments. However, the returns it seeks are not in profits, but in advances in education, environmental protection, rural development, poverty alleviation, human rights, healthcare, care for the disabled, care for children at risk, and other fields.[1]

Like Bill Drayton, Ashoka is a lean organization that punches well above its weight. Its 120 staff members have assembled a global network that includes thousands of nominators and supporters who search regularly in their countries for people who will cause major, positive system change: who will become "references in their fields," who will "set or change patterns" at the national and international levels.

This book chronicles the efforts of some of these people. It tells the stories of leading social entrepreneurs in Asia, Africa, Latin America and the United States (most of whom were identified through Ashoka's network) as well as some other individuals who are no longer living but whose ideas are very much alive in the world, such as Florence Nightingale and James P. Grant.

Numerous organizations identify and support social entrepreneurs today, but I have chosen to use Ashoka as a vehicle to trace the emergence of social entrepreneurship because it is the only organization that has been actively monitoring this phenomenon at the global level for more than twenty years. Additionally, its "search and selection" process remains the most rigorous system I have come across for identifying pattern-setting innovators at relatively early stages in their careers. In a story with strands that extend into many lands, Bill Drayton is like the spider at the center of the web. And so, it is fitting that we begin with him.

Bill Drayton looks like someone you might expect to find in a library on a Saturday night. He is inordinately thin. He wears out-of-fashion suits, thick glasses, and wallabees. His hair is limp, his skin a little pale, his tie generally askew. Yet his eyes convey a sense of excitement about life, a seemingly boundless fascination with the world that is reminiscent of a young child's curiosity. This quality is counterbalanced by a highly conservative deportment. Drayton has the manners of a Victorian gentleman. When greeting someone, he offers a courtly three-quarter bow. When indicating the way, he extends his arm in the manner of a butler. He seems constitutionally incapable of passing through a doorway first. And he speaks in soft, patient tones, having been taught by his parents that to speak loudly is to imply that what you have to say is not that important.

Listening to Drayton, you get the sense that you've stumbled upon a magical secret or, to quote a friend of his, Marjorie Benton, an "orchid in a crack in the pavement." He has a remarkable intellect and an uncanny ability to absorb information. At times, he seems oblivious to this ability, and he tends to assume that others are equally informed about such things as the rise and fall of the Mauryan dynasty, the social dynamics in Nagaland, or the circumstances that led to the drafting of the Magna Carta. But he is genuinely modest. And although, in a conversation, he is as likely to refer to, say, Philip II of Macedon as he is to George W. Bush, he does so without a hint of pretense. The effect is not to make you feel undereducated, but rather to get you excited to dig out your history books.

Drayton has worked as a lawyer, a management consultant, and a government administrator, but over the past quarter century, his main preoccupation has been traveling around the world looking for individuals who are working to bring about systemic social change. Along the way, he's had thousands of detailed conversations with these people and has made it a matter of utmost importance to keep track (with little notebooks and a microcassette recorder) of the things they are doing that work and the things that don't.

Ted Marmor, a friend of Drayton's who teaches at the Yale School of Management, recalled a comment made by one of Drayton's college professors years ago: " 'You've never seen anything like this fellow. It looks like a heavy wind would get rid of him—but he's got the determination of Job and the brains of a Nobel laureate.' " Marmor added his own assessment of Drayton: "This wispy, carefully controlled, blue-suited fellow has got enormous power. And connected to it is a shrewdness about the way institutions operate and the world really works."

I first met Drayton in 1996, a few months after the publication of a book I had written on the Grameen Bank of Bangladesh.[2] Given my writing interest, a friend who had worked at Ashoka suggested that I interview him.

The Grameen Bank had pioneered and popularized a methodology for extending small, collateral-free loans for self-employment to some of the world's poorest people.[3] Founded in 1976 by a Bangladeshi economics professor named Muhammad Yunus, by 2003 the bank had lent $4 billion to 2.8 million Bangladeshi villagers, 95 percent of them women. With the additional income that Grameen's working-capital loans bring millions of villagers are better able to feed their families, build tin-roof houses (that keep them dry during the monsoons), send their children to school, and accumulate assets for old-age security.

During the 1980s and 1990s, Yunus demonstrated that Grameen-style "micro-credit" enabled poor families to overcome poverty on a massive scale. He played the leading role advancing a global movement—the "micro-credit revolution"—which has produced waves of change in international development. By 2002 more than 2,500 micro-credit programs were reaching 41.6 million of the world's poorest families.[4]

In my book, I had focused on three questions: How did the Grameen Bank come to exist? How did it work? And how did the idea of micro-credit spread worldwide?

What I discovered was that Yunus had worked without pause for two decades to develop Grameen's credit delivery system, and to institutionalize and market his idea. Countless people have contributed to the success of micro-credit—competent staff, enlightened donors, courageous borrowers—and many other organizations have pursued the idea independent of the Grameen Bank. But it is unlikely that micro-credit would have grown into a major global movement without Yunus's vision, single-mindedness, persuasiveness, and energy.

I concluded my book by saying that if societies wanted to see more innovation of this sort, they would have to channel more support to entrepreneurs like Muhammad Yunus. At the time, I did not know that that was what Bill Drayton had been doing for fifteen years.

Before joining the Environmental Protection Agency (EPA) in 1977, Drayton had attended Harvard College, studied economics at Oxford University and completed a J.D. at Yale Law School, then worked for five years at the management consulting firm McKinsey & Company. He chose to specialize in economics, law, and management because he saw each discipline as a key tool to effect social change.

To get Ashoka going, he called up some colleagues whom he believed possessed the values and skills that would contribute to a strong institution.

"Bill called one day and said, 'I want to incorporate this organization. Will you be on the board?'" recalled Julien Phillips, a colleague of Drayton's from McKinsey's public practice, who had been an early Peace Corps volunteer in Peru and had served as chief deputy director of the Department of Health under Governor Jerry Brown in California.

"I had a kind of leftist—but not socialist—idea of social change heavily influenced by the civil rights movement," recalled Phillips. "When I was in the Peace Corps I barely knew what an entrepreneur was, and to the extent I did it was something *not very good.*

"I hesitated. Bill said, 'It won't take much time for a while. I just need some names on an incorporation paper and we'll talk later about what it might involve.'"

Drayton enlisted a few other colleagues with whom he had been discussing the idea for years: Ashok Advani, an Oxford classmate from Bombay (now called Mumbai) who had founded *Business India*, the country's pioneer business journalism magazine; Anupam Puri, another Oxford classmate who had worked in McKinsey's public practice on a broad range of health, education, and welfare issues; Stephen Hadley, a classmate from Yale Law School who had served in the navy and as a member of the National Security Council staff under President Ford; and Bill Carter, an EPA colleague who had completed a Ph.D. in Chinese studies and spent years working in Indonesia.[5]

Drayton thought hard about what to call his organization. "I thought it shouldn't belong to any one tribe or group, which ruled out a name in any one language like English," he recalled. "I also had a belief that the parochialism of Europe and America was a blinder that was hurtful. It never occurred to me to create a nonsense word like Exxon or Kodak. So the solution seemed to be to name it after a person."

He had four heroes: Thomas Jefferson; Mohandas Gandhi; Jean Monnet, the architect of European unification; and the Indian emperor Ashoka, who unified much of South Asia in the third century B.C. and pioneered innovations in both economic development and social welfare. Drayton considered Ashoka to be one of history's most tolerant, global-minded, and creative leaders.

He opted for Ashoka: Innovators for the Public. (In Sanskrit, *Ashoka* means the "active absence of sorrow.") For the organization's logo, Drayton chose an oak tree. Not only is an oak a tough tree, resistant to drought, that sets down long, deep roots, it is a "wonderful, spreading tree" affording much shade, that is often used as a meeting place in villages. It also reminded Drayton of the proverb: "From little acorns do great trees grow."

During their Christmas vacations in 1978 and 1979, Drayton and his colleagues took exploratory trips to India, Indonesia, and Venezuela to figure out how to design a program to spot social entrepreneurs when they were still relatively unknown and predict the ones most likely to achieve major impact in the decades ahead. (To market test the idea, they focused on three countries of different sizes with dissimilar cultures.) Drayton wondered: "Was it possible to create a system that would, with high reliability, spot major pattern-changing ideas and first-class entrepreneurs before either were proven?"

Over a two-week period, Drayton and his team would meet with sixty or seventy people. "We'd go and see someone for breakfast, two people during the morning, someone for a late lunch, someone for afternoon tea, and then dinner," Drayton recalls. "We were systematic about it. We would go and see anyone who had a reputation for doing something innovative for the public good. And we kept asking questions: 'Who in your field, as a private citizen, has caused a major change that you really respond to? How does it work? Is it new? Where do we find this person?' Then we'd go and see that person and ask the same questions and get more names. We'd turn each name into a three-by-five card, and as the weeks went by, we'd begin to get multiple cards on people. At the end we had mapped out who was doing what in the different fields."

One early concern was that an organization specializing in collecting information about local reformers would arouse suspicions of CIA or KGB involvement. But the signs were reassuring. "We found people very accessible," he recalled. "We found lots of examples. We came away thinking, 'Boy, these people are something,' and seeing that it was really the right time to do this."

Social entrepreneurs who would achieve the impact that Ashoka was seeking were rare, so it made sense to start looking in the biggest countries. In 1979, of the six most populous countries in the world, Brazil, China and the Soviet Union wouldn't tolerate social entrepreneurship.

Bill Drayton interviewing Ashoka fellow Vivik Pandit,
who has sharply reduced debt slavery in western India

Gloria de Souza

(Social entrepreneurs make dictators uncomfortable.) The United States was too expensive. Indonesia was a possibility, but the political situation would be tricky. That left India.

Drayton hired a representative in India and enlisted a committee of local volunteers to oversee the program. Initially, board member Ashok Advani arranged for office space in Delhi. Nominators and electors agreed to donate their time (as they still do). Funding came from friends, especially three with private foundations, and Drayton's pocket. They started with about $50,000.

By 1981 Drayton had collected hundreds of three-by-five cards, and Ashoka was ready to hold its first "selection panel."

The first fellow elected was Gloria de Souza, a forty-five-year-old elementary school teacher in Bombay whose dream was to transform education across India. De Souza had been teaching for twenty years. Nothing pained her more than to walk through a school hallway and hear students repeating in unison: "Here we go 'round the mulberry bush." To her, this rote learning—a holdover from the colonial era—was the very sound of minds being deadened.

In 1971 de Souza had attended a workshop on experiential and environmental education that opened her eyes to new educational opportunities. When she tried to get her colleagues to try out the methods, however, their response was cool. "It sounds great," she was told. "But it's not for India. The philosophy is good but it's totally impractical for us."

She decided to try it herself. She set aside her textbooks with their references to robins, bluebirds, and willow trees and took her students outside to learn about local birds and plants and explore questions such as: "Why do the monsoons come and go?" In lessons, she began substituting Indian names like Arun and Laila for Rover and Kitty. She took students on excursions to monuments such as the Gateway of India to learn about architecture and history, and she explored democracy through school elections. Teachers and administrators criticized her for using her students as guinea pigs, but the students' responded enthusiastically.

Over the next five years, de Souza tried and failed repeatedly to get the Jesuit school where she was teaching to adopt her methods. By the time Drayton met her, she had finally persuaded the teaching staff and administration to give them a try and was in the process of spreading her work to a second school. "I had finally been able to show teachers how it was possible to teach this way without making it too labor intensive for them," de Souza told me. "I also discovered that the best way to build up teachers' confidence is to tell them all the stupid things you did."

A private Jesuit school is far from the real India, however. The real challenge would be to carry experiential education to the Bombay public school system—and beyond. Drayton inquired if de Souza had considered her work in the context of Indian society as a *whole*.

She had.

"Do you know that 70 percent of the kids in Bombay want to emigrate?" she said to Drayton. "Something is *deeply wrong* in our society. And I think I can do something very important with this idea. If we can help children grow up learning to think rather than memorize and repeat, learning to problem solve, learning to be creative, learning to be actors rather than acted upon, we can create a generation that will be very different. And India will be very different. And that's a revolution."

From Drayton's point of view, there was nothing particularly novel about environmental education. The approach was well established in the United States, Canada, and Europe. "If you talked to Gloria and you just looked at environmental education you might say 'ho-hum,'" he said. His interest was not just de Souza's teaching ideas, but her ability to adapt them to India's specific circumstances—then market them.

How did she plan to get administrators, teachers, parents, and students in a rigid, authoritarian system to buy into her curriculum and teaching methods? How did she intend to make them attractive and nonthreatening? "It would be a challenge even if we had teacher-to-student ratios of one to twenty and reasonably equipped teachers," de Souza said. How to make the methods accessible to a poorly trained teacher in a public school in Bombay with sixty students in a classroom teetering on the edge of chaos?

These questions were what Drayton called the "how-tos"—the sorts of questions that theorists hate and entrepreneurs live for. De Souza was a gifted teacher, but success in this realm would demand salesmanship and resourcefulness and thick skin and a level of commitment bordering on obsession. These were the qualities Ashoka was looking for, and Drayton and his colleagues believed that they had found them in Gloria de Souza.

In order to disseminate her approach, de Souza said she would have to quit teaching and devote herself to the task full time. Ashoka granted her a four-year living stipend, a total investment, at the time, of about $10,000.

The following year, in 1982, de Souza founded an organization called Parisar Asha, Sanskrit for "hope for the environment," and began building a team to spread her ideas. In a few years, she was able to demonstrate that her Environmental Studies (EVS) approach significantly increased students' performance. (One independent evaluation found that students learning with EVS scored twice as high on reading comprehension tests and mastered writing and mathematics three times faster than students taught by the rote method.) By 1985 de Souza had persuaded Bombay's municipal school board to introduce EVS in 1,700 schools through a pilot program. Within three years, almost a million students were learning with her methods. By the end of the 1980s, the Indian government had incorporated EVS into its national curriculum, making it India's official standard of instruction in grades one through three.[6]

Today, more than twenty years later, de Souza is still the driving force behind Parisar Asha. In the intervening decades, her work has influenced a generation of teachers and curriculum developers in India. Each year she improves her curriculum, extends her work to more cities, and looks for ways to adapt the methods to different environments, such as rural and tribal areas.

The Light in My Head Went On

Fábio Rosa, Brazil: Rural Electrification

In 1982, at the same time that Gloria de Souza was launching her Environmental Studies curriculum in India, Fábio Rosa, twenty-two, a recent graduate in agronomic engineering, was trying to deliver electricity to poor people in Brazil. It all began when Rosa received a phone call from one of his university classmates inviting him to come to Palmares do Sul, a rural municipality in Brazil's southernmost state, Rio Grande do Sul, an area famous for its beautiful grassy plains—the pampas—inhabited by gaúchos, Brazil's cowboys.

Rosa didn't know that his friend's father, Ney Azevedo, had just been elected mayor of Palmares. Azevedo had previously been the technical director at the state's rice institute, and one evening, over dinner, he and Rosa got into a long conversation about the possibilities for improving life for local villagers. After listening to Rosa's ideas, Azevedo offered him the post of secretary of agriculture.

Although Rio Grande do Sul is one of Brazil's wealthiest states, Palmares was a depressed area, reminiscent of the Mississippi Delta. The municipality had recently been cobbled together. When Rosa showed up for work his first day, he found no city hall, no records, no municipal employees, not even a pickup truck. A local priest let him work out of a church. Rosa dropped off his boxes and set out to talk to the villagers.

What he heard surprised him. Politicians in Rio Grande do Sul were always talking about building roads. But when Rosa asked farmers about their priorities, nobody mentioned roads. They spoke about educating their kids and escaping poverty and holding onto their farms. They didn't want to move to the city. But unless they could find a way to boost their farm incomes, they would soon have no choice.

The primary wealth in Palmares was the irrigated rice crop. Ninety percent of the land was lowland, good only for rice production. And Rosa quickly discovered that the villagers had a big problem. Rice needs a lot of water to grow, but wealthy landowners owned most of the dams and irrigation channels, and they set the price of water high. Rosa found that small farmers were paying as much as a quarter of their production costs on water, triple the world average.

"Without water there was no production," Rosa explained. "And without production there was no wealth. The whole political situation was determined by this fact."

Looking for ideas, Rosa read a book written by a Brazilian agronomist who had traveled to Louisiana in the 1940s and documented how rice plantations were irrigated with artesian wells. It made him wonder: "Could something similar work in Palmares?" First they would have to get the water out of the ground—and the only way to do that cheaply was with electricity.

That was a problem. Among the many differences between Brazil and the United States—countries of comparable size—is that Brazil never had a government works projects comparable to the Rural Electrification Administration, the New Deal agency that brought electricity to 98 percent of U.S. farms between 1935 and 1950.

Brazil's electrification standards had been designed under a military regime to serve cities, industry, and large farms. In the 1970s, a short-lived abundance of credit for rural electrification led Brazil's utilities to rely heavily on expensive technology. The cost of providing electricity to a single rural property in the early 1980s had soared to $7,000, five to ten years' income for a poor farmer.[1]

"The electric companies install lines with excess capacity, forcing small and medium landowners to pay huge sums for power they won't use," Rosa explained. As a result, the lines weren't built. Today 25 million Brazilians have no access to electricity: no refrigeration, no lights, no computers.[2] In short, no future. That was seemingly the case in Palmares, where Rosa found that 70 percent of the rural population—about 9,000 people—had no electricity.

Watching the TV news one evening, Rosa happened on an interview with Ennio Amaral, a professor at the Federal Technical School of Pelotas, in a municipality a few hours south, who had developed an inexpensive rural electrification system. Rosa knew that as a candidate for mayor Azevedo had campaigned on the promise to bring electricity to all of Palmares. "I was committed to it," Azevedo told me, "but I didn't know *how* to do it." So when Rosa mentioned Amaral's interview, the mayor handed him $20 and keys and said: "Take my car. Go there tomorrow."

Rosa was impressed by Amaral's approach. By contrast to conventional power distribution systems, which employ three wires ("three-phase"), Amaral employed a high-tension "monophase" current system suitable for modest energy consumption, in which a single wire carried the current through a transformer to a house and the system was grounded in the soil. Amaral further reduced costs by substituting cheaper materials for expensive ones: wood instead of cement poles, steel rather than copper wire, and steel-and-zinc conductors in lieu of aluminum ones. He used fewer poles and smaller transformers and employed ordinary people from the community as builders.

"The light in my head went on," Rosa said. "With cheap electricity, poor farmers could drop wells and irrigate their land. Then they would be free from the tyranny of water."

Fábio Rosa is an easygoing and affable person, with a disarming smile and a precise mind. He is the sort of person you would be lucky to encounter in an airport lounge while waiting an hour for a flight. That's about how long it would take him to explain the basics of rural electrification, rice farming, managed cattle grazing, the causes of landlessness, and the connection between poverty and the destruction of the environment. Afterward, you'd get on your flight and look out the window and the land below would seem more fragile and more beautiful.

Rosa's mother, Nice, was a school teacher with an irrepressibly cheerful disposition. His father, Geraldo, was a methodical thinker who managed a bank branch in Porto Alegre. Both Nice and Geraldo had grown up on farms, and Rosa's childhood tales revolved around life on the pampas. His mother's forebears had all played in a family farm orchestra, an image that enchanted Rosa. "Can you imagine?" he said to me. "A small orchestra in a farm lost in the vastness of the pampas at the end of the nineteenth century!" His father's parents had raised cattle and cultivated rice, and Rosa loved to hear the story of the 1929 market crash when cattle and rice prices plummeted, but his grandfather refused to lay off a single farmhand.

As a child, Rosa's favorite pastime was playing in his backyard with toy cows and fences, designing mini-irrigation systems and dams. Later, carrying on the musical tradition, Rosa taught himself to play guitar. For a number of years, he considered becoming a professional musician, but, in the end, his first love—of cows and dams and fences—won out.

Fábio Rosa

* * *

Returning from Pelotas, Rosa was eager to see if Amaral's approach could be used to power an irrigation system. First, he prepared a hydrogeological survey to see if there was sufficient underground water throughout the municipality to irrigate rice. "There was water," he recalled. "It was not too deep: an average of twenty-three meters below the surface. There was enough. It was of good quality for irrigation. The door was open."

Amaral had spent a decade developing his system. It was fully operational. But state and federal energy interests had prevented him from extending it beyond a test site. "He kept running into what you might call a 'small-big' problem," Rosa explained. "What he had invented worked beautifully, but it was illegal."

In Brazil at the time, state electric companies determined technical standards. If a system didn't comply with the "norm," the company wouldn't turn the electricity on. The state electric company in Rio Grande do Sul saw no reason to change the norm. Rosa disagreed. "If the government has no money and the technical standard is expensive," he explained, "then you *have* to change the standard."

Rosa needed authorization from the state electric company to experiment with Amaral's system. For help, he turned to Ney Azevedo, who was friendly with a number of senior government officials in Rio Grande do Sul. With Azevedo's influence, Rosa was granted permission to proceed.

Ennio Amaral went to Palmares to advise Rosa. Before he left he said: "I'm sending you my best student—a really loyal guy." A few days later Ricardo de Souza Mello, an electrical technician, showed up in Palmares, and he and Rosa have worked together ever since.

Rosa got hold of an abandoned ambulance. He put in a new motor and lashed the doors with rope. That became Mello's official vehicle. The two men went to work developing a plan to spread Amaral's system to a few hundred households. Mello focused on the technical details while Rosa met with farmers. Would they help build the system? The farmers had been promised electricity many times before; they were skeptical. But they assured Rosa: If wires, poles, and transformers actually materialized, they would put them up.

Next: How to sink the wells?

The traditional woodpecker-style drills used to bore artesian wells ran on three-phase electricity, which was unavailable. But Rosa discovered that water pressure pumps, operating on diesel fuel, loosened the subsoil enough to force polyethylene tubes down to the water level. That problem was solved. However, the water pumps needed to bring the water to surface also ran on three-phase power. Rosa had no solution to that problem, but he was confident that one would present itself.

And it did. "After we dropped a few wells, the water pump solution appeared," he explained. The natural ground pressure brought the water to an average depth of four meters, shallow enough for a monophase electric pump to carry it the rest of the way to surface.

Low-cost irrigation was beginning to look like a distinct possibility.

One of the other major problems facing farmers in Palmares was "red" rice. Red rice is like a weed. Its seeds multiply quickly. If land is continually cultivated, eventually the red rice will destroy the desired rice crops. To inhibit the weed growth, small farmers cultivated only one-quarter of their land each year, leaving the remainder fallow for three years before replanting.

Rosa had a better solution. Farmers could flood the fields before planting the rice and keep them saturated while the rice grew. The soil would be deprived of oxygen, preventing red rice seeds from germinating. The trick would be to *pregerminate* the domestic rice plants in prepared beds and transplant them to the submerged paddies. Then only the desired rice would grow.

In Palmares, this kind of rice farming, known as water seedling, had been impractical because water was so expensive. But cheap irrigation changed everything. "Using the saturation system," Rosa explained, "we could multiply the land that each farm could use by a factor of four."

He put it together like an equation: inexpensive electricity + shallow artesian wells + monophase pumps = cheap irrigation. And cheap irrigation + water seedling = more efficient land use, increased income, a rural future.

Rosa created a municipal department to train locals in the new rice farming methods and added a credit mechanism so they could take loans to prepare their land, sink wells, and pay for irrigation.

"Finally," he said, "we had a complete system."

After drafting his plan, Rosa traveled to Rio de Janeiro to present it to the Banco Nacional de Desenvolvimento Econômico e Social (BNDES), the $50 billion federal agency responsible for long-term national development funding. "I showed them the cost structure and they jumped," he recalls. "It was like selling sweets to children."

Rosa found a strong supporter in Aluysio Asti, one of BNDES's project analysts. Asti, who later nominated Rosa to Ashoka, was no fan of wishful thinking; he liked good data. Rosa had lots of it. He had charts showing farmers' expenditures, costs of materials, well capacities, expected rice yields and prices, with studies to back everything up. Based on his analysis, the bank's investment would be repaid in four years.

It was obvious to Asti that Rosa was organized and determined. What particularly impressed Asti was Rosa's initiative. "Just to have an agricultural development department in a small municipality in Rio Grande do Sul was itself an innovation," he told me. "Especially an agricultural department that actually worked with small farmers."

Rosa told Asti: "If we don't succeed with this project, the people of Palmares will find their own solution: the worst solution for everybody. They will flee to the cities."

In recent decades, like the Okies in *The Grapes of Wrath*, millions of rural Brazilians, in search of work, had abandoned their land in favor of urban shantytowns, causing massive social upheaval and sending unemployment and crime rates skyrocketing. To the extent that the Brazilian government was responding to the problem, it was attacking the symptoms—for example, trying to resettle the landless on government-owned land, at best a short-term solution. Rosa, by contrast, was attacking the root cause. And, if he was successful, Asti saw, he would have something valuable to show the country.

Asti recommended financing for the project.

The major obstacles remaining were resistance from the state electric company, Companhia Estadual de Energia Elétrica (CEEE), and political opposition from cement and aluminum cartels. "We didn't need contractors to carry out the work," Rosa recalls. "The whole thing could be done by the community with one technician hired by the mayor's office. It was practically an autonomous system. And the state company knew that if we succeeded in Palmares, it could lead to other things."

To mobilize political support for rural electrification, Rosa met with journalists and visited mayors in neighboring municipalities, urging them to lobby the state assembly. Meanwhile, he purchased wire and contracted with two companies, which agreed to manufacture the miniature five-kilowatt-amp transformers that Amaral's system required. Mello created a schedule for installations. The farmers had agreed to supply trees from their properties for electric poles. Rosa found they could get by with three poles per kilometer, one-quarter the number that the government required. And he found a way to extend the life of the wood from three to thirty years by saturating the poles in creosote, a chemical solution. Everything was set to go when he received a letter from CEEE withdrawing permission.

Ney Azevedo immediately telephoned Jair Soares, the state governor, who called a meeting with Rosa, Azevedo, and the president of CEEE. Rosa has a vivid recollection of the encounter. As he recalls, the president of CEEE, hoping to put an end to the Palmares project, offered to cut a deal with Azevedo, promising to provide electricity to rural areas of Palmares through the conventional grid if Azevedo would abandon Rosa's project.

Rosa smiled when he recalled Azevedo's response: "Ney said to him, 'But could you do that for the whole state?' And he had to say, 'No.' Then Ney said, 'I don't sell my opinion so cheap. You have to think about this problem and try to solve it throughout the state—and throughout Brazil.'"

BNDES then informed the state government that its funding would be cut if CEEE stood in the way of the Palmares project. Not long after the meeting, the state energy minister arrived in Palmares by helicopter, with a contract authorizing Rosa to proceed. "I remember this meeting as if it happened yesterday," Rosa told me. "I was very emotional signing this paper. I still guard it very closely. But we would have other David and Goliath battles."

As a selling point, Rosa had told the villagers that his plan could provide a household with electricity for about the price of a cow. Two years later, in 1988, he and Mello delivered on the promise: 400 rural families were hooked up to the electric grid at a cost of $400 per family, less than one-seventeenth of the government's figure of $7,000. Seventy-five percent of the farmers bought water pumps; 80 percent bought refrigerators or television sets. Others bought rice processing machines, electric lights, fences, and water heaters.

Initially most farmers were reluctant to change to water seedling, but those who did were rewarded. Incomes jumped from $50 to $80 a month to between $200 and $300 a month. For Rosa, the most compelling finding was that almost a third of the households served—130 out of 400—were people who had returned from the city because of the Palmares project. This was a striking development: It showed that, contrary to assumptions, it was possible to slow the flood of rural-to-urban migration, allowing the cities more time to absorb the millions squatting on their hillsides.

Rosa made sure that journalists and politicians heard about the Palmares project. Soon technicians were visiting from other states. "For a small municipality recently created to have visitors coming from around Brazil was something very exciting," recalled Azevedo. The government of Rio Grande do Sul asked Aluysio Asti, from BNDES, to coordinate a meeting on rural electrification so Rosa and Mello would have the opportunity to explain how the project could be expanded.

But CEEE was not ready to accept a major change to its distribution norm. "At this meeting, all the Ph.D.s and masters from the state company were on one side—and Ricardo [Mello] and I were on the other," Rosa recalled. A debate ensued. Rosa argued that a new legal distribution standard was needed. The CEEE officials countered that his results were inconclusive. "What you've done in Palmares, you won't be able to do anywhere else," they said.

After that meeting, CEEE refused to budge for almost a year. Eventually, however, the Palmares project caught the attention of Rio Grande do Sul's newly elected governor, Pedro Simon, who had vowed to expand rural electrification in the state. BNDES was offering loans to spread Rosa's system. Finally, in 1989, CEEE gave in. Rosa's technical standard was officially approved as the *025 Norm*. "At last," Rosa recalled, "we could say we weren't breaking the law."

In 1999 I visited Palmares do Sul with Rosa. In the intervening decade, Rosa had moved to Porto Alegre and broadened the focus of his work to the rest of Brazil. As we drove by rice plantations and fields with buffalo cows grazing, Rosa was uncharacteristically quiet. The land was flat, the horizon visible all around.

Because of term limit laws, Azevedo could not run for mayor again after his six-year term expired in 1988. The townspeople of Palmares (who had electricity) elected a conservative candidate who proceeded to shut down Rosa's departments, dismiss his technicians, and divert the loans he had negotiated. Recalling the events, Rosa commented: "We don't have the mechanisms yet for democratic government. Each emperor comes in and destroys everything that preceded him.

"It feels very sad coming back here," he added.

We drove in silence for a while, then Rosa tapped my arm and pulled over to the side of the road. "Look," he said, pointing to a little gray box hanging on a pole. "Monophase."

I got out to take a closer look. A single wire strung over thin poles led a quarter mile to a farmhouse.

"Just one wire," he said. "You see?

"Ennio Amaral made his first five-kilowatt-amp transformer in a milk can."

Back in the car, Rosa was happy again. As we continued, he interrupted our conversation periodically with "Look, monophase," and "Look, over there, monophase."

We visited Paulo Sessim, one of the first villagers served by the Palmares project. Sessim came out of his house when he heard the car pull up and smiled broadly when he recognized Rosa. He pulled Rosa toward him with a warm handshake. "It's been a long time," he said with unmistakable affection. He invited us in and served us cold drinks. I was grateful for his refrigerator. I could hear the TV in the next room.

I told Sessim I was writing about Rosa's work.

"Before the electricity," he offered, "we used to have dances and there would be candles and kerosene lamps in every corner of the building. When you would touch the face of the girl you were dancing with, black grease would rub off."

Sessim wasn't talking about the 1930s, but the 1980s. The townspeople and well-to-do farmers had had electricity for years. "When you entered a poor family's house," Rosa recalled, "you could hear the sound of the wind moving in the wires. Below, people would be using gas lamps."

"When Fábio first spoke to us about electricity," commented Sessim, "we said, 'It will never happen here.'"

Now he couldn't imagine how he had lived without it.

A short distance from Sessim's home, Rosa showed me the stone memorial that locals had erected in memory of Ennio Amaral, who had died of cancer at the age of forty-five, a few months before construction had begun on the Palmares project. A plaque read:

> In the fight for an ideal, we face those who are deceptive, envious and incompetent. The man who is firm pays no mind to such people and wastes no time counting them. For he who marches toward the light need not worry about what occurs in the darkness.
>
> To Prof. Ennio Amaral, who through his genius, idealism and perseverance, made it possible for poor people in the fields to gain access to electric energy benefits—our eternal recognition and gratitude.

"Ennio was a very pure man," Rosa said thoughtfully as we returned to his car. "One of the most impressive human beings I've ever met."

In 1988, after all his work, Rosa found himself out of a job. He wanted to continue expanding the Palmares project, but he needed to make money. He'd also just gotten married. He didn't even know how he would describe himself in a résumé. He was an agronomist, but his work went beyond agriculture. He was an engineer, but technical issues occupied only a fraction of his time. He'd been working in government, but he wasn't a civil servant. Much of his time was spent persuading people to try new things.

Then Aluysio Asti, from BNDES, nominated him to Ashoka.

When Rosa met Drayton, he found a new way of looking at himself. "Bill made me see that I was a social entrepreneur," Rosa told me. "He showed me that my role was to take things beyond theory and find practical solutions for all the problems that emerged along the way."

Ashoka's stipend—$9,600 a year—gave Rosa enough of a financial cushion to continue his work. He traveled around Rio Grande do Sul promoting rural electrification. He leased land to experiment with rice planting techniques. He knew that BNDES had offered the state $2.5 million in loans for rural electrification, on the condition that he oversee the project. He waited until CEEE finally came around.

After the 025 Norm was approved, Rosa organized a meeting of mayors from forty-two municipalities. In each municipality Rosa had surveyed terrain, developed plans for electrical distribution, and identified local champions to organize the community. Between 1990 and 1993 he and Mello implemented Pro Luz (Project Light), carrying electricity to 25,000 low-income rural dwellers. Working with corn, soybean, and milk farmers, they demonstrated the widespread applicability of the Palmares project. With inflation, the installation cost per household had jumped to $600.[3]

One of Asti's colleagues at BNDES put Rosa in touch with Fernando Selles Ribeiro, a professor at the University of São Paulo, which housed the country's best electrical engineering department. After studying Rosa's experiences, Ribeiro established a resource center for low-cost electrification, with the 025 Norm ensconced as its central standard.[4] "That put an end to the ongoing conflict that our standard wouldn't work or would work only in one place," Rosa recalled.

In 1991 BNDES instituted a special credit line to promote low-cost rural electrification based on the 025 Norm. Other states picked up the model. For a short time the prospects for Brazilians without electricity looked bright. But the following year, with the economy spiraling out of control, the Brazilian government slashed social spending and BNDES terminated its credit line.

To Rosa, the idea that the government would withdraw support for a cheap, proven system that alleviated poverty, spurred economic growth, and forestalled rural exodus was incomprehensible. But this was the second time that government had brought years of his work to a halt.

"I felt like Sisyphus," he said.

And he resolved to rid himself of the burden of working through the government.

In 1992 he established a for-profit company—Sistemas de Tecnologia Adequada Agroeletro (Agroelectric Adequate Technology Systems), or STA Agroeletro—and began spreading photovoltaic solar energy (which converts light to electricity) across Brazil. "It's much quicker than spending ten years of my life arguing with the government," Rosa explained.

Solar energy—clean, renewable, decentralized, easy to install—has always had one major drawback: high cost. Rosa saw that to make it cost effective, he would have to package it with something else—the way he'd packaged Amaral's monophase system with irrigation in Palmares.

Having grown up in a family of gaúchos, Rosa knew that one of the major problems in rural Brazil was inadequate fencing for animal grazing. Because of the high cost of conventional fencing, cattle farmers used fences sporadically. The result was overgrazing, which translated into lower farm yields and degradation of pastureland. However, Rosa saw that if *electric* fences were used—if solar energy were sold as a package with inexpensive polywire and fiberglass posts—it would bring down the price of the fencing by 85 percent. Farmers would receive electricity, increase their farm production, and improve land management all at once. Brazil has a vast cattle stock; the potential market was enormous.

Using this business model, within five years, STA Agroeletro installed 700 solar electric and fencing systems in sixteen Brazilian states. Rosa traveled from the pampas in the south to the Amazon rain forest in the north, to the *cerrados* (savannah) in central Brazil, to the dry *sertão* (arid lands) in the interior of Bahia, to the semiarid northeast. He was away from home two to three weeks each month. His wife, Liege, frequently asked him to cut down on his traveling. Each time Rosa came home early from the office on a weekday, his son João Pedro inquired: "Are you leaving again?"

Away from home, Rosa spent his days in the sun installing solar panels, pumps, and lights, measuring paddocks, and running wire. At night he slept in farmhouses. By the mid-1990s STA had a six-month backlog of work, and Rosa had gained national recognition as a leader in the delivery of low-cost solar energy.

While Rosa built up STA's business, he continued to promote the 025 Norm, offering his services as a consultant to state governments. Even without BNDES's special credit line, state governments continued to pursue rural electrification. In 1996 Rio Grande do Sul launched Pro Luz II, a $34 million plan, based on the 025 Norm, to carry electricity to 160,000 more people. For political reasons, the state company declined Rosa's help. Later that year the government of São Paulo State launched a $240 million rural electrification project based on Rosa's system to provide electricity to 800,000 people.

In 1997, when I first interviewed Rosa, he had just been recruited as a consultant on the São Paulo project and was optimistic. Two years later, however, he reported that Pro Luz II and the São Paulo project had both

Bringing solar energy to rural Brazil

fallen short of their goals. In Rio Grande do Sul, the state company had extended the system to about 40,000 rural dwellers. In São Paulo state, the project was reaching a quarter of its intended recipients. In both places, Rosa said the problem was lack of motivation and follow-through. "The technicians were trying to make the project work from their offices," Rosa said. "You have to *go* there."

By 1999, however, the political landscape in Brazil had shifted. Under pressure from the International Monetary Fund, Brazil's state governments divested their utilities. In 1997 Rosa had told me that he would have to work quickly because rural electrification would be abandoned by the power companies once they were privatized (it is more profitable to serve cities), and privatization had come more swiftly than he expected. As a result, rural electrification by the power companies had slowed to a trickle. "For years I have shown the government how to respond," Rosa said. "I had become well respected in Brazil. But since privatization, the people I knew are gone. Everything is different."

When Rosa spoke of this—yet another—setback, he didn't seem discouraged or bitter. "The context and the environment have changed," he went on. "But the necessity of my work is the same. I am an entrepreneur, and as an entrepreneur, I am always possessed by an idea. If it doesn't go well, you haven't come to the end. You have to do more work. If you haven't succeeded, the work goes on."

But what about seventeen years of his life?

"Yes, I am very angry," Rosa conceded after considerable prodding. "Every time I think about it, I get angry, I feel like shouting out at the top of my lungs. But I try to transform the feeling into a positive force: into solutions."

I didn't feel sympathy for Rosa. What I felt was a thrill at the way he experienced life: Despite all the problems, he still saw himself as the central mover of events. And the effect it had on me, as I'm sure it had on many people he'd met along the way, was to make me want to help him.

By the late 1990s Rosa had installed solar electric systems across Brazil. He had traveled to almost every corner of the country and talked with thousands of people about their problems, and the stories he heard were strikingly similar. Everywhere, he encountered farmers whose farm yields and incomes were declining.

Nationally, millions of poor people could no longer subsist on their land. A major new political movement—the Movimento Sem Terra (landless movement)—had spread across Brazil. In the mid-1990s, in response to pressures brought by this movement, the Brazilian government had launched an ambitious land reform program that, by 2002, had distributed 18 million hectares of land to a half million families.[5]

Unfortunately, the government hadn't taken the steps to provide electricity to these people or help them establish viable farms. In Rio Grande do Sul, for example, the government simply resettled many of the *sem terra* (landless people) in the pampas, where they proceeded to plow the grasslands to plant rice, wheat, corn, and soybeans. Such farming practices destroy the soil composition that protects natural pastures from wind and water erosion. The result has been environmental degradation and a perpetuation of poverty.[6]

Across Brazil, most of the families resettled by the government are struggling to support themselves. A quarter abandon their land within two years; the remainder barely hang on. In some regions, almost half have quit.[7] The problems are fundamentally the same ones that Rosa encountered in Palmares.

This downward economic-environmental spiral is not unique to Brazil or to the pampas. In fact, the pampas, as grasslands, have a global significance. Grasslands are the earth's second largest ecosystem, occupying vast areas of Europe, Asia, Africa, Australia, and the Americas. Like rain forests, grasslands are endangered, but they are rarely managed, and in many parts of the world they are seriously degraded. In addition to their inherent value as pasturelands and wildlife habitats, grasslands are major water catchment areas. Allan Savory, an authority on holistic resource management, has called water the "Achilles' Heel" of modern industrial and postindustrial civilizations. He writes: "[I]ts quantity and quality are determined by the state of the land on which it falls."[8]

Looking for ways to address some of these problems, Rosa again sought guidance in an old book: *Grass Productivity*, a classic 1957 text written by André Voisin, a French farmer and biochemist who was legendary for spending hours on his farm in Normandy watching his cows graze.

Voisin had made the breakthrough discovery that the key factor in grazing was time.[9] If animals grazed in any one area too long, or if they returned to an area too soon after grazing, they overgrazed.

Voisin came up with a system called rational or managed grazing, in which a pasture is subdivided into numerous paddocks (fenced-in areas) and animals are rotated from one to another in a regular fashion. He established precise guidelines to govern this process.

Managed grazing had many benefits, Voisin demonstrated. Farmers could reduce operational costs, cut their dependence on inorganic fertilizers and grain supplements and reduce soil erosion, while boosting milk and meat yields. Animals tended to forage evenly and spread their own manure over the land. Biodiversity increased and cows' health improved. Rather than being subjected to confinement feeding, where conditions cause cow stress and illness, cows could wander around outside and rest in the shade of trees. Farmers required less machinery, saving on fuel and making it safer to work alongside their children.

Voisin's techniques were implemented in France and New Zealand. Managed grazing was later adapted to rangelands in Africa. In recent decades it has spread in Canada and the United States, particularly in Wisconsin, where it is known as management-intensive rotational grazing (MIRG) and, having proven to be more cost-effective than feedlot production, is one of the fastest growing dairy farming practices.[10] However, when it was introduced in Brazil in the 1970s, the results were disappointing and the idea was abandoned.

Rosa suspected that people hadn't taken the time to work out the bugs. He thought: If he could demonstrate that Voisin's system worked in Brazil, he would be able to influence grassland management and government resettlement policy. "It is *unbelievable*," he told me, "that in millions of hectares of natural grasslands—protected from snowfalls and extreme drought—no one has taken the care to design an organic pasture grazing system."

Why hadn't Voisin grazing worked in Brazil?

The key to the system is rotation. "You can only do it if you can create many small paddocks at low cost," Rosa said. "And you can only create many small paddocks at low cost if you use electric fencing, and, in Brazil, you must have the appropriate technology to deal with the land, climate, plants, and lightning."

Once again it was necessary to delve into the details. When Voisin's methods were first attempted in Brazil, the electric fencing systems were imported from Europe. But in Brazil's subtropical climate, plants grow taller than in Europe—tall enough to touch an electric fence and drain the current. A cow will "respect" an electric fence with 2,500 volts; sheep will respect an electric fence with 3,500 volts. Both Rosa's machines and the European ones put through 6,000 volts, Rosa explained. But when plants touched the wire with European machines, the current dropped to 2,000 or even 1,000 volts. So Rosa and Mello designed machines in which the current dropped only to 5,500 volts.

Then there were regionally specific modifications. In central Brazil, for example, the soil has low conductivity, which means that higher voltages are required. "How did we figure this problem out?" Rosa asked. "From the Palmares project!"

Other modifications were required because Brazil has one of the world's highest incidences of lightning. And then there were all sorts of pasture plants and cattle species to learn about. Details, details, details. All of it was different from Europe, Argentina, Uruguay, New Zealand, and North America.

Rosa put together another equation: solar energy + polywire + fiberglass posts = inexpensive electric fencing. And inexpensive electric fencing + Voisin managed grazing = higher yields, sustainable land use, a rural future.

Within a few years Rosa had installed dozens of successful solar/electric fencing/Voisin managed grazing systems in ten states, enabling farmers in Bahia to raise goats, restoring cattle pastures in the state of Rio de Janeiro, helping buffalo farmers produce organic milk and buffalo mozzarella cheese in the state of Paraná. In most cases farmers saw their yields double or triple. In instances where the land had been particularly degraded, the new system produced 500 percent gains.

"We have now demonstrated results in every type of Brazilian environment, and other agronomists are beginning to do the same," Rosa told me in 2001. There was still resistance to the idea, he added, but that was to be expected. "It's difficult to say that something doesn't work for thirty years and then say, 'Oh, I was wrong.'"

But this time Rosa didn't have to worry about the government. The system was spreading through market demand. "Farmers want to do it," he said. "It produces organic milk and meat. And now the world, especially Europe, is willing to pay for it."

During the 1990s, land devoted to organic farming worldwide increased tenfold. The organic food market has global revenues in excess of $22 billion.[11] Brazil's cattle farmers want in, and Rosa plans to help them.

In 2001 Rosa stepped down from STA to build up a nonprofit organization that he had established a few years before, the Instituto Para O Desenvolvimento De Energias Alternativas E Da Auto Sustentabilidade (Institute for the Development of Natural Energy and Self-Sustainability), or IDEAAS.

STA had served as a vehicle to test market and refine a set of practical models. Now, through IDEAAS, Rosa sought to apply those models in poor areas where the for-profit model did not fit.

Initially he planned to concentrate on Brazil's three southernmost states, Rio Grande do Sul, Santa Catarina, and Paraná, which he knew best and where grassland degradation was intensifying. He further narrowed his focus to the southern half of Rio Grande do Sul, where 250,000 people lacked electricity, then targeted 13,000 poor families.

Next he conducted a market study. One key finding was that more than half of the families in his target area spent at least $13 each month on diesel fuel, kerosene, and batteries. "We saw that the amounts that people spent monthly on nonrenewable energy could be transferred to pay a monthly fee for a renewable energy supply, equipment, and service," Rosa explained. In other words, most of the families could afford solar energy at commercial rates provided they were given the option to rent it or pay it off slowly—over five to seven years on average. Villagers who spent less than $13 a month could also gain access to solar energy, Rosa added, but they would need longer-term financing and additional services. "For these people it isn't enough to bring electricity," he explained. "It's also necessary to improve their incomes and change their production models by introducing appropriate technology."

Rosa recruited a team of technicians, businessmen, lawyers, and journalists to help him think through the strategy. To reach the full market would require a mix of for-profit and nonprofit distribution channels, with some clients being served by STA at market rates and others being served at subsidized rates by IDEAAS.

They came up with two projects. The first, which Rosa named the Quiron Project, was a nonprofit venture to boost incomes of approximately 7,000 poor families while safeguarding the environment through a combination of solar energy, organic animal production, managed grazing, and other methods of resource conservation. (Gaúchos are attached to the image of the centaur in Greek mythology, and Quiron—Portuguese for Chiron—was the only centaur distinguished for wisdom rather than brute force.)

The second project, which Rosa dubbed The Sun Shines for All, was a for-profit venture to deliver solar energy, initially, to 6,100 rural families who did not have electricity but could afford to pay for solar panels through a rental system. Rosa estimated that the project could break even between months 42 and 48 and produce a 20 to 30 percent return for investors in addition to providing social and environmental benefits (e.g., switching from kerosene to solar lighting would translate to better health for families as well as reduced carbon emissions).

Rosa was particularly excited by the findings of his market study because it indicated the potential to reach a large number of people through a business format. "If an investment in solar energy will pay itself off in five to seven years, that means that it will be possible to attract investment capital," he explained. "This is very important, because it is not possible to imagine bringing electricity to poor people around the world with only philanthropic dollars."

* * *

As I listened to Rosa's plans, I thought about the archaeology of social change: how in each generation people build on the foundation laid by previous generations. As a result of the micro-credit revolution, advanced over the past twenty years by the Grameen Bank and others, poor people in developing countries are today recognized as acceptable credit risks. The Grameen Bank has financed more than 570,000 tin-roof houses, providing ten- and fifteen-year mortgages that Bangladeshi villagers pay off with installments as low as $1 a week. The notion that institutions can establish reliable, long-term credit relationships with poor people across the world is no longer radical. It has been proven. And if it works with houses, it can work with solar panels, or cell phones, or any other productive asset.

This is an important idea. "Installment buying literally transforms economies," notes Peter Drucker. "Wherever introduced, it changes the economy from supply-driven to demand-driven, regardless almost of the productive level of the economy."[12]

Consider that 2 billion people—30 percent of the world's population—are currently without electricity and about half of them could afford solar power at commercial prices today if they had the opportunity to rent it or pay it off in installments.[13] Bringing electricity to remote rural areas around the globe would not only transform economies, it would transform education and healthcare. It would transform agriculture. Access to electricity is often a precondition for farmers to switch from nonsustainable, low-yielding agricultural practices to sustainable, higher-yielding ones. Global rural electrification also would relieve the population stress on the world's megacities, reducing the urban discontent that is so easily exploited by advocates of violence.

In 2001 Rosa was one of the first forty social entrepreneurs honored by the Geneva-based Schwab Foundation for Social Entrepreneurship, which supports "outstanding social entrepreneurs" worldwide.[14] Later that year Rosa also won a $50,000 Tech Museum of Innovation Award from the San Jose Tech Museum for applying technology to benefit humanity. Five winners had been chosen from 400 nominees from fifty countries.[15]

I sent Rosa an e-mail, asking how it felt to win.

"It was fantastic!" he wrote back. "When I was walking to receive the prize, lights in my eyes, in my mind in high velocity went the past: the grids, the transformers, the solar panels, Ennio, Ney, Bill Drayton.

"Afterward, when people were silent, it was time for me to say something. I was very nervous. I said: 'I spent my younger days in distant areas bringing electricity to rural people in Brazil. I love technology. I believe it is the principal force to bring change to humanity. Every project I have seen at this gathering is marvelous. When we use our intelligence and knowledge to serve people, humanity has hope. We are the hope, we are the future.'"

Rosa is forty-two as of this writing. He still travels ten to twenty days a month, but would like to cut back. He wants to spend more time with his children. "I can no longer work two days nonstop without sleep," he says.

In 2002 he informed me that the Solar Development Group, based in Washington, D.C., had agreed to invest in The Sun Shines for All. He also had received support for the Quiron Project from the Avina Foundation and Canopus Foundation and was planning to seek financing from the World Bank's Community Development Carbon Fund, launched in September 2002. (The fund channels private investment to development projects with an emphasis on renewable energy. Investors receive carbon "credits," which can be traded or used to comply with environmental laws. The idea builds on a foundation that, as we will see, was initially laid by Bill Drayton when he was an assistant administrator at the EPA.)

Rosa was completing technical studies and designing the delivery and service models for both projects. He planned to have the market research completed and seventy test sites installed by August 2003. Twenty-one years after he had begun his work in Palmares, he wrote in an e-mail: "Now I see again that it will be possible to reach all groups with sustainable models and designs—I am starting again!"

The Fixed Determination
of an Indomitable Will

Florence Nightingale, England: Nursing

When Drayton calls someone a leading social entrepreneur, he is describing a specific and rare personality type. He doesn't mean a businesswoman who gives jobs to homeless people or devotes a percentage of profits to the environmental movement. He doesn't mean someone running a nonprofit organization who has developed a business to generate revenue. He means someone like Florence Nightingale.

Most people know a little about the "lady of the lamp" who tended to British soldiers during the Crimean War. But what did Florence Nightingale really do? Why are nursing students still assigned Nightingale's 1860 book *Notes on Nursing: What It Is and What It Is Not?*[1]

In *Eminent Victorians*, biographer Lytton Strachey observes that, as children in the nursery, while Florence Nightingale's sister displayed "a healthy pleasure in tearing her dolls to pieces," young Florence already displayed "an almost morbid one in sewing them up again." As a girl, Nightingale was driven "to minister to the poor in their cottages, to watch by sick-beds, to put her dog's wounded paw into elaborate splints as if it was a human being." She imagined her family's country home turned into a hospital "with herself as matron moving about among the beds."[2]

In 1845, at the age of twenty-five, Nightingale expressed a desire to work as a nurse in Salisbury Hospital. But when her father, William, a wealthy landowner, was informed of the low moral standards then associated with nursing, he forbade his daughter to take the position. For a woman of wealth and social standing in Victorian England, seeking work was odd enough; seeking work as a nurse was almost unimaginable. At the time a "nurse" implied "a coarse old woman, always ignorant, usually dirty, often brutal . . . in bunched-up sordid garments, tippling at the brandy bottle or indulging in worse irregularities."[3]

Nightingale was devastated by her family's refusal. Still, she found ways to apprentice herself. On family trips to London and European capitals, she toured hospitals, slums, schools, and workhouses. Privately, she studied the history of hospitals and convalescent homes and devoured reports from sanitary authorities and medical commissions. After a friend sent her a copy of the yearbook of the Institution of Protestant Deaconesses at Kaiserswerth, Germany, which trained girls of good character to nurse the sick, Nightingale fought with her parents for four years until she was permitted to take the training course.

When a suitor made an offer of marriage, Nightingale declined. She was torn between her "passional nature" and her "moral" and "active nature." Although she found her suitor attractive and intellectually stimulating, she felt the need to remain independent to pursue her work—even though her family still opposed it. "In my thirty-first year," she wrote, "I see nothing desirable but death."[4]

In 1853, at age thirty-three, Nightingale was finally permitted to accept an unpaid position as superintendent of the Institution for the Care of Sick Gentlewomen in London, where she gained a reputation as an excellent administrator. Then, in the fall of 1854, English soldiers were dispatched to Crimea, on the north coast of the Black Sea, to fight alongside Turkish forces at war with Russia. Through the advent of war journalism, the English public began receiving reports about wounded soldiers in the Crimean campaign being left to die without basic medical attention.

In response to the public outcry, on October 15, 1854, Nightingale's friend, Sidney Herbert, secretary at war, sent her a letter asking if she would take charge of nursing in the military hospitals in Scutari, a district of Istanbul. Herbert's words were prescient: "If this succeeds . . . a prejudice will have been broken through and a precedent established which will multiply the good to all time."[5]

Nightingale had already sent a letter to Herbert offering her services; within six days she had assembled thirty-eight nurses and departed for Constantinople. When she arrived in Scutari on November 4, Nightingale encountered a catastrophe: total system collapse. The barracks and general hospitals contained almost 2,400 sick and wounded soldiers. They lay in filthy clothes along four miles of cots. Not only were basic surgical and medical supplies unavailable, the hospital barracks were infested with rats and fleas, and the wards stank from underground sewage. Water was tightly rationed. Cholera, typhus, and dysentery were endemic, causing deaths almost at the rate of one in two—deaths that Nightingale found were not even being properly recorded in hospital registers.

The army surgeons thought it preposterous that the War Office had dispatched a boatload of civilian women to the rescue, and they promptly informed Nightingale that her nurses would not be permitted to enter the wards. However, within days, the doctors had no choice but to solicit Nightingale's assistance following the Battle of Inkerman, when more than 500 soldiers, suffering from wounds, malnutrition, exposure, dysentery and scurvy, began lining the hospital corridors on straw litters. "In all our corridor, I think we have not an average of three Limbs per man," wrote Nightingale.[6]

Immediately Nightingale set out to fix the system that was producing such a high death toll. She requisitioned 200 scrubbing brushes and saw to it that the wards were cleaned and the soldiers' clothes were taken outside for washing. She visited the army purveyor to see what could be done about the supply shortages. When he proved uncooperative, Nightingale took over his job, using the £30,000 (raised from private donations) that she had brought with her. When she discovered that supplies were being held up in Turkish customs, she persuaded the War Office to straighten out the problem. She raised additional funds from private sources in England and built a warehouse for supplies. When she received advance word of an impending battle, over the surgeons' objections she authorized the construction of a new ward.[7]

With a combination of tact, good sense, political influence, and calm authority, Nightingale reorganized the military hospitals in Scutari. She introduced meticulous record-keeping, built new kitchens and laundry rooms, and made sure that soldiers ate with sterilized cutlery, washed with fresh towels and soap, and wore clothes that had been laundered in boiled water. She made nightly rounds to comfort patients, speaking in a "soft, silvery voice."[8] She established reading rooms, recreation rooms, classes and lectures, and even got soldiers to send remittances home, a feat the army had deemed impossible. Soldiers stopped cursing when Nightingale was in earshot. Their morale soared. They came to adore her. In February 1855 the death rate in the British army hospitals in Scutari was 43 percent; by May it had dropped to 2 percent.[9]

"Certainly she was heroic," Strachey wrote. "Yet her heroism was not of that simple sort so dear to the readers of novels and the compilers of hagiologies—the romantic sentimental heroism with which mankind loves to invest its chosen darlings: it was made of sterner stuff.... It was not by gentle sweetness and womanly self-abnegation that she had brought order out of chaos in the Scutari Hospitals, that, from her own resources, she had clothed the British Army, that she had spread her dominion over the serried and reluctant powers of the official world; it was by strict method, by stern discipline, by rigid attention to detail, by ceaseless labor, by the fixed determination of an indomitable will."[10]

After the war, Nightingale returned to England a national heroine. But she declined all public receptions and accepted only those invitations—such as an interview with Queen Victoria—that could advance her work, which she now determined was to improve the health of the British army.

Because of poor sanitation, ventilation, and food in army barracks, mortality rates among soldiers in England were nearly double those for civilians. "[Allowing such a high mortality rate] is as criminal ... as it would be to take 1,100 men per annum out upon Salisbury Plain and shoot them," Nightingale wrote.[11] The weapon she wielded in this battle was not a lamp, but an extensive collection of health statistics.

As a young woman, Nightingale had pleaded with her father to teach her mathematics. She was deeply influenced by the development in her day of the theory of probability, particularly the work of the Belgian statistician Jacques Quételet, who is regarded as one of the founders of modern social statistics. Nightingale believed that statistics were a means of discerning the will of God.

After returning from Turkey, she worked with the leading statistician in England, William Farr, and produced and printed at her own expense an 800-page book entitled *Notes on Matters Affecting the Health, Efficiency and Hospital Administration of the British Army* (1858), which featured an extensive statistical analysis of the causes of sickness and death in the army. Nightingale was a pioneer in the use of graphical tools (such as polar-area or "pie" charts), which she employed to dramatize the need for change. She went so far as to frame her statistical charts and present them to officials in the army medical department and War Office.[12]

Nightingale didn't do these things in person. In fact, she rarely ventured outside her home. Having suffered from a bout of Crimean fever during the war, she suffered thereafter from frequent fainting fits and chronic physical exhaustion, and remained bedridden much of the remainder of her life. Yet from her sofa, she greeted countless visitors, and issued an unending stream of orders, memos, and letters to a group of devotees.

She operated principally through her friend and political ally Sidney Herbert, who pushed for the establishment of a series of Royal Commissions to investigate health in the military and in society. As a woman, Nightingale was not permitted to sit on these commissions, but she guided their recommendations and ensured that they were carried out. Due to her efforts, the army established a medical school and statistical department and remodeled barracks across the country. Among other things, Nightingale taught the British army about the salutary effects of

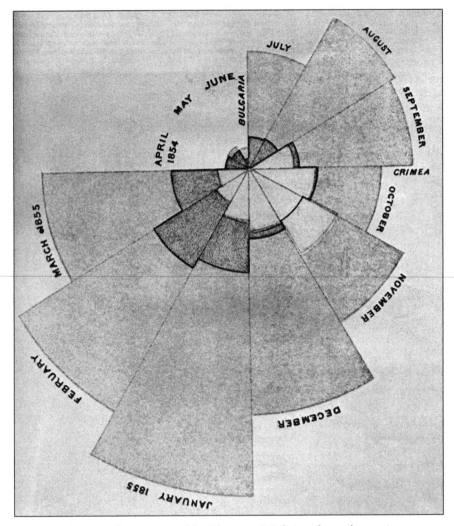

Polar-area diagram used by Florence Nightingale to dramatize death rates in British military hospitals during the Crimean War

sunlight, pure water, and clean kitchens. In two and a half years, the mortality rate among troops in England was cut in half.[13]

Nightingale later applied the same strategy in India, where the death rate for British troops was *six* times higher than the rate for civilian young men in England. Through sanitary reforms, between 1863 and 1873, the annual mortality rate of soldiers in India was reduced by 75 percent.[14]

In 1859 Nightingale published the first edition of *Notes on Hospitals*, which would go on to revolutionize the theory of hospital construction. In 1860, with the support of contributions from the public, she established the Nightingale Training School for Nurses, based on the principle that nurses should receive instruction in teaching hospitals while residing in homes that formed moral character. In so doing, Nightingale began the process that transformed nursing into a modern, respectable profession. Over the next four decades the number of nurses in Britain increased from 28,000 to 64,000. Perhaps more telling, by the end of the nineteenth century, nursing had been reclassified in the British Census from the list of occupations headed "Domestics" to the list headed "Medicine."[15]

Nightingale never recovered from the Crimean fever she suffered while in her thirties. For five and a half decades after her return to England until her death in 1910, she continued to experience fainting fits and often was too weak to stand. Nevertheless, during her life, she authored an estimated 12,000 letters and 200 books, reports, and monographs.

In accordance with her wishes, Nightingale did not receive a national funeral and was not buried in Westminster Abbey.

"The first thought I can remember, and the last," she wrote, "was nursing work."[16]

As a child, I imagined Florence Nightingale to be sweet and gentle, which she was not. I certainly never thought of her as an administrator, statistician, or lobbyist. I still can't get used to thinking of her as an "entrepreneur," although she certainly fits the original definition, having increased the "productivity" or "yield" of healthcare resources by many orders of magnitude. In addition to blazing a trail for nurses, Nightingale established standards for sanitation and hospital management that have shaped norms worldwide.

Given the march of medical science over the past 150 years, one might imagine that these changes would have occurred with or without her. That is impossible to say. What we can say is that the existence of knowledge and the widespread application of knowledge are very different things. If knowledge alone were enough, millions of children would not still be dying each year of dehydration due to diarrhea. (Stopping these preventable deaths was the obsession of James P. Grant, whose work is detailed in Chapter 19.)

Changing a system means changing attitudes, expectations, and behaviors. It means overcoming disbelief, prejudice, and fear. Old systems do not readily embrace new ideas or information; defenders of the status quo can be stubbornly impervious to common sense, as Nightingale's many battles with British army officers can attest. In his classic analysis of politics and power, *The Prince*, Niccolò Machiavelli observed: "[T]here is nothing more difficult to carry out, nor more doubtful of success, nor more dangerous to handle, than to initiate a new order of things. For the reformer has enemies in all those who profit by the old order, and only lukewarm defenders in all those who would profit by the new order."[17]

This may be one reason why society needs ethically driven social entrepreneurs like Florence Nightingale to break out of negative patterns and to initiate new orders of things. It takes concentrated focus, practical creativity, and a long-term source of energy to advance a system change and to ensure that the change becomes well rooted in institutions and cultures. Certain people, because of the quality of their motivation—their inexplicable obsessions, their action and growth orientation, their unwavering belief in the rightness of their ideas—seem particularly well suited to lead this process.

A Very Significant Force

Bill Drayton, United States: The Bubble

Bill Drayton was born in New York City in 1943. His father, William Drayton Sr., who descended from an English aristocratic family, was something of a maverick. In 1901, at the age of nineteen, William, inspired by Teddy Roosevelt, dropped out of Harvard College to become an explorer. He spent years doing mapping and archaeological research in the Sahara and gold mining in British Columbia.

Drayton's mother, Joan, grew up in a middle-class family in Melbourne, Australia. A gifted cellist, Joan played in the Melbourne Symphony Orchestra as a teenager. At age nineteen, during the Depression, she journeyed alone to New York with the dream of becoming one of the world's top cellists. Although she had played professionally, when she saw that she would never play at the level that satisfied her, she quit performing and began channeling her energy into a program that spotted promising young musicians and arranged their debut performances at New York's Town Hall.

"Both my parents gave themselves permission to pursue their dreams in life, to do something really excellent that was theirs," Drayton told me. "They looked very conservative and establishment, but they were quite willing to do radical things."

In grade four, Drayton launched his first venture, *The Sentinel*, a two-page class newspaper that soon grew into a thirty-two-page monthly magazine. He recruited a team of writers and illustrators, persuaded local merchants to advertise in the magazine, and got it distributed to several New York City elementary schools.

The Sentinel was a defining experience. "I wasn't very good at sports,"

Drayton recalled. "I suffered through baseball and soccer. But this stuff I was quite good at. It gave me an outlet to be forceful, creative, and be in control. So I gravitated to it."

As a high school student attending Phillips Academy in Andover, Massachusetts, Drayton established the Asia Society and turned it into the school's most popular student organization. He took over the school's literary magazine, *The Mirror*, and reinvigorated it. He joined the National Association for the Advancement of Colored People (NAACP), and in 1957, at the age of fourteen, organized a boycott of the local Woolworth store to protest its discriminatory practices. When school administrators threatened him with disciplinary action, Drayton went around stapling signs to trees denouncing segregation, then dispatched letters to elected officials. In response to one of his letters, the headmaster of Phillips Academy received a telephone call from Hubert Humphrey, then a U.S. Senator from Minnesota, who had called to defend the boy's right to demonstrate. Humphrey won a fan for life, and Drayton learned that it pays to write letters.

Drayton loved history, particularly Indian history. He had been fascinated by India since he had first come upon a description of Kashmir in a grade-four geography book. As a teenager, he was profoundly influenced by the ideas of Gandhi, who had led India to independence just a decade earlier. As the civil rights movement gathered momentum in the United States, Drayton watched with intense interest as Martin Luther King Jr. began emulating Gandhi's tactics of nonviolent resistance.

What most fascinated Drayton about Gandhi were his "how-tos": *How* did Gandhi craft his strategy? *How* did he build his institutions? *How* did he market his ideas? Drayton discovered that Gandhi, despite his other-worldly appearance, was fully engaged in the details of politics, administration, and implementation.[1]

Over the years Drayton came to believe that Gandhi's greatest insight was recognizing early in the twentieth century that a new type of ethics was emerging in the world—an ethics grounded not in *rules*, but in *empathy*. It was a change that was necessary as human society grew increasingly complex. In the past, when people lived in homogenous communities and rarely moved far from their birthplaces, rule-based ethics had been adequate to govern human relations. But the world had become too fast-paced and interconnected for rule-based ethics. There were too many interactions in which rules were outdated and belief systems clashed. The new circumstances demanded that people become more ethically self-guiding: People had to be able to put themselves in the shoes of those around them. Those who could not navigate situations in which rules were changing or could not master the skills of empathetic understanding would find themselves unable to manage their behavior wisely and ethically; increasingly, Drayton asserted, they would be seen as "loose cannons" and marginalized within society.

Gandhi wasn't responsible for these changes, but he recognized them. "It was a deeply egalitarian transformation. Empathy had become a powerful new force in the world," adds Drayton. "And Gandhi fashioned political instruments that made that new force really have *political bite*. He saw that what you've got to do is make people face up to the fact that they are not treating other people equally. Once you do that, they can't continue doing it and still respect themselves."

How did he do it?

Gandhi's 1930 Salt March was perhaps the greatest example of his strategy in action. The ostensible goal of the march was to protest the salt tax and the British law that prohibited Indians from making their own salt. The plan was for Gandhi to walk 241 miles to the sea to pick up some salt from natural deposits—an illegal act—at which point the British would arrest him. Gandhi knew that the salt tax had been bitterly despised since the time of the Moguls.[2]

"It just makes the hair on the back of your neck stand up when you visualize what he did," explains Drayton. "It was illegal for the press to cover. But by walking to the sea, of course everyone in India knew about it and there was drama building up from day to day. And of course the British arrested him, and there then was this incredible wave of thousands of people [more than 60,000] being arrested for this very simple act of making salt. In the Bombay salt flats, wave after wave of the Congress Party workers would come up and be hit over the head and shoulders by this very violent metal-tipped hinged club. You can almost hear the thump of these hinged clubs on the unprotected bodies of the Congress workers. They would fall to the ground and other Congress workers would come up with stretchers and women would help take them off. And then the next line would come along. This was an incredible demonstration of self control and strength and nonviolence. And it confronted the British and the world with a morality play. It was part of the process of getting Indians to feel that they were not inferior. Quite to the contrary. Not that they are superior, but that this is a superior *ethic*. It's a universal ethic but one that, historically, is especially characteristic of Indian society. And to the British, of course, he was saying, 'This is an ethic that you as a society of laws, in fact, believe in.' Now please live up to your beliefs."

* * *

After high school, Drayton enrolled in Harvard College. He remained marginally involved in the civil rights movement, organizing busloads of students who integrated picket lines in front of segregated businesses in Maryland.

As his interest in India deepened, he became fascinated by the ancient emperor Ashoka, who ruled from 269 to 232 BCE.

Ashoka had undergone a stunning transformation early in his reign. After enlarging his empire through war and unifying much of the Indian subcontinent, he suddenly became stricken with remorse. He renounced armed conquest and, for the duration of his life, propagated the values of nonviolence, proper treatment of servants and animals, and generosity toward all beings.[3]

In Drayton's view, what distinguished Ashoka from other historical figures were, again, his "how-tos." Ashoka established what was effectively the world's first large-scale class of civil servants devoted to public welfare. These workers built up India's Grand Trunk Road, an ancient travelers' route extending from Afghanistan to West Bengal, placing watering sheds, rest houses, and shade trees along much of its length. They established hospitals for people and animals, food-for-work programs in the spirit of today's workfare, and land settlement programs comparable to the Kibbutzim in Israel.

Ashoka was also a global-minded leader, fostering long-distance trade and dispatching ambassadors to other empires. He played a seminal role in the spread of Buddhism. In fact, the oldest independent evidence of the existence of Buddhism are Ashoka's inscriptions.[4] Although himself a Buddhist, Ashoka tolerated other religious sects and guaranteed freedom of religion throughout his empire.

"He was a practical creator on as giant a scale as anyone in history," comments Drayton. "He realized the economic power of the continental scale empire and he used that power for social purposes."

At Harvard, Drayton established a weekly gathering that he called the *Ashoka Table*, inviting prominent government, union, business, and church leaders—"people running real things"—to off-the-record dinners at which students had the opportunity to ask "how things really worked."

In the summer of 1963, Drayton, then twenty, finally made it to India. Before leaving, he sought advice and introductions from numerous India experts, including Bayard Rustin, the U.S. civil rights leader who had counseled Martin Luther King Jr. in Gandhian nonviolence during the Montgomery bus boycott of 1955–56.

Rustin gave Drayton a letter of introduction to Jaya Prakash Narayan, one of India's leading political figures, who in turn put him in touch with Vinoba Bhave, the social reformer known as India's "walking saint."[5] Bhave had been one of Gandhi's key disciples. After Gandhi's assassination in 1948, Bhave continued to seek ways to promote nonviolence and self-reliance, and he chose to focus on land reform.

Bhave didn't believe that the government could achieve land reform peacefully. For him, the way was to change people's hearts. So, in 1951, he launched his *bhoodan* (land gift) movement, which later grew into his *gramdan* (village gift) movement. Although he was fifty-five at the time and suffered from malaria and a stomach ulcer, Bhave began walking across India, ten to twelve miles a day, teaching villagers about nonviolence and exhorting them to transfer portions of land to a cooperative ownership system to support landless people and "untouchables," the poorest of India's poor.

By 1960 Bhave's efforts had led to the voluntary redistribution of 7 million acres of land, an area larger than Massachusetts, Delaware, and Rhode Island combined.

Drayton traveled to Orissa, in eastern India, to join Bhave's encampment for a few weeks. Each morning Bhave and his group of fifteen to thirty "constructive workers" set out walking at 2:30 A.M. After a few hours they would stop and silently observe the sunrise. For Drayton, these walks during the cool morning hours were "completely magical."

Then Bhave and his colleagues would continue to a designated village. As they drew close, Drayton would watch as multitudes converged from all directions. When Bhave reached the village boundary, the local leaders would lead him under a palm arch and offer him the "light of the village" (a ceremonial honor). Then Bhave would hold a silent prayer service only for children. "You could hear a pin drop," Drayton recalled. "I have never seen such large numbers of children—thousands—behave that way so consistently."

Bhave's volunteers would then break into groups and negotiate with locals for "village gift."

In the heat of the afternoons, sitting together on a *charpoy*, a small bed or couch, Drayton would question Bhave about nonviolence. "Vinoba was very patient with me and adjusted to my level of understanding," he recalled.

It was clear that Bhave was a sophisticated thinker. He could be as calculating as any beltway insider. Yet he remained, at his core, a humble man, and villagers responded overwhelmingly to him. "He had a—

force—about him," Drayton said, not quite satisfied with the word "force." "He was not only a political liberator, but a psychological liberator. He knew he had the ability to reach out and help people make heroic life decisions in a large part through his example. And like all good leaders he made people feel bigger, not smaller. I came away with great respect for him. I understood his intelligence on the analytical level. And I saw him as a living saint.

"Today I would probably see him as a social entrepreneur."

As Drayton's interests in Gandhi, King, Ashoka, and Bhave converged, another influence was soon added. As an undergraduate at Harvard, Drayton took a class with David C. McClelland, who had recently published his landmark book *The Achieving Society*, which, among other things, explored the motivational qualities of entrepreneurs.

McClelland, a psychologist, defined three dominant human motivations—need for *power*, need for *affiliation*, and need for *achievement*—and developed techniques to measure them. What most interested him was the need for *achievement* which he found correlated with entrepreneurship.

McClelland found that individuals with a high need for achievement tended to be less influenced than others by suggestions as to what they should do, think, or believe. They were "oriented forward in time toward longer-range goals, even when that means foregoing immediate pleasures."[6] They were less conforming and cared less about public recognition. What influenced them most in engaging problems were facts. They preferred the counsel of experts to friends.[7] They were not gamblers. They tended, in fact, to be conservative in games of chance and daring in games of skill, at which they usually overestimated their chances of success. While others viewed entrepreneurs as risk takers, McClelland noted that they did not see themselves this way. They typically accepted challenges only when they perceived that there was an acceptable chance of success and when the main determinant of success was their skill.[8] And, contrary to common assumption, McClelland asserted that entrepreneurs were motivated primarily by the sense of achievement rather than a desire for money. Profits were important because they gave the entrepreneur "definite knowledge" of his or her competence.[9] But real satisfaction for the entrepreneur came from making the world conform in a very specific way to his or her will.

In much of this, Drayton recognized himself.

* * *

After graduating from Harvard, Drayton studied economics, public finance, and history at Oxford University, then enrolled in Yale Law School, where he founded Yale Legislative Services, a program that matched students with lawmakers in six states to help them craft intelligent social policy. At its peak, the organization involved a third of the law school's student body.

During this period, the late 1960s, Drayton also suffered a series of personal losses. His mother, Joan, passed away suddenly from cancer; his older cousin, Thornton, who had been like a second father to him, suffered a stroke that left him barely able to communicate; and in early 1969 Drayton had to sever an eight-year relationship with a Czech woman whom he had met on a trip to Eastern Europe in 1960. (After the Soviets invaded Czechoslovakia in 1968, Drayton believed that continued contact with the woman and her family would have placed them in jeopardy.)

Drayton responded by concentrating his energies and thoughts in the area where he could exert most control: his work.

"I just buried it all," he told me. "I didn't want to have any more of it."

During the first half of 1970s, he worked chiefly in McKinsey & Company's public practice ("to learn how institutions work," he says), taking leave to teach at Stanford's Law School and Harvard's Kennedy School of Government. As a management consultant, Drayton focused on public issues such as housing, unemployment, and minority economic development. He led a team that reworked the mechanism for environmental enforcement in Connecticut, removing the incentive for polluters to tie up cases in courts—the major hurdle in enforcement. (A number of those changes became part of U.S. environmental statutes.)

"Everything that Drayton did he worked to solve fundamentally," recalled Carter Bales, who hired him for McKinsey. "He taught me to look for the nonobvious ways to gain leverage times ten on an issue."

Drayton's achievements in Connecticut combined with his political contacts—he had worked on several campaigns—led to his appointment as assistant administrator of the Environmental Protection Agency (EPA) in 1977. That was when he began pushing through the "bubble."

When I asked Drayton to explain the "bubble" to me, he explained that he would first have to provide a little background information about pollution regulation. "Imagine a factory, an auto plant," he began.

"It gives off particulates and hydrocarbons, basic air pollution, *bad stuff*. There might be a hundred different processes in the plant that release air pollution: paint-spray booths, degreasing operations, and so forth. The way the regulatory system works is that there is a process that goes into motion for paint-spray booths, for degreasing operations, and for all the other ninety-eight sources that give off hydrocarbons, and each one of those processes involves a long administrative procedure: proposal, comment, revision, and so forth.

"The typical outcome is a regulation that applies to all paint-spray booths across the industry. In the meantime, a separate group of people are producing a regulation on a different time schedule for degreasing operations—which also deals with hydrocarbons—but they are focused on a different technology.

"The net result is a hundred different regulations that apply to a hundred different processes in the same plant that were written by different teams of people at different times that don't take one another into account.

"Now, the cost of removing one pound of hydrocarbons from the air differs markedly from one process to another. It is not uncommon to find a cost differential of a hundred to one. So, say in one process it costs $100 and in another it costs $1.

"It is immediately obvious that if you allow the factory to come back to you with a counterproposal so that if they can get more of the $1 pounds out they can stop taking $100 pounds out, they are saving an *oodle* of money. They have a big incentive to do this. One good thing that happens is that this lowers the cost of achieving any given level of pollution reduction. Lowering the cost means lowering political opposition. It also means eliminating a lot of crazy—i.e., politically costly—examples that inevitably come out of the application of rules to concrete cases."

The bubble was the framework that would make this possible. The basic idea was to imagine a bubble over a factory. Within it engineers had to limit total emissions in accordance with the law. The difference was that they could make proposals to the government about how to do it. They could offset one internal source against another, provided that the net result was as clean and enforceable as the government's standard. And any savings was theirs to keep.

The bubble wasn't a new concept. Economists had been debating its merits for years, but the discussion remained theoretical.[10] In 1977, when Drayton, age thirty-three, arrived at the EPA, he resolved to make it real. "I came to the EPA with a very strong sense that the environment was

Bill Drayton explaining the "bubble" at an EPA press conference, 1979

built on a politically flawed and failing foundation," he explained. "I had experienced 'environmental reaction' in Ohio, Connecticut, and New York City. The field was on the defensive more than able to move ahead. Without a change in the underlying political balance, as long as the cost of pollution reduction and abatement increased, the inevitable consequence would be increased human exposure to pollution."

As Drayton saw it, the key to changing the political dynamic was to make it more attractive for business to fight pollution than to fight the EPA. One way to do this was to give plant managers and engineers—the people in the best positions to develop new pollution control technologies—economic incentives to do so. The prebubble regulatory system had not only failed to create such incentives, it had created negative incentives. "The last thing in the world that anyone from industry's side wanted was someone to find a new and better way of controlling pollution because then, given the law, they'd all have to go and spend money to implement it," explained Drayton.

The bubble didn't have to be confined to one factory. Depending on the natural sink of the pollutant, a bubble could encompass all the factories in a state or a country or even the world. Greenhouse gases need to be controlled at the global level, so what is needed is a system that encourages people to search for greenhouse gas–reduction opportunities anywhere on earth: a system that allows a company in, say, Ohio to clean up a smoke-spewing factory in Calcutta, or maintain a forest in Honduras, in exchange for not having to make a less significant change at home that might be ten times as costly. The mechanism to make it happen, Drayton believed, was a tough regulatory framework that freed the market to work.

There were many obstacles involved in putting the bubble into practice. Above all, the idea had to be sold. Many environmentalists were flatly opposed to using the market to achieve public policy goals. Hardliners did not feel that the government should have to consider the costs of pollution control.[11] Many in the EPA's air pollution program saw the bubble as a cave-in to big business, and some of the enforcement staff saw it as a budget threat. Nevertheless, in 1979 the bubble and pollution trading became U.S. environmental policy. Brian J. Cook, who chronicles the battle in his book, *Bureaucratic Politics and Regulatory Reform: The EPA and Emissions Trading,* details how Drayton, through his stubbornness and tenacity, his ability to recruit allies, and his mastery of the details, championed the bubble, pushing it through the system, changing the way the EPA worked, and gaining a "foothold" for the idea that is "not likely to be shaken."[12]

But it didn't end there.

In January 1981, following the election of President Ronald Reagan, Drayton left the EPA. That August he was contacted by a Republican senator on the Senate Environmental Committee, a Republican official at the Office of Management and Budget, and an employee in the EPA's personnel office, all of whom informed him (in confidence) that the Reagan administration was planning to destroy the EPA.

The administration had proposed a cascade of cuts that, within twenty months, would have reduced the EPA's budget by two-thirds. Reagan's new EPA administrator, Anne Gorsuch, was also planning personnel changes that would have resulted in 80 percent of the employees in the EPA's headquarters being fired, demoted, downgraded, or reshuffled—destroying the web of experience and relationships that made the institution effective.[13] The details were buried in a 3,000-page budget plan that the senator had leaked to Drayton as well as boxes of files Drayton had gotten hold of from the personnel office.

Having served as the EPA's head of planning and chief budget officer, Drayton understood the implications of the Reagan administration's plan. "They were essentially dismantling the key decision-making processes," he explained. "They couldn't win the policy fight, so they were going to destroy the institution. It was a very clever attack. The laws don't matter if you don't have the institution to enforce them."

The budget cuts were coming at a time when the EPA needed more, not less, money to do its job. In the late 1970s, Congress had passed a wave of new environmental laws regulating the use and disposal of toxic pollutants. The EPA's workload had effectively doubled. Under Gorsuch, however, life in the agency had become so unpleasant that staff attrition was running at 32 percent a year.[14]

"There I was sitting with all this information," recalled Drayton. "I don't like conflict. Fighting to defend something doesn't turn me on. I like to build things. But I had spent a good part of my professional life building the environmental institution at the municipal, state, and federal levels. And what they were doing was illegitimate; it was just *wrong*."

He contacted a *New York Times* reporter, Philip Shabecof, who wrote a front-page story.[15] The following day the *Washington Post* responded with its own front-page story.[16] And the ball was rolling. Drayton then set up an organization called Save EPA and began building a network of environmental managers to help. He set up a peer-review Facts Committee, which soon identified a sharp decline in enforcement cases sent to the Justice Department, as well as drops in voluntary compliance—both indications that the budget cuts were taking a toll on the environment.

The long-term impact of a budget cut does not lend itself to gripping journalism. However, Drayton put together a strong case to show that the cuts would effectively double Americans' exposure to toxic pollutants by 1990.[17] During the autumn of 1981 he spent six hours each day on the phone selling this case to editors, journalists, and environmentalists, triggering newspaper articles and editorials across the country. He even got industry magazines, such as *Chemical Week,* to recognize the dangers, by arguing that, in the absence of enforcement, companies that flouted environmental laws would enjoy a competitive advantage over those that abided by them in good faith. This would lead to an increase in pollution from industry and, inevitably, a public backlash. Drayton also cautioned that the Reagan-Gorsuch program could cause the EPA, under future administrations, to "swing back vigorously," becoming more rigid and adversarial with business.[18]

He funneled Save EPA's analysis to Democrats on the Hill, along with strategy briefs on how to exploit the Reagan administration's weakness on the environment. That October Congress hastily convened a hearing on the issue. Then, in January 1982, as Congress reconvened, Save EPA went on the offensive. "We planned a 'Let's destroy their credibility' week," Drayton recalls. They prepped ABC news for an exposé. Drayton met with Garry Trudeau, and for a week the destruction of the EPA was the subject of the *Doonesbury* comic strip. Drayton also met with Russell Train, who had been the EPA administrator from 1973 to 1977, and showed him a list of people who had been squeezed out of the agency. Train wrote an op-ed piece for the *Washington Post* under the headline "The Destruction of EPA."[19]

"It was a catalytic week," Drayton recalled. "We were able to tip the presumption in our favor. The general assumption afterward was that something really bad and probably illegal was going on."

Over a secret breakfast meeting, as Drayton recalls, one of Reagan's advisors confided: "Political people don't care about the environment. But they're not against it. They just want to win politically. So you just have to make it obvious to them that this is going to be political torture until they stop."

Drayton took the advice. For the next three years, as soon as the administration unveiled its budget plan, Save EPA was all over it: getting advance copies of the figures, analyzing them, showing the impact on the environment, and getting the message to the press. Eventually the Senate acted to halt further budget cuts to the EPA. Meanwhile, Congress discovered serious abuses of power within the agency, and Gorsuch was forced to resign. It was no victory to be sure: The EPA had lost a third of its funding (some of which was restored under George Bush Sr.'s presidency).

"They did tremendous damage," Drayton says. "But it could have been a lot worse."

By the late 1990s, it was reported that the emissions-trading provisions in the 1990 Clean Air Act had brought significant reductions in sulfur dioxide pollution, the source of acid rain.[20] By 1997 emissions trading had become one of the central features of the Kyoto Protocol, the leading international framework to address global warning.[21] In July 2003 the European Parliament agreed to launch the world's first international global emissions-trading market, which will be used to curb carbon dioxide emissions from 10,000 companies (responsible for 46 percent of

Doonesbury Comic Strip, January 25–28, 1982

emissions in the European Union). The market, which will begin operating in January 2005, is the centerpiece of the EU's strategy to meet its commitments under the Kyoto Protocol (which include an 8 percent reduction from 1990 emissions levels by 2010). The emissions-trading market is expected to reduce the costs of achieving this target by 35 percent.[22]

"Concepts that Bill was advocating twenty-five years ago, that were considered radical cave-ins by the environmental movement, are today advocated by nearly everybody as better ways to control pollution," explains Jodie Bernstein, the former director of the Federal Trade Commission's Bureau of Consumer Protection, who worked with Drayton at the EPA. "Bill was a very, very significant force in changing the way the government went about carrying out the environmental mission."

After I met Drayton, I began researching the bubble and emissions trading. I went through newspapers and magazines and searched the Internet. I found hundreds of reports and articles on the subject, but very little linking Drayton to the initial demonstration and marketing of the idea. It would have been easy to conclude that emissions trading was one of those ideas whose "time had come." There was no indication that it had been fought for with dogged persistence by an unusually determined and creative individual.

Why Was I Never Told about This?

In the early 1980s, while Drayton was managing Save EPA and working at McKinsey half time, he continued making regular trips to India to build Ashoka. In 1982 he traveled to Indonesia to begin laying the groundwork for a second-country launch. In Indonesia, under the dictatorship of Suharto, social entrepreneurship was far riskier than in India, so Ashoka's first consideration was: Do no harm.

Ashoka's board member Bill Carter had taken an exploratory trip to Indonesia in 1980. He put Drayton in touch with Fred Hehuwat, the founder of the Green Indonesia Foundation, one of Indonesia's first private environmental organizations. "He was getting away with it," recalled Drayton. "But we knew it was going to be a tricky environment. We had to go through the most amazing hoops to get approval to operate there." With Hehuwat's help, Drayton set out on another marathon series of meetings and accumulated a new stack of three-by-five cards.

In India Drayton had encountered unforeseen problems. The local volunteer committee that he had formed to oversee Ashoka's program turned out to be riven with conflicts. In Indonesia he made special efforts to assemble what he hoped would be a more compatible committee, but he ran into similar problems. He also discovered that Indonesian cultural sensitivities made it difficult to say no to anyone. Ashoka had to find some way to turn down candidates without its nominators and staff "losing face."

Another delicate matter was money. Drayton didn't want Ashoka to be lumped into the "funder" box. He and his staff struggled to avoid using the words "grant," "donor," or "foundation" because he felt such terms were associated with negative perceptions—lack of trust, an expectation of not being treated as a peer—that were unfavorable to building a collaborative fellowship. "Financial relationships are very troubling, because it means that the other relationships are not 100 percent voluntary," notes Drayton. He also didn't want to have the unintentional effect of helping fellows to create institutions that might not be "financially realistic."

After much consideration, it was decided that fellows should receive "stipends" to cover personal expenses, allowing them to quit their jobs and focus full time on their ideas. The standard for duration was "long enough to give the social entrepreneurs the opportunity to launch and begin marketing their ideas and establish their own financial base." Stipends could run anywhere from under a year to four years, but the average length turned out to be three years. The amounts were pegged to social-sector salaries in each country, with some flexibility to accommodate fellows' specific needs, such as if a fellow needed to hire a special care worker to look after a disabled child. Ashoka placed no restrictions on the use of stipends; they were not investments in a project but in a person.

Back home, Drayton had his own funding problems. At foundation offices, eyes glazed over when he spoke of "social investments" in "entrepreneurs." It didn't help when he likened Ashoka's approach to venture capital. As board member Julien Phillips recalled: "We were worried: 'If we use the term 'entrepreneur,' would we turn everybody off who's sort of leftist-inclined? Or was the whole point to help people reevaluate and give new value to entrepreneurial qualities when they're not used in pursuit of profit?"

Without support from large foundations, Drayton and the board members pursued individual leads. One of Drayton's college friends, Mack Lipkin, provided early funding and introduced him to two other funders, John Klingenstein and William Golden. Golden, a successful investment banker who has played a pivotal role shaping America's scientific institutions, was a particularly important ally. However, when Drayton first approached him for support, Golden's response was: "I don't believe in India. I believe in *you*."

One group that appreciated Drayton's approach was his McKinsey colleagues. In 1982 two McKinsey consultants, Thomas J. Peters and Robert H. Waterman Jr., published the runaway business best-seller *In Search of Excellence*, which looked at some of the most successful American companies. Although the authors had not originally intended to write a book about leadership, they couldn't avoid the fact that many of the companies they examined seemed "to have taken their basic character under the tutelage of a very special person" and had done so "at a fairly early stage of their development."[1] Moreover, Peters and Waterman found that excellent companies systematically supported "idea champions" within their ranks, granting latitude and channeling resources to unconventional thinkers who demonstrated unusual creativity and perseverance. They quoted the management expert Peter Drucker, who had observed: "Whenever anything is being accomplished, it is being done . . . by a monomaniac with a mission."[2]

Drayton said the same held true with social change: The way to promote innovation was to nurture idea champions. "Let's find these people," he said. "We should be investing in them now—when they are shaky and lonely and a little help means the world."

It was slow going.

"For the first five years of Ashoka," Drayton recalled, "I could not get one public foundation in the United States to support us with one cent. *None.* It was not that this is a bad idea or because I was inarticulate. It was not because I was not well known. I had just come out of being assistant administrator at EPA and had a good reputation from that. Not one of them would risk any money on this idea. How could they *miss* it?

"This is the experience of our fellows over and over and over again."

Then, one afternoon in October 1984, Drayton received an unexpected telephone call informing him that he had been awarded a MacArthur Fellowship, worth $200,000 over five years. William Golden had nominated him. "It was the last week of the Mondale campaign, which was a very sad and trying period for me," Drayton recalled. "I had just spent several years on the Save EPA effort trying to stop the Reagan administration from tearing down everything that we had built, and now the election was looking hopeless for the Democrats. It was wonderful timing."

Not long afterward, Drayton went on leave from McKinsey and hit the road. He was soon traveling seven or eight months of the year, spending weeks at a time in cities and villages in India and Indonesia, interviewing candidates, building a nominator network, and developing a reliable "search and selection" process for social entrepreneurs.

Drayton was meticulous about quality, and he was willing to go slowly to find the right people. "For a long time, we sort of limped along in terms of very small and low paid staff and a very low rate of growth," recalled board member Julien Phillips. "And if you didn't know Bill, you could imagine that this was going to be an invisible marginal endeavor forever."

But from the outset, Drayton seemed to have more belief in his vision than in what was actually on the ground at any one time. That, at least, is how it appeared to Michael Northrop, a twenty-six-year-old Princeton graduate whom Drayton hired in 1985 to run Ashoka's operation in Washington, D.C. Northrop had just come off a two-year stint as a corporate finance analyst. He was captivated by Drayton and agreed to join him. At the time, Ashoka had a few volunteers on staff in Washington and a global budget of about $200,000. By the end of 1985, it had elected just thirty-six fellows.

Northrop found that Drayton had the ability to make it seem as if he had an army behind him, when the reality was closer to a couple of foot soldiers. Like many entrepreneurs, the sheer force of his belief in his ideas seemed to lend them a quality of inevitability. He was also like a "magician pulling rabbits out of a hat" when it came to generating new funding leads and contacts. But Ashoka desperately needed a stronger organization in Washington to back him up. So Northrop focused on systems. He worked on fundraising, strengthened the organization's database of fellows, created budgeting tools, and, with the little money he had, built up the staff. He was joined by Miriam Parel, a Brazilian woman who had studied business management and civil engineering, and Michael Gallagher, a friend of a friend who had studied cultural anthropology and just returned from a Rotary fellowship in Cameroon.

For Northrop, working closely with Drayton was simultaneously thrilling and exasperating. Drayton was extraordinarily creative and was willing to give his young staff considerable responsibility, but he was also a perfectionist and stubborn as they come. He was also extremely frugal with Ashoka's budget. He was particularly concerned about maintaining a culture of thriftiness given the wastefulness of so much foreign aid.

So when Northrop wanted to buy computers, Drayton asked why typewriters weren't good enough. When a better photocopier was requested, Drayton insisted that a cost-benefit analysis first be conducted.

There were many such frustrations. But, at the end of the day, Northrop stuck around because he believed that Drayton "really had developed a methodology that could find the most valuable human resource that exists in the world." And Northrop could think of no better opportunity to contribute to the well-being of the planet than by helping to institutionalize and support that system.

In 1984 Ashoka got a break when Peter Goldmark—who became head of the Rockefeller Foundation in 1988—was asked by the Rockefeller Brothers Fund (RBF) to help craft its strategic plan. Goldmark had been an early supporter of Ashoka. Not long afterward, RBF became the first "blue-chip" foundation to support Ashoka. Although not one of the larger foundations, RBF was well respected. Once RBF had given its support, other foundations became more receptive. "This may sound crazy," says Drayton, "but they made it safer for other people. The risk factor had been cut in half because everyone could now say, 'We made the same mistake that RBF did.'"

The timing was propitious. In 1985 Brazilians had elected their first civilian president in twenty years and Drayton was eager to expand into Latin America. In 1986 he and Miriam Parel traveled to Brazil to scout for leads. Having learned his lesson, Drayton vowed: "No more committees." This time they would find one suitable country representative and just start electing fellows.

They were lucky to find Leni Silverstein, a feisty American anthropologist who'd lived in Brazil for years. Silverstein, forty-two, had received a Ph.D. from the New School for Social Research in New York, specializing in the Afro-Brazilian religion of candomblé. Having developed the first graduate gender studies course in Brazil and inaugurated the Ford Foundation's women's programs in the country, Silverstein also would bring a much-needed feminist perspective into an organization then dominated by men. Soon after an interview with Drayton in a Chinese restaurant, she was running Ashoka Brazil out of her home in Rio.

"It was totally nuts," Silverstein recalled. "People were coming to my house at all hours of the day and night to inquire about Ashoka. I had two daughters. My husband was getting very upset."

Silverstein had access to an apartment that she could use as an office, but it needed a phone—and installing a line in Rio cost $2,000. When she asked Drayton for the money, he resisted.

"We had a horrific fight," Silverstein recalled. "We were in a taxi. I told the driver to stop and I got out of the car and said: 'If you don't buy me a phone, I quit!'"

Silverstein got her phone. By the end of 1986, Ashoka had elected its first Brazilian fellows.

Back in Washington, Ashoka's young staffer Michael Gallagher had been listening to Drayton talk about social entrepreneurs for a year, but it was only after he had attended his first selection panel in Brazil that he "got it." "That was an 'aha' experience for me," he recalled. "I saw that Bill had deeply thought through the question: 'How do you find these people?'" Gallagher took it upon himself to document Ashoka's process for interviewing and screening social entrepreneurs.

* * *

In 1986 Brazil was emerging from the long enforced shadow of military rule. Social entrepreneurs were beginning to turn up everywhere—in the Afro-Brazilian community, in the gay community, in the disability community, in the women's movement. "It was perfect timing," recalled Candace Albertal Lessa, who succeeded Silverstein as Ashoka's Brazil representative in 1988. "Brazil was just opening up to democracy. The NGO [nongovernmental organization] network was moving toward social change organizations rather than just political movements. There were a lot of lonely people with no money, and suddenly Ashoka came in funding people who were taking provocative stances vis-à-vis the status quo.

"But people were also skeptical," Lessa added. "At first, they thought Ashoka was like the CIA. Who was this strange American coming in and interviewing everyone?"

That was the initial concern of Peter Lenny, a left-leaning, Portuguese-English interpreter based in Rio de Janeiro who received a call one day requesting an "emergency replacement" for a finicky North American.

Lenny's first job with Drayton was a five-hour interview with a stonemason from a village in the south of Brazil. "He'd developed this novel way to convert low-class housing into a reasonable neighborhood," Lenny recalled. "In the end, he wasn't selected; he wasn't really a social entrepreneur. He didn't have the awareness of the potential of his own idea."

In time Lenny got over his skepticism. As he continued working with Drayton, he began to recognize patterns in the way he interviewed people. He saw that Drayton would press forward with, say, a peasant farmer who knew how to work with people, but he tended to shy away from academics. One of Drayton's acid tests was to ask a how-to question in very specific practical terms in order to see if the person would respond in similarly practical terms (good) or go off on a tangent or give a theoretical answer (not good).

The experience did more for Lenny than teach him how to recognize social entrepreneurs. If not for Ashoka, Lenny says he probably would have left Brazil and returned to live in England.

In the mid-1980s Lenny, like many Brazilians, had begun to lose hope in Brazil's future. After the dictatorship fell, the media turned its focus to corruption, inflation, and crime. It seemed unlikely that free elections and a new constitution would produce genuine social change. "Brazil is very big," Lenny says. "You don't hear about anything that happens at the microlevel. The whole idea that there was this ongoing social activity—these people doing great things—was just totally invisible. No one from the middle class sets foot in a *favela* [slum]. And if you hear anything about any sort of social change organization, it's just through the strangest chance, through your maid or a taxi driver."

Through Ashoka, Lenny discovered the work of social entrepreneurs across Brazil, people like Mary Allegretti, who was working to protect the Amazon rain forest from deforestation, while ensuring a livelihood for local Indians and rubber tappers; Silvia Carvalho, an early childhood educator in São Paulo, whose organization, Crecheplan, was improving day care for poor children; Marilena Lazzarini, who had launched a consumer protection movement with her organization, Instituto Brasileiro de Defesa do Consumidor (IDEC); João Jorge Rodrigues, who was turning the percussion band Olodum, in Salvador, Bahia, into a vehicle to activate the political consciousness of Afro-Brazilians; Suely Carneiro, an Afro-Brazilian woman whose organization, Geledés, was laying the foundation for a black women's movement; Ana Vasconcelos, whose Casa de Passagem was focusing national attention on the problem of female child prostitution; Ismael Ferreira, whose cooperative, Associação dos Pequenos Agricultores do Município de Valente (APAEB), was connecting poor sisal growers in rural Bahia to international markets; Normando Batista Santos, whose network of community-run schools were reaching remote areas in northeast Brazil; Vera Cordeiro, who had founded the Associação Saúde Criança Renascer to address a hidden gap in the health-care system; and Fábio Rosa, who was delivering electricity to poor people in rural Brazil.

"Suddenly," recalled Lenny, "I had this view of *another* Brazil—nation-wide—in all sorts of areas—through Ashoka's selection process. And what I saw in a short while I wouldn't have seen if I'd lived in Rio and read the newspapers for ten years.

"And I thought, 'Why was I never *told* about this?'"

Ten—Nine—Eight—Childline!

Jeroo Billimoria, India: Child Protection

As the plane approached the runway, I pressed my face to the window to survey the massive shantytown below. It looked like a sea of rotting wood and rusting tin. I had traveled to Bombay to interview Jeroo Billimoria, the founder of Childline, a twenty-four-hour helpline and emergency response system for children in distress. Millions of children in India live on the streets and work as underage laborers. As I scanned the sprawling slum, I imagined emergency calls ringing in to Childline from similar slums across the city—thousands of calls—reporting injuries, abuse, abandonment, assault, tuberculosis, dysentery, jaundice, AIDS—and I could not begin to fathom how, in the chaos of Bombay, such a system could possibly work.

According to the reports on my lap, however, Childline had begun operating in Bombay in 1996; in 1998 it had branched out to other cities. By March 2000 it was operating in eleven cities. By 2002 it was in thirty.

I had spoken to Jeroo once by phone before my arrival to firm up the details of my visit. (I refer to her by her first name, as she is generally known.) It sounded as if she were standing in a schoolyard at recess. She asked for my flight information. "I'll send one of the street boys to the airport to pick you up," she yelled over the din. "He'll take you to the beach. We're having a conference. You're lucky. You'll get to meet all the boys."

As promised, Laxman Halale, twenty-one, whom Jeroo had met in a boy's shelter years earlier, was waiting at the terminal brandishing a yellow Childline poster. He had run away from home at the age of eleven and had been a Childline "team member" since 1996. He hoisted my bag

Jeroo Billimoria

like a veteran porter and hailed one of Bombay's black-and-yellow bowler-hat taxis. Soon we were stuck in a brown haze of horn-blaring traffic.

After two hours, we arrived at a camp with bunk houses and a view of a golden sunset over the Indian Ocean. The taxi stopped in front of a dining hall. I heard laughter and applause and the buzz of conversations in many languages: English, Hindi, Bengali, Telugu, Tamil, Marathi. Inside, a group of eighty people, most of them youths who had lived for years on the streets, kneeled, squatted, and sprawled across one another. They were in a large circle. All attention was fixed on Jeroo, thirty-six, in

69

the center, barefoot, dressed in a *salwar kameez* and *dupatta* that waved like a cape as she moved.

"When contacting police, at what level should you call?" speaking in Hindi, she was asking the youths.

"Don't go to senior officials. Go to constables or ward boys," a young man from Jaipur replied.

"We have workshops with police," Jeroo said. "We must work more closely with them. What else?"

"When you go to a police station," added a Calcuttan, "you need to find a particular constable who is sensitive to children and begin working with him first."

"It's important to begin working first with the constables who are child sensitive," Jeroo reiterated.

The conference was a training workshop for Childline "team members" from across India. The team members were Childline's front line. Backed up by social workers, the youths responded to calls, providing information to other street youths, transporting street children to shelters, hospitals, or police stations, documenting calls, and working with Childline partners to match children with necessary services. Not only did they carry out much of Childline's work, they defined the organization's priorities and policies.

"How do you deal with a case of HIV or a death?" Jeroo asked. "What if the hospital refuses to treat the child? What if police are unwilling to intervene?"

"The police commissioner is a member of our Childline Advisory Board (CAB)," explained a member of the Nagpur team. "So this makes it easier to work with them."

"Yes! Yes! Good! Every city has a CAB," Jeroo said. "This is one of the most important aspects of Childline. If you have a problem, the CAB can help.

"Remember," she added, speaking slowly. "Childline *cannot* work in isolation. We used to think we were great people—that we could do everything alone. Now we know better. Now we set up the CABs to facilitate things. The CABs include government officials, health department officials, railway officials, police officials. We work with them. When they begin to see that Childline can do what they cannot do and that Childline will make their jobs easier, they begin to readily cooperate."

She paused for a minute to let the information sink in, then proceeded with the next question: "Now, what do we do in a case of child abuse?"

"We rescue the child," said a team member from Madras (now called Chennai).

"First, we ensure the child's safety," Jeroo concurred. "What do we do with the abuser?"

"Our job is to rescue the child," explained a staff member from Madras. "It's not our job to deal with the abuser."

Jeroo spun around. "No!" she said. "We *must* deal with the abuser!" She scanned the circle to make sure everyone saw how serious she was.

"First, we have to rescue the child, get him or her to a safe place, and later try to rehabilitate him or her with the family. Our policy is that institutionalization is the last resort. But we will also make sure that people who abuse children get punished. *We will make sure they are locked up if necessary.* Offenders must not go scot free. And we'll go and get some compensation for the child. Set up a trust for the child. The offender *must* be made to pay.

"Childline is not a charity service or a welfare service," she added. "It is a *rights* service. We are not helping 'poor children.' I want to take the word 'poor' out of our vocabulary. If we take a charity approach, we will be here for 50,000 years and nothing will be different. We are a child rights service. Childline has to play the lead role in this!

"Now, what is the *most* important thing to remember in Childline?" Jeroo said, turning 360 degrees.

"EVERY CALL IS IMPORTANT" came the response from eighty voices.

"Every call is important," Jeroo echoed.

"A child may call us and it may seem like a prank," she said. "Or the child may speak abusively. But it is equally likely that the child is testing us to see whether we will take him or her seriously and deal with him or her politely. Someone who calls and hangs up may be testing us too.

"And remember," she added with a grin, "it may be *me* calling. You know I call up to test Childline. Sometimes I call and I say bad words or speak angrily to test out the service—and very often people speak bad words back to me!"

The hall erupted in laughter.

"So the next time you answer an angry caller, remember, it might be me!

"Now," she went on, "what is the first thing you do if you make a mistake?"

"ACKNOWLEDGE IT" came the group's response.

"Yes," Jeroo said. "Acknowledge it. Tell others you made the mistake. Then correct that mistake.

"Be passionate," Jeroo added, "but make decisions with your heads.

"Remember our mission: The child comes first. We don't work for the government. We don't work for any organization. We work for the child. The child comes first."

Jeroo paused to let it all sink in.

"Now, there are 400,000 most vulnerable kids living on the streets," she continued. "These are the main target kids we want to reach. How are we going to reach them *all*?"

From Hyderabad: "We have to tell them."

Another boy from the Hyderabad group, standing, clutching a stick by his side, spoke up. "I have lived on the streets, and I don't want other children to go through what I went through. So I make it a point to tell other children I meet about Childline. I have a little book which I always keep with me, and every time I tell a child I get them to sign my book and I give them a Childline sticker. I have four hundred names in my book."

Jeroo raised her hands and applauded.

"We have to reach out to all these children," she said. "But we have to think *how* we are going to do this. We are going to talk about this tomorrow morning. Not the professionals or the staff. This question is only for the children who have lived on the street and know what life is like. How are we going to reach them all? I want you to think about this tonight.

"Now finally, it's time to eat."

The group erupted in applause.

After dinner I spoke with Venkahnababu Vidyanagar, the boy with the stick and the notebook with four hundred names. He was eighteen. One leg was lame from polio. He came from the state of Andhra Pradesh in southern India and spoke Telugu, which for our talks was translated first into Hindi and then into English.

Venkahnababu had been abandoned by his parents when he was thirteen because they were too poor to care for him. He had lived on the streets of Hyderabad for a year shining shoes and working in a tea stall, where the owner let him sleep. Then he went to Bombay and was befriended by boys who lived in a railway station. They helped get him into a boy's shelter. After hearing about Childline, he became a team member, earning 1,200 rupees (about $30) a month, which he liked to spend on "fancy clothes" and movies. He loved *Titanic*.

Street kids, explains Jeroo, are savvy and tough, but in many ways naive. "They're easy to manipulate, and they have a strong chivalrous streak.

Young women can easily lure them into marriage. They want very badly to be loved. Many get married suddenly and in nine months *flat* there will be a baby. I am constantly telling the boys in the office that they *must* not get married right away. I tell them if they get married, I will *kill* them."

When I asked Venkahnababu if he had any contact with his family, he said no. Then he told a story: Several months earlier a stranger had approached him saying that Venkahnababu's mother was sick. The man said he needed 800 rupees (about $20) for medicine. Venkahnababu had had no contact with his mother since the day he had been abandoned. Still, he gave the man the 800 rupees. After that, the man returned twice; each time Venkahnababu gave him some more money.

A dozen team members huddled around as we spoke. When I asked Venkahnababu if his mother received the money, he said he didn't know. None of the other boys interrupted Venkahnababu; no one said, "He's cheating you," a thought that ran through my mind. I asked Venkahnababu if he wished to see his mother. "I might visit her sometime in the future," he said. "But only when she's feeling better. I am afraid to see her sick in bed." He looked at the ground, indicating that he wished to end the conversation.

On that cue, Deepak Kumar stepped forward. Deepak, also eighteen, grew up "somewhere in Punjab" and ran away from home at age ten after receiving a beating from his father. He ended up at a train station in Delhi, where some boys befriended him and taught him how to earn money by collecting and selling bottles and broken glass. A policeman picked him up and he was sent to a juvenile home, where the master administered beatings with a variety of implements, including a cricket bat. Deepak escaped and returned to the train station in Delhi. Eventually a friendly social worker helped him get into a good shelter. As a Childline team member, Deepak felt that his work was "worthwhile and important."

That night everyone gathered on the beach for what the boys described as a "cultural event." The stars were bright; the sea roared. Signs along the beach warned of a deadly undertow. The boys built a mammoth bonfire. Everyone joined hands in a circle and danced around the fire crossing over their feet and kicking their legs high in the fashion of a hora. There was no hanging back; a bystander was immediately swept into the celebration by many hands. After a while the dancing turned chaotic, with the boys knocking into one another with increasing gusto ever closer to the flames. In the excitement of the moment, they appeared not to have a worry in the world.

* * *

Jeroo Billimoria grew up in a prominent Bombay family in which the dominant profession was accounting. Her father, Mehervan—an accountant in a manufacturing firm—was cautious and conservative. Her mother, Homai—a social worker who counseled low-income children in public schools—was adventurous and liberal. As an undergraduate, Jeroo studied commerce. She was leaning toward a career in accounting but her father's death, when she was twenty, caused her to reevaluate her life plans.

Jeroo Billimoria with some of the children Childline works to assist

"My father was a very kind man," Jeroo told me. "He felt very strongly that you should focus on giving of yourself. And I found out after his death, despite his being so unwell—he had a heart and a lung condition—that he had helped many people living on the streets anonymously. We had queues of people who came to pay their respects. Even my mother did not know that he had silently supported these people through the years."

She decided to switch to social work. She enrolled in the Tata Institute of Social Sciences (TISS), India's premier college of social work, to do postgraduate studies and then studied nonprofit management at the New School for Social Research in New York City. In New York she also got involved with the Coalition for the Homeless, a nonprofit group that assists people living on the streets and in shelters. "I was very moved by the spirit of survival among the homeless," Jeroo recalled.

In 1989 she returned to India and traveled for six months before joining TISS as an instructor. A number of her graduate students were placed as social workers in Bombay's shelters. When Jeroo visited them, she found herself drawn to the children, especially to their honesty and resilience. "Street kids are tough and they speak their minds," she explains. "When they are sad you know it, and when they are happy or angry, you know it. It's very clear, but they don't hold on to it."

They needed to be acknowledged in small ways—by a smile or a touch—and they were easily hurt when they felt ignored. They were also very proud. Many of the street children worked hard to support their families in the villages. They would tell the social workers: "Don't take pity on us. We can earn our own money."

The children called Jeroo "Didi," an affectionate term for an older sister. In turn, she found herself developing a strong protective feeling for them. She gave out her home phone number—to be used in cases of emergency—but soon she was receiving calls on a daily basis. "That's when I learned how much street kids love the phone," she recalled. Sometimes the kids called just to say hello, sometimes they called because they were feeling sad and lonely. But when the calls came in the middle of the night it was because one of the kids had been injured, or fallen ill, or had been beaten up by an adult, often by a policeman.

Jeroo found that it could take days to find the necessary assistance for a child. Bombay had many children's agencies, but they had no mechanisms for working with one another or with the government. Jeroo approached several organizations and proposed the idea of coordinating services but found little enthusiasm for the idea. She decided to drop it for the time being. "The climate for networking among NGOs wasn't there yet," she recalled. "Or maybe I wasn't ready to take it on."

Instead, in 1991 she founded an organization called Meljol (Coming Together) to bring together children from diverse backgrounds to work, side by side, on projects with tangible social benefits: building playgrounds, cleaning up schools, campaigning against smoking. "The goal was to create an alternative mindset for children to give them a sense of their own power," she said.

By 1993 Jeroo was still receiving late night calls. It was obvious that the children needed an emergency service. This time she decided to see if she could convince the Bombay police to initiate one. After the police turned her down, she approached the government telecommunications department to explore the possibility of creating a toll-free number for children's assistance. "I went to the DOT [Department of Telecommunications] and just hung out and met people and asked how to do this," she recalled.

At the suggestion of one of the DOT's public relations officers, she arranged a meeting with the general manager. She brought along Armaity Desai, then the director of TISS. "The general manager said, 'We'll think about it. We'll get back to you,'" Jeroo recalled.

In the meantime, Jeroo followed up with letters to DOT officials in Bombay and Delhi. With the backing of TISS, the request made its way up to the Ministry of Telecommunications. The ministry was doubtful that children would use a hot line. However, Jeroo had conducted her own survey and almost all of the street children said they would use the service. "Today in India we have women's hot lines, hot lines for disability and drugs," Jeroo explains. "But in 1993 it was an absolutely new concept."

In fact, such a service had become feasible only because of three recent developments: (1) Public telephones had been widely installed in India's major cities; (2) the number of child service organizations had exploded; and (3) the government was receptive to the idea of forming partnerships with citizen groups.

The next major step, Jeroo concluded, was to improve coordination. The hundreds of child service organizations in Bombay were scattered. They didn't talk to one another. They also varied in quality. Some did wonderful work; some were incompetent; some were compassionate; some were abusive. It was hard enough for a full-time social worker to find the right assistance for a child in need. How was a street kid, a police officer, or a concerned citizen to know where to look for help? What was needed, Jeroo saw, was a system that would allow anyone who came across a child in distress anywhere in Bombay to take simple and immediate action to assist the child.

Jeroo recruited a team of students to compile a directory of child service organizations in Bombay. They listed a hundred organizations, including twenty-four-hour shelters and long-term residential institutions; organizations that offered legal, health, psychological, and educational services; organizations that provided disability rehabilitation, vocational training, and treatment for addiction; and many others. Next Jeroo set up meetings to encourage participation in a new network: Childline.

She put together a budget and set out to raise start-up funds. For the first year, she needed 250,000 rupees, about $6,000, to establish two call centers staffed by fifteen people. Initial support came from the Ratan Tata Trust and the Concern India Foundation. In May 1996 the government telecommunication department granted Childline use of the telephone number 1098. And a month later, with fourteen organizations having signed on, Childline was officially launched.

To create awareness about the service, Childline staffers, team members, and volunteers, mostly street children, targeted railway stations, bus stations, slum areas, bazaars, and hospitals. They organized fairs and outdoor plays. They encouraged youths to distribute yellow 1098 stickers and to test out the number, reporting any problems. They asked older street youths to teach younger ones. Jeroo wasn't crazy about "1098," but the kids taught her to say it as "Ten—nine—eight—Childline."

Childline's telephones are housed in organizations with twenty-four-hour shelters for emergencies. In Bombay, one such shelter is run by Youth for Unity and Voluntary Action (YUVA) and located near Dadar Train Station. In the front room of the YUVA shelter is a desk where the phones are manned. The day I visited, I met team members Ravi Saxena, Samir Sabu Sheikh, and Rupesh Kumar.

Ravi, nineteen, had run away from the city of Bhopal at the age of ten. "When I fell sick, there was no one to help me or take me to the hospital," he said. "In Childline, I have helped more than three hundred children." Samir, twenty, had gotten lost at age six and lived on the streets until he was put in a government home at age nine. And Rupesh, eighteen, had run away from his home in the state of Bihar at age ten to

Childline team member Manohardas spreading the word

escape an alcoholic father. All three were studying to take their tenth-grade exams. Each earned $30 to $40 a month from Childline.

The team members worked eight-hour shifts. They had each fielded hundreds of calls, and they each had dramatic stories to tell. One of Ravi's stories was particularly moving.

"Some boys called up Childline," he explained. "They said: 'There is a little girl in the station. She is standing all alone with no clothes on. Someone has thrown hot water on her. She has a burn all over her chest, stomach, and legs.'

"So a Childline volunteer went to take her to the hospital. But at the station, a drunk man came by and said he was her father. It turned out he was just a strange man who lives in the station. He wanted to use her to beg. The policeman wanted to hand the girl over to him.

"We had to go to the police station and argue and argue, explaining that the police couldn't just hand over the child. She needed medical care and the man was clearly drunk. Finally they gave in and we took her to the hospital to treat her burns. Then Childline petitioned the court to declare her destitute so she could be adopted. Now she's living in a children's institute. It takes about a year to get her adopted. She's small so she won't be difficult to get adopted. She didn't know her own name. We named her Seema."

During its first year Childline fielded 6,618 calls. More than 70 percent came from children and youths. Many called to chat, sing songs, ask questions, share feelings, and offer insults. The opportunity to make a free phone call was itself a major attraction.[1]

"It's their service," Jeroo reminded everyone. "They're testing us out."

Eight hundred fifty-eight calls were for direct emergency assistance: medical problems, need for shelter, abuse, repatriation of missing children, protection from police, and death-related services.[2] More than half of these calls were received between 5:00 P.M. and 10:00 A.M., when most children's agencies are closed. "I thought that we'd get a lot of calls about police abuse," Jeroo recalled, "but the boys said, 'No, you'll get a lot of health-related problems.' We weren't geared for that."

At first the calls came from children living on the streets. After some time Childline began receiving calls from concerned adults and children working as domestic servants in middle-class homes. "Initially I didn't want it to become a middle-class service," Jeroo recalled. "I wanted it focused on the street level. But then we got two cases from concerned adults about domestic child labor. One was about a girl named Sarita, who'd been severely beaten. She had cigarette burns all over her body. It showed us that people often observe abuse, but turn a blind eye because they don't know who to contact and don't want to get involved with the police. I saw that it was necessary to create awareness about the service amongst larger sections of the population."

The first year was all about making mistakes and correcting them, identifying gaps and filling them. Team members were having trouble locating callers, so a system of standard questions was introduced to note the time of call, specific landmarks, and the clothes the child was wearing. Childline volunteers were issued yellow T-shirts and caps.

After receiving angry calls because phones were not connecting to 1098 and the proprietors of pay phone concessions were being uncooperative, Childline enlisted street children to test phones around the city. The Department of Telecommunications also issued letters informing all pay phone managers that they were obligated to allow children to call 1098 at any time.

Team members who were having difficulty gaining the trust of runaways received trainings from social workers in telephone interaction.

Each month children were invited to Childline's "open house" to learn about the service and suggest improvements. Case by case, the system improved.

Meghana Sawant, the first of Jeroo's students to become an official Childline staff member, recalled a policy decision that was enacted after the death of an eighteen-year-old boy. "A call came in from a boy who had tuberculosis," she explained. "A team member went to take him to the hospital. But he said, 'I don't want to be admitted to the hospital. I'll be fine. If I need help I'll call Childline again.' So our team member left this boy on the platform. After three or four days, the boy expired. His friends who are very frequent callers started making abusive calls. They informed other people that Childline is a useless organization. So we went back to the place where our team member let the boy stay sick. His friends were very angry. They said, 'We don't want to have anything to do with Childline.' We and the team member apologized and said we made a mistake. We asked the boys to tell us what we should have done. They were still very angry. But after they calmed down, they gave a suggestion: 'If the boy says that he doesn't want to be hospitalized or go into a shelter then you should inform *us*, his friends. Let us know that you have left him on the street.'

"We thought that was a good suggestion," Sawant added. "So now that is our policy."

One night a call came in at 1:30 A.M. reporting that a boy had been hit by a taxi. A Childline team member rushed to the scene and took the child to the hospital only to be accosted by a policeman for seeking admission for a boy unknown to him. Jeroo had been pulled out of bed many times in such situations, and she'd learned not to be confrontational with police or hospital officials. "That was a big learning experience," she said. "It got you nowhere."

This time she contacted the Coordination Committee for Vulnerable Children, a municipal body, and Unicef, the United Nations agency charged with promoting the well-being of children, and got them to sponsor a conference, inviting members of the Juvenile Welfare Board and the Juvenile Aid Police Unit to learn about Childline.

Her goal was to build awareness about both 1098 and India's Juvenile Justice Act, which extends protections to all children under the age of eighteen.[3]

At the conference, Jeroo noticed that the police officials became receptive when they began to see that Childline would simplify their jobs. They agreed to participate in more workshops. Eventually Childline and the

Bombay police established a partnership, with the Juvenile Aid Police Unit issuing special identification cards to Childline team members.

Hospitals were another challenge. Medical staff regularly turned away kids who were dirty, without identification, or unaccompanied by an adult.

So Childline trained its staff in basic first aid and instituted a policy of cleaning up children before taking them to the hospital. Meanwhile, all staffers received training in Indian law, which stipulates that a public hospital cannot deny care to anyone in need of medical attention. Additional workshops were organized to sensitize hospital staff.

As word about 1098 spread, the network grew. Newspaper articles brought in tens of thousands of rupees in public contributions. Jeroo persuaded a local college of social work to develop a two-month telephone counseling course for staffers. She raised additional funding. Then, one day at the airport, she bumped into an executive from Tata Consultancy Services, one of India's leading management consulting firms, and persuaded him to help. His firm could design a database to track calls.

In November 1997 Jeroo took an unpaid leave from TISS to devote herself to Childline. Her plan was to create a national child protection system. Shortly thereafter she was elected an Ashoka fellow.

In February 1998 Jeroo sent a letter to Anand Bordia, the joint secretary of India's Ministry of Social Justice and Empowerment, proposing that the Indian government help extend Childline to other cities. "From the very beginning, I had envisioned Childline as a national service," Jeroo explained. "I knew we had to get the government involved. But first we needed to demonstrate it. And we needed documentation and statistics."

That June Childline organized a gathering, in conjunction with the government, inviting 117 people from twenty-nine cities to explore the potential for spreading the service. At the time, Childline had responded to 14,000 calls. It had arranged direct assistance for 3,505 children, including medical services (2,126 cases), shelter (988), information and referral to other agencies (249), repatriation (49), emotional support and guidance (39), protection from police harassment (30), protection from abuse (23), and death-related service (1).[4]

The government's rationale for supporting Childline was compelling. The service was doing many of the things that the Indian government had committed to when it ratified the United Nations Convention on the

Rights of the Child in 1992, such as promoting children's access to healthcare, justice, shelter, and education.⁵ Childline also had the hallmarks of a twenty-first-century organization. It was integrated and decentralized. It blended technology and human services. It linked government, business, and citizen groups to maximize efficacy. And, best of all, it was low cost, involving almost no bricks and mortar. Just about everything that Childline needed to work was already on the ground. At essence, Childline was about turning a city into a team.

Why not a country?

By the workshop's end, Anand Bordia and a colleague, A. P. Singh, the deputy secretary of the Ministry of Justice and Social Empowerment, agreed to help spread the service to ten cities. A month later Maneka Gandhi, India's minister of social justice and empowerment, declared that she wanted to see Childline in every Indian city with a population above 1 million (twenty-three cities) by 2002.⁶

It took only a few days to sketch out the general plan for national expansion. Childline would operate like a franchise, with decentralized management, but with a uniform brand, operating procedures, and standards. It would remain a free, national twenty-four-hour service. The word "Childline" would always be written both in English and translated phonetically into regional languages. (India has eighteen officially recognized languages.) The logo and the phone number would remain the same everywhere.

Each city would select organizations based on local needs but conform to a uniform structure: A "nodal" organization, a noted academic institution like TISS, would facilitate operations, training, documentation, and advocacy. "Collaborating" organizations, like YUVA, the shelter where I met Ravi, Samir, and Rupesh, would respond directly to calls. "Support" organizations would handle follow up, and "resource" organizations would assist with long-term needs.

Each city would have one Childline coordinator. The government would make grants to Childline partners to pay salaries for Childline social workers and team members placed in them. Each organization also would have to raise its own funds for Childline. Franchisees would receive training and promotional materials, a call-tracking database (in development), and, initially, one year's funding for out-of-hospital medical assistance to children.

Seeking to avoid conflicts with officials, Jeroo decided that Childline would not begin working in a city until the police commissioner and

senior healthcare officials had furnished written commitments of cooperation. Additionally, each city would be required to establish a Childline
Advisory Board made up of senior officials in the police and health
departments, the Juvenile Welfare Board, the Department of Telecommunications, and other key agencies.

Another policy that Jeroo adopted was that any business that wanted
to publicly associate itself with Childline at the national level would have
to commit to a full partnership. It would have to offer business expertise
and ongoing assistance—not just write checks.

Nationally, Childline would have a central office in Bombay to oversee
expansion, set standards, monitor results, allocate funds, and advocate
for better children's services.

Today the national hub of the Childline India Foundation is located in a
yellow municipal school in central Bombay, in a classroom crammed with
old mattresses and board games and a bunch of wild kids. "Our office is
a madhouse, *really*," Jeroo told me on the drive over after the beach conference. "I have to warn you. People will jump on you. We have three
kids who are high on glue. We tell them not to do it, but at least they
come in; otherwise they'd be on it eight hours a day."

Moments after we arrived at her office, Jeroo shifted into work mode.
She sat down cross-legged on the floor and took over one of the office's two
phones. A young boy crawled onto her lap, and she curled an arm around
him. Periodically—as when the secretary of the Ministry of Social Justice
and Empowerment called—she brought her fingers to her lips and whispered "shhh," but the gesture had no discernible effect on the noise level.

The room next door housed a quiet, squeaky-clean office, equipped
with networked computers and air conditioning, courtesy of Tata Consultancy Services. But Jeroo preferred the madhouse. "I think this office
gives you a sense of what Childline is all about," Jeroo said. "Everything
is happening—despite what may seem to be the case."

Meghana Sawant was testing the new ChildNet computerized call-
tracking system. Prakash Fernandes, sitting cross-legged on an old mat-
tress, was drafting the expansion plan. Both had been students of Jeroo's
at TISS. On the floor, also sitting with a child on her lap, was Neelam
Kewalramani, city coordinator for Childline Bombay, who was reviewing
a call report.

I asked Neelam how she had come to Childline. "I was working in a
nine-to-five job at the Indo-American Society, in a lavish setting, as a
counselor for students who wanted to go abroad for higher studies," she

Inside the Childline India Foundation office in Bombay

said. "These were mostly wealthy pampered kids. I thought: 'Do these people actually need me?' I realized I wasn't getting much satisfaction from my life. I said, 'Neelam, you're not meant for this.' A teacher referred me to Childline. I came to an open house here and I saw these kids enjoying themselves. I saw the volunteers. I was taken away by it."

Within six months of the June 1998 workshop, Childline had expanded to Delhi, Nagpur, Hyderabad, and Calcutta. Drawing on her contacts in Bombay's business community, Jeroo pulled in various corporate partners, including the advertising firm Ogilvy and Mather, which helped Childline develop a national branding and marketing campaign.

In each new city, the launch was similar. Local organizations began by meeting informally. With guidance from the Childline team, they formed a core working group. Then a Childline Advisory Board was assembled. Next the working group conducted a needs assessment survey and feasibility study and compiled a resource directory. After consulting with the advisory board, the NGOs determined who should staff the phones and who should provide follow-up support.

The central office screened all partner agencies, a critical role. "Initially in Bombay we worked with any organization," Jeroo explained. "But we made a lot of mistakes." One Childline office had to be shut down due to corruption. Another agency was dropped from the network because it refused shelter to disabled children. Others did not meet Childline's standards of care. "Now we look first at commitment and motivation," Jeroo added. "We make sure the organization has a crisis culture and a child rights orientation. We like to choose younger organizations that are self-sustaining and already working on children's issues. We don't want to build something new."

Prakash Fernandes, who handled much of the preparatory work in new cities, added: "In a collaborating agency, the first thing we look at is: Are they responsive and free with kids? We talk to the staff. It's very rare that we look at their reports—because they can put anything on paper. We look at how they *really* work. What are their processes? Intake policies? Are they flexible? Would they be willing to accept a child at 2:00 A.M.? What if the child doesn't have documentation?"

After the structure was defined, the phones were activated and the DOT communicated with pay phone operators across the city. Then, after locals had had two weeks' experience handling calls, a staffer from the national office came to conduct a ten-day training. Two or three months later, if all went well, the local franchise called a press conference and launched an awareness campaign. The national office monitored franchises closely for several months and, thereafter, through spot checks.

There were always problems. One of the most common was when a local organization claimed full credit for Childline. "In the NGO sector, a lot of people, especially senior people, don't like partnering," explains Jeroo. "My biggest task is making *everyone* feel that they own Childline."

By the spring of 1999, Childline had launched 1098 in Calcutta and Madras and was preparing to start up in Patna. Groundwork had begun in Bhopal, Bhubaneshwar, Calicut, Coimbatore, Guwahati, Gwalior, Jaipur, Lucknow, Panjim, Pune, Trivandrum, and Varanasi. (In one year Jeroo and her colleagues visited nineteen cities.)

There was a slight problem with the government, however: In six months, only one check had arrived. "It was a big crisis," Jeroo recalled. "For almost a year, we had no money from the government. I give hats off to the NGOs. We survived because we chose solid organizations. Even when there was no money they could carry the project on. And we kept talking with everybody, saying 'We're all in this together. . . .'"

Three times Jeroo had to turn to wealthy individuals to avert collapse.

In May 1999 Childline was registered as a government initiative and given national control over 1098. Jeroo persuaded the government to select a board of directors comprised of individuals who had demonstrated strong commitment to Childline, a key factor in the organization's success.

Within twelve months Childline was operating in fifteen cities and preparatory work had begun in another fifteen. It had fielded a half million calls.[7]

The ChildNet database system was an unusual computer program: It had been designed for users who were easily distracted and often semiliterate. It guided team members with picture and voice commands in English, Hindi, and regional languages. "Street kids really don't like to document things," Meghana Sawant explained. "And even when they do document them, there are often important elements missing."

The new system, which addressed the problems, proved extraordinarily useful for analyzing call patterns. For example, it enabled Childline to track specific hot points within cities. If a high number of health-related calls were coming from a particular railway station, Childline could advocate for a medical booth to be installed in that station.

As Childline expanded to new cities, the call-tracking system also emerged as an important source of child protection information. National data showed that the biggest killer of street children was tuberculosis, but regional call patterns revealed a variety of local problems. In Jaipur, for example, Childline received reports of abuse in the garment and jewelry industries. In Varanasi, there were reports of children being abducted to work in the sari industry. In Delhi, many calls came from middle-class children. In Nagpur, a transit hub, there were frequent reports of children abandoned in train stations. In Goa, a beach resort, a major problem was the sexual abuse of children by foreign tourists.

ChildNet also proved to be India's best resource for repatriating missing children. With franchises in most of India's major cities and a centralized database that stored information about children, it was suddenly possible to repatriate children who turned up a thousand miles from home. And because Childline was a government initiative, its data carried an official imprimatur. It is an inspired combination of technology and human management that today allows telephone calls from children across India to be systematically analyzed to inform government policy.

Despite many high-level pledges of cooperation, Childline found that police, health, and railway officials across India remained largely ignorant about and indifferent to 1098. So Childline designed a series of training workshops, and, in June 2000, in conjunction with the government's National Institute of Social Defense and seventy-eight partner organizations, launched a National Initiative for Child Protection.[8]

The goal was to make police stations, hospitals, schools, and train stations more "child friendly" by educating officials about the law, introducing them to street children, and teaching them about Childline. One of the features of the campaign was the presentation of awards by children to child-friendly police stations and hospitals.

Because empathy begins with understanding, the training began with children explaining to officials what their lives were like. They role-played encounters with police and hospital employees. The interactions were followed by discussions about children's rights and Indian law.

Despite much fanfare, the government came through with little funding for the National Initiative for Child Protection. As they had done before, Childline's partners drew on their own resources, conducting more than 700 training programs with officials across the country.

The majority of participants in these programs reported to Childline that, in the future, when they encountered children in distress they would call 1098. Many of them regularly had experiences like that of a policeman in Calcutta who one day came across a young girl wandering naked alone in the streets. The policeman admitted to Childline that, if he hadn't completed the training course, he might have ignored the problem—not knowing how to help the child and not wanting to take an action that might create significant paperwork for himself. Instead, he simply dialed 1098 and was immediately referred to a shelter with social workers and an educational program. He took the girl there. He even bought her crayons and a coloring book.

By the fall of 2002 Childline had spread to forty-two cities, with preparatory work under way in another twelve. Mature franchises were now directly paired with start-ups to speed training. In addition, preparatory activities had become more sophisticated. "We do much more training with the police, health departments, Department of Telecommunications, and the chair of the Childline Advisory Board," Jeroo said. "And we don't launch formally until the service has been in operation for at least six months."

The network had more than 120 organizations directly implementing the Childline service and over 2,000 providing assistance. By October 2002 Childline had fielded 2.7 million calls.[9] The Ministry of Justice and Social Empowerment had consulted with Childline during the drafting of its most recent Five Year Plan. The government also had incorporated several Childline recommendations in revisions of India's Juvenile Justice Act and mandated Childline as a lead child protection agency.

In 2001 Jeroo received international recognition for her work from the Schwab Foundation for Social Entrepreneurship. Later that year she made the decision to step down as Childline's executive director. She remained on board until May 2002, easing back from her 100-hour workweek and watching how things progressed without her. Some of Childline's board members felt her decision was premature. But she believed that Childline's expansion had become a technical challenge and felt her energy could be better applied elsewhere.

"Most people think I resigned because I got married," she wrote in an e-mail in March 2002, a month after her wedding. "But the truth is I needed a new challenge. And I believe, in principle, that a founder should leave after five to seven years. It has to do with my understanding about the social sector and has a lot to do with the principle of detachment and *dharma*.

"I am a lousy administrator and I hate routine and systems. I was bad for the long-term sustainable growth of the organization. And most important there was an inner voice which said it was time to go."

Her new plan is to build an international consortium of child help lines. In August 2001, Childline had convened a gathering in Pune, India, which brought together seventy-nine child protection advocates from nineteen countries to advance the global use of children's help lines. Jeroo is now exploring ways to link existing help lines in the United Kingdom, the Philippines, Zimbabwe, Slovakia, Pakistan, South Africa, India, and other places, to set up a global "help desk" for these services, and to establish global standards. She has recently launched a new organization—Child Helpline International (CHI)—and, to build initial momentum, has invited groups from more than forty countries to CHI's first "international consultation" of child help lines, to be held in Amsterdam in October 2003.

In 2002 I asked Jeroo what she had learned from her work with Childline in India. She thought for a moment, then replied: "If I have to summarize it in one line, it would be, 'Learning to let go.' Everything will not be exactly the way you want it. You have to let people take charge. The best thing is not to have a picture of what you want, but to have basic principles.

"Anyway, I don't take ownership for Childline. It happens because it has to happen. It is not because of me."

The Role of the Social Entrepreneur

O ver the past century, researchers have studied business entrepreneurs extensively. They have analyzed their orientation to action, to risk, and to growth; they have explored the entrepreneur's "personal-value orientation" and "internal locus of control" and searched for clues to explain the entrepreneur's propensity to seek out and exploit change.[1] Not only have business entrepreneurs been thoroughly studied, but their talents have been nurtured by value systems, government policies, and a wide array of institutional supports.[2]

In contrast, social entrepreneurs have received little attention. Historically, they have been cast as humanitarians or saints, and stories of their work have been passed down more in the form of children's tales than case studies. While the stories may inspire, they fail to make social entrepreneurs' methods comprehensible. One can analyze an entrepreneur, but how does one analyze a saint?

The study of social entrepreneurs has not been neglected for lack of examples. In the United States, an abbreviated list of well-known innovators might include: William Lloyd Garrison (abolition), Gifford Pinchot (environmental conservation and management), Horace Mann (public education reform), Susan B. Anthony (women's voting rights), Jane Addams (social welfare and juvenile justice), Asa Philip Randolph (labor rights for African Americans), and Ralph Nader (consumer protection). However, while much has been written about the various movements these people helped to build, their methods have not received the rigorous, cross-industry scrutiny that is common to the study of business entrepreneurs.

The difference in the treatment of business and social entrepreneurs seems to reflect different attitudes about the role of individuals in the

90

business and social arenas. In the business sector, individuals have long been recognized as engines of change. It was only a few decades after Adam Smith published *The Wealth of Nations* in 1776, which set down the basic tenets of market-based economics, that Jean-Baptiste Say identified the special role of entrepreneurs.

By contrast, theories of social change have concentrated more on how ideas move people than on how people move ideas. Émile Durkheim, one of the founding fathers of sociology, was concerned with the process by which "social facts"—institutions, customs, collective sentiments—act on individuals to shape behavior.[3] Sociologists identify many forces in social change—demographics, technology, economics, social movements, political processes—but with the exception of Max Weber's treatment of the "charismatic leader," they spend little time discussing the role of individuals.

In social change theory, ideas take center stage and people remain in the audience. The thinking is captured succinctly in Victor Hugo's famous adage: "There is one thing stronger than all the armies in the world, and that is an idea whose time has come."

The problem with this statement is that it gives too much to ideas. It fails to account for the fact that ideas compete for attention and legitimacy and the ones that gain ascendance do not win the day on their merits alone.

Ideas whose times have come are all around us. Given the widely shared concern about global warming, for example, one might imagine that "environmentalism" is an idea whose time has come. Today in the United States, it often seems to be an idea whose time has come and gone, to judge from the fact that millions of people drive sport utility vehicles (SUVs) that are highly polluting and less fuel efficient (not to mention more dangerous for both their own passengers as well as those in other vehicles) than the cars that were on the market twenty-five years ago.[4]

The idea that the world's children are entitled to basic health protection was accepted in principle decades ago. However, it took an individual named James Grant, whose story is detailed later, to *make* child survival an idea whose time had come.

An idea is like a play. It needs a good producer and a good promoter even if it is a masterpiece. Otherwise the play may never open; or it may open but, for lack of an audience, close after a week. Similarly, an idea will not move from the fringes to the mainstream simply because it is good; it must be skillfully marketed before it will actually shift people's perceptions and behavior.

This is especially true if the idea threatens the powerful or runs counter to established norms or beliefs. In his book, *Leading Change: The Argument for Values-Based Leadership*, James O'Toole, an expert in management and leadership, observes that great thinkers throughout the ages agree that "groups resist change with all the vigor of antibodies attacking an intruding virus." O'Toole examines a number of cases in which a potentially beneficial institutional change was resisted and finds that the resistance occurs when a group perceives that a change in question will challenge its "power, prestige, position, and satisfaction with who they are, what they believe, and what they cherish."[5] He asserts: "The major factor in our resistance to change is the desire not to have the will of others forced on us."[6]

If ideas are to take root and spread, therefore, they need champions—obsessive people who have the skill, motivation, energy, and bullheadedness to do whatever is necessary to move them forward: to persuade, inspire, seduce, cajole, enlighten, touch hearts, alleviate fears, shift perceptions, articulate meanings and artfully maneuver them through systems.

While researching this book, I looked at a variety of changes that had occurred in different fields and found a pattern. Frequently, when I traced the change back to its source, I found an obsessive individual working behind the scenes—a person with vision, drive, integrity of purpose, great persuasive powers, and remarkable stamina.

The origin of the modern postal system is a classic example.

The system was introduced in England in 1840 by Rowland Hill, a then-unknown British schoolmaster and inventor whose ideas initially met with hostile opposition and ridicule.[7] Hill had noticed that postal revenues in England failed to increase between 1815 and 1835 although the country's economy had grown considerably. Searching for an explanation, he spent five years on his own time studying the cost structure of mail delivery.

At the time, the average price to mail a letter in England was 12 cents, which put the service out of reach for most of the population. The price was a function of handling costs. Because postal clerks priced letters according to their weight, enclosures, origin, and destination, each letter had to be studied individually: Clerks would hold letters up to lamplight to count the number of enclosures before consulting price tables and recording each transaction in a log. Additionally, letters were paid for at the time of receipt; if the intended recipients rejected them, no money was collected.

Through his analysis, Hill demonstrated that the costs for conveyance of mail were actually minor in comparison with handling and administrative costs. He began thinking about ways to simplify the system and came up with the idea of charging a uniform price for all mail in Great Britain (initially a penny for a half ounce) and a prepayment system: an adhesive postage stamp.

Hill's proposal met with virulent opposition from the postal bureaucracy. Senior postal officials condemned it as "preposterous" and a "wild and visionary scheme." But his call for a "Penny Post" struck a populist chord and eventually won the endorsement of leading newspapers, which stood to benefit from reduced postal fees. After a protracted political battle, the government authorized Hill to implement his system.

Hill then embarked on a two-decade battle within the postal authority to reorganize the collection and delivery of mail so that the service could handle a dramatic increase in volume and justify the trust that prepayment implies. It took several years for the system's merits to be demonstrated. However, by 1843 the idea had already spread to Switzerland and Brazil. From 1838 to 1863 annual mail delivery in England rose from 76 million to 642 million letters. To cite one example of the impact of the Penny Post on commerce, in 1839 the annual amount transmitted via money orders in England was £313,000. By 1863 the amount was £16.5 million, more than a 5,000 percent increase. Among those for whom Hill's system was a godsend was Florence Nightingale, author of 12,000 letters.

Another behind-the-scenes innovator was John Woolman, an eighteenth-century American Quaker whose impact on American society remains largely unrecognized. Among those most active in the campaign to end the slave trade in the United States were the American Society of Friends, or Quakers, who voluntarily emancipated all their slaves between 1758 and 1800.[8] Although individual Quakers had been preaching against the evils of slavery since 1680, Quakers did not actually abandon the practice of slaveholding in large numbers until Woolman, a tailor and part-time preacher living in Mount Holly, New Jersey, took it upon himself to travel the country talking them out of it.[9]

In 1743 Woolman set out on a series of extended walking journeys that, over the decades, took him across New Jersey, Maryland, Rhode Island, and Pennsylvania, where large numbers of Quakers lived. Like Vinoba Bhave in India, Woolman traveled only by foot ("that I might have a more lively feeling of the condition of the oppressed slaves") and wore only undyed cloth (dyes came from slave plantations in the West Indies). In his soft-spoken but unyielding way, he persuaded Quakers to free their slaves and encouraged them to make slaveholding illegal in their states.[10]

Another remarkably skillful and influential "idea champion" who fits this mold was Jean Monnet, the architect and driving force behind the unification of Europe. Monnet, who is relatively unknown in the United States, was a lifelong proponent of internationalism, a man who spent virtually his entire adult life building one institution after another to allow, or *compel*, nations to work together to solve common problems. During World War I, as a private citizen without office or title, Monnet initiated joint planning for the distribution of supplies and resources between France and England.[11] During World War II, he organized the combined resources of the Allies. The economist John Maynard Keynes said that Monnet's influence, which led President Franklin Delano Roosevelt to dramatically increase American production of airplanes early in World War II, "probably shortened the duration of the war by a year."[12]

After the war Monnet sought to ensure lasting peace in Europe. He conceptualized and hammered out the details of the European Coal and Steel Community and the European Common Market, precursors to the European Union. It's easy to forget that, until the mid-twentieth century, Europe was one of the most dangerous places on earth. Its current stability owes a great deal to Monnet's vision, energy, and persuasiveness. There may be few individuals in the twentieth century who played a greater role determining the course of European politics and international affairs.

Even urgent life-saving ideas need champions. Consider blood pressure. Prior to 1970 people rarely thought about high blood pressure, a major contributor to strokes and heart attacks. Today millions of people regularly visit the doctor to monitor blood pressure. In his book, *Lifespan: Who Lives Longer and Why*, Thomas J. Moore explains how a relatively unknown American woman orchestrated this change.[13]

In 1966 a leading researcher on blood pressure, Edward Freis, discovered that a drug he was testing offered significant protection for moderate or severe hypertension. Freis immediately halted his study and rushed to publish his findings in the *Journal of the American Medical Association*. For four years, little changed. Then, in 1970, after completing a second phase of research, Freis published another study. This time he got a one-sentence mention on Walter Cronkite's evening television news, which caught the attention of Mary Lasker.

Lasker, who died in 1994 at the age of ninety-three, wasn't a doctor. Moore describes her as a "wealthy, stylish, energetic widow." (She had been married to the advertising magnate Albert Lasker.) Dr. Jonas Salk, who developed the first safe and effective vaccine for polio, called her a "matchmaker between science and society."[14] Lasker liked to describe herself as a "self-employed health lobbyist." Elsewhere in the media she is described as a "dowager," a "philanthropist," an "art dealer," and a "socialite," all of which serves to illustrate the trouble we have characterizing social entrepreneurs.

Mary Lasker was, in fact, the driving force behind the creation of the National Institutes of Health and, for five decades, the leading proponent for increased government funding for biomedical research in the United States.[15] Descriptions of Lasker—her zealotry, her fierce, unbending commitment to her self-appointed mission—are reminiscent of Florence Nightingale.

After reading Freis's studies, Lasker persuaded officials in the Nixon administration to plan a national campaign to educate the public about blood pressure treatment. She founded an organization, Citizens for Treatment of High Blood Pressure, which began producing an onslaught of messages about "the silent killer." She persuaded her friend Eppie Lederer, a.k.a. Ann Landers, the well-known advice columnist, to write about blood pressure; lobbied Congress to introduce funding for blood pressure education in high schools; and worked with pharmaceutical companies to get the word out to doctors. Within a few years, "the nation's attitude toward high blood pressure was transformed."[16]

Lasker's marketing efforts probably saved countless lives. But they also may have been premature given that, at the time, many unanswered questions remained about blood pressure. Indeed, Lasker has been criticized for her single-minded passion for cures at the expense of other treatments and other avenues for medical research. (Lasker was also the force behind the U.S. government's "war on cancer," which many scientists today consider to have been misconceived.[17])

For these reasons, it's important to acknowledge the power of the Mary Laskers of the world and pay attention to them. No matter how well intentioned they may be, they can make mistakes, and those mistakes will be greatly amplified by the force of their entrepreneurial ability.

Lasker's blood pressure campaign is a straightforward example of marketing. But marketing doesn't necessarily involve communicating through the media. The essence of good marketing is ensuring that anyone on the path to your destination who can foil your plans by saying no says yes. And if that isn't possible, it means finding another path.

"When you're working through a change," explains Drayton, "you've got to lay out all the steps in the process across the top and all the key actors down the sides. And when you're designing it, you have to think about each step for each of the actors. And if you've got an actor who is not going to like what's happening in that step, you've got a big problem."

Consider another, more hidden, healthcare innovation in the United States: improvements in the administration of anesthesia. Between the 1960s and 1980s, a death due to anesthesia error occurred once or twice in every 10,000 operations. With anesthesia administered 35 million times a year in the United States, that translated to 3,500 to 7,000 avoidable deaths each year—many of them during minor procedures. In a *New Yorker* article entitled "When Doctors Make Mistakes," medical reporter Atul Gawande chronicled how Ellison C. Pierce, an anesthesiologist, changed the standards in his field.[18]

Pierce grew up in North Carolina and attended Duke Medical School in the early 1950s. He began documenting deadly anesthetic mishaps in the 1960s, but his focus on patient safety intensified after friends took their eighteen-year-old daughter to the hospital to have her wisdom teeth pulled and the young woman died while under general anesthesia because the anesthesiologist mistakenly inserted the breathing tube into her esophagus instead of her trachea, a common error that is usually quickly corrected.

In 1972 Massachusetts General Hospital hired a man named Jeffrey Cooper to develop machines for anesthesiologist researchers. Cooper spent hours observing anesthesiologists and noticed a lack of standardization in the machines: In half of them, a clockwise rotation of a dial decreased the concentration of anesthetics; in the other half, it increased the concentration. He interviewed anesthesiologists to search for patterns in how mistakes were made and, using a technique developed by aviation experts called critical incident analysis, studied 359 errors. He published his findings in a 1978 paper entitled "Preventing Anesthesia Mishaps: A Study of Human Factors."[19]

As Gawande reported: "The study provoked widespread debate among anesthesiologists, but there was no concerted effort to solve the problem."[20] In 1982 Ellison Pierce was elected vice president of the American Society of Anesthesiologists. After ABC Television's 20/20 aired a segment on the dangers of general anesthesia, Pierce seized the opportunity to move his field in a new direction. He established a committee on patient safety and pulled in respected colleagues. Then he teamed up with Cooper and persuaded the Food and Drug Administration to produce a preanesthesia machine checklist and a series of patient safety videos for anesthesiologists and persuaded pharmaceutical companies to pay to distribute the videos to every anesthetic department in the United States. Then he and Cooper brought fifty anesthesiologists from around the world to Boston for the first international symposium to focus exclusively on anesthetic patient safety, a meeting now held biannually.

Pierce then established the Anesthesia Patient Safety Foundation (APSF), raising money and embarking on an extended tour of meetings with surgeons, nurse anesthetists, anesthesia equipment manufacturers, insurance companies, pharmaceutical companies, government officials, and senior figures in the American Medical Association—every group that had a role to play in the solution. "Through APSF, we were able to work without restrictions and hierarchy," Pierce told me. "It was much better than trying to work changes through existing organizations, which were so staid and rigid." APSF launched a newsletter, which today has 60,000 subscribers, and began channeling grants to researchers focusing on patient safety.

As a result, the workload for anesthesiology residents was curtailed to prevent errors caused by fatigue, with residents precluded from administering anesthesia on days following overnight on-call shifts in the hospital; machines were redesigned, with dials standardized and safety locks added; and monitoring devices for early detection of problems became standard. As the error rate dropped, so did malpractice insurance premiums for anesthesiologists. In 1995 Pierce, speaking at the annual meeting of the American Society of Anesthesiologists, noted that 139 papers had been submitted under the topic: "Patient Safety, Epidemiology, History, and Education." Ten years earlier the category hadn't even existed.[21] By the time of Pierce's address, the death rate due to anesthesia-related errors had dropped to one in 100,000 to 200,000 cases.[22]

Today dozens of organizations are involved in anesthesiology patient safety and APSF's example has galvanized patient safety in other fields, such as surgery, internal medicine, and obstetrics. "There has been an explosion of activity in this field," notes Pierce, who remains APSF's executive director as well as an associate professor at Harvard Medical School. "We were pretty much alone for eighteen years."

"What Sort of a Mother Are You?"

Erzsébet Szekeres, Hungary: Assisted Living
for the Disabled

For the first three months after her son, Tibor, was born in March 1976, Erzsébet Szekeres managed two hours of sleep each night. Tibor's crying was unendurable. It didn't seem to come from a baby but from another world.

Szekeres took Tibor to doctors, but didn't learn that he was mentally and physically disabled until he was almost two. The diagnosis was later given as microcephalus, an abnormal smallness of the head, and severe mental retardation. The doctors doubted that Tibor would live beyond the age of four.

As Tibor grew, it became clear that he would never speak. At night he needed to be rocked continuously. If Szekeres paused, he would scream. "I felt so exhausted. I didn't know if I could endure it," she recalled. "For three years after the diagnosis, my life was all apathy and fear."

Her marriage began to deteriorate. Her husband was ashamed of Tibor. Her parents and in-laws offered little support. The best decision, everyone advised, would be for Szekeres to place Tibor in an institution. It was crazy for an attractive, intelligent woman to sacrifice her career—and her life—to take care of a "deformed" child.

Seeking help, Szekeres spent hours in hospitals and government offices in Budapest. Whenever doctors examined Tibor or consulted with one another, they told Szekeres to wait outside. When she asked to see Tibor's medical reports, the doctors said: "If you need to know something, we'll tell you." Once, when she tried to leave Tibor in a nursery to be watched for a few hours, she was scolded because he wasn't toilet trained. "What sort of a mother are you?" the attendant asked sharply.

* * *

In 1982, about the time Tibor turned six, Szekeres felt a change come over herself. As she began to believe that he would survive childhood, her apathy diminished and she began to think more deeply about the meaning of his disability. She thought about her grandmother, a happy, loving woman who had been blind since childhood, yet had run a large cooperative. As a young girl working with her grandmother in the garden, it had never dawned on Szekeres that her grandmother had a disability.

"I started to think about what Tibor's disability meant for us," she recalled. "One day I got a piece of paper and drew a chart with two columns." In the left column, she listed things that Tibor would never be able to do. In the right column, she compared his situation to that of a nondisabled person.

In the left column, she wrote, "He will never marry," and next to it wrote, "A lot of people never marry." Below that, in the left column, she wrote, "He will never learn to cook," and beside that wrote, "A lot of people never learn to cook." Then: "He will never learn to wash clothes," and beside that, "A lot of people in society don't wash their clothes.

"Through this process, I began to see that disabled people are not qualitatively different from nondisabled people; they are quantitatively different. There are simply more things that disabled people will not be able to do in their lives compared to nondisabled people."

Szekeres is a round-cheeked, large-boned, graceful woman who comes across initially as guarded. She doesn't smile easily, but her attentive eyes give a hint of her inordinate capacity for empathy. Years before Tibor's birth, her dream had been to open a guest house with a beer garden, a place where travelers could feel at home. After Tibor turned six, she began dreaming of creating a place where he could feel at home. There was nothing for him in Hungary. The state solution for people with severe disabilities was institutionalization for life. "I knew that it was up to me to create a place for my kid to live and work," Szekeres told me, "a place for him in society."

She has done much more that that. In the intervening years, she has created a network of twenty-one centers across Hungary that provide vocational training, work opportunities, and assisted living to more than 600 multiply disabled people. Her facilities have shaken up the mental health and disability establishment and challenged the standard practices in her field.

Erzsébet Szekeres and her son, Tibor

* * *

In October 2000 I visited the Pilisvörösvár Social Home, a state-run institution for the mentally and physically disabled in a town outside
Budapest. Once inside I was escorted along a narrow, cramped hallway,
along which men and women padded aimlessly, wearing ratty hospital
gowns and pajamas, murmuring and sputtering to themselves. Their hair
was shaggy, their faces smeared with snot. I smelled sweat, urine, halitosis,
and cigarette smoke. I felt as if I had entered a world in which all spirit
had atrophied.

Although it was noon, many residents were still in bed. Many sat
immobile on benches staring into space; others followed me with their
eyes as if I were an alien creature. One woman rushed up and started
singing a loud song a few inches from my face until another resident
pushed her away. Within ten minutes, I saw two residents who had to be
restrained by attendants.

According to my escort, the institution had 111 residents, 71 women
and 40 men. They were pressed together like laboratory rats in an area
that, to my eyes, was suitable for thirty. Small rooms contained as many
as ten bunk beds. The walls were decorated with cartoon duckies and

Inside the Pilisvörösvár Social Home

horsies. When I asked a nurse why the rooms were painted like nurseries (all the residents were adults), I was told: "They have the mental capacity of children."

My escort bypassed a room. When I asked if I could look inside, she hesitated but relented. In the room, I found a man in a caged bed, squatting like a chimpanzee. He appeared to be in his twenties. "He'll walk around and eat everything," the attendant said to justify his confinement.

Across the room was a man half wrapped in bandages like a mummy. "This patient would masturbate all day if we did not stop him," the nurse explained.

The next stop was a locked basement room, the size and shape of a tool shed. This was the "intimacy" room, where couples could enjoy privacy.

"They come down here and get it over with," my escort said.

It was clear to me that the sole function of the Pilisvörösvár Social Home was containment. The intimacy room notwithstanding, no consideration was given to the residents' emotional lives. There were no real attempts to help them develop social skills or pursue interests. The assumption seemed to be that the residents were not really human, or were oblivious to their conditions, so why bother? Szekeres had told me that sexual and physical abuse was common in the state institutions. I had no reason to doubt her. At Pilisvörösvár, however, the problem didn't seem to be individual abuse, but abuse by a system that was stuck in the dark ages.

In the early 1980s, when Tibor was six, Szekeres joined the National Association for the Disabled, hoping to pressure the Hungarian government to improve services for disabled people. She found the process frustrating: A totalitarian government is not easily lobbied. Besides, Szekeres was more of a crafts- and tradeswoman than an activist. She had worked as a ceramist, carpet weaver, and seamstress, managed a Metro station in Budapest, and supervised a department in a clothing factory.

While staying home to care for Tibor, she had begun supplementing her income by taking on piecework from the clothing factory. Each night, after she got Tibor to sleep, she would sew underwear into the early-morning hours.

Through her involvement with the disability association, Szekeres began helping other parents like her, as well as some disabled people, earn extra income by doing similar work. Before long she had an informal cooperative business running out of her basement. She got people to pool capital, then purchased materials from the factory and brought them to different homes. When the work was finished, she collected and distributed the profits. All of this was illegal.

In 1982 the government passed a law that permitted the creation of private industrial ventures, including economic work cooperatives and independent contract work associations.[1] That year, while passing through a town called Csömör, on the outskirts of Budapest, Szekeres came across an abandoned farming cooperative. "I sniffed around and got information from the head of the town council," she recalled. She sent a letter to the farmers' cooperative: "I would like to create a center on this parcel of land where handicapped young folk could work, learn and live, keeping their human dignity," she wrote—and was amazed when her request was granted. Immediately she thought, "I had better do something good with this land. What sort of person would I be if I did not make something of it?"

To explore the idea, she formed a working group with other parents and moderately disabled people, but the group fell apart. She formed another group. That one fell apart too. She formed a third group. It fell apart too. Each time she sank into a depression. Yet each time she summoned the strength to try again, reminding herself: "If I give up, what will happen to Tibor?"

Finally, the fourth group—thirteen moderately disabled youths and another parent—held together.

For three years, little changed. Legally, they had little scope to do business because only state-owned enterprises were permitted to engage in wholesale trade. But Szekeres sensed that change was coming. In the meantime, she familiarized herself with the welfare, health, and employment ministries. She met with special educators and factory directors and researched work suitable for people with mental, hearing, orthopedic, and visual disabilities. Then, in 1986, the Hungarian government passed a law legalizing wholesale trade for private businesses.[2]

By then Tibor was nine. He required twenty-four-hour supervision. If Szekeres was going to take advantage of the new law to build her cooperative, she would have to find a place for Tibor to live. "I had reached an emotional stage where I just couldn't take care of him all the time," she said.

She was dismayed by her options. In one institution, she found a single nurse in charge of a hundred residents. At another, she could smell the stench outside the gates. Eventually she found what appeared to be a clean facility in Göd, a small settlement north of Budapest.

Her plan was to build the cooperative and add a small, supervised group home for Tibor and others. "I thought I'd be able to take Tibor out in a few years," Szekeres said. "But it didn't work out that way."

With a start-up loan from two disability organizations, Szekeres established Összefogás Ipari Szövetkezet (the Alliance Industrial Union), choosing the prosaic name to avoid attention from the authorities.

For three more years, things progressed at a snail's pace. "It was work, work, work, and nothing much happened," Szekeres recalled. "We had this piece of land but no money to do anything with it. I had a crappy fourteen-year-old Russian car. And I was still organizing the work and taking it to everybody's home."

Then, in 1989, after "applications, applications, applications, layers and layers of applications," to the Welfare Ministry, the Ministry of Employment, the Ministry of Finance, to foundations, companies, and individuals, Alliance finally received its first major funding from Hungary's Ministry of Welfare.

"When I hold lectures," Szekeres told me, "I tell people, 'If you really believe in something, you just have to *do it and do it and do it*, because if I had given up one month prior to 1989, I would have ended up with nothing.'"

The funding—subsidies for employing disabled people—allowed her to reach out to more disabled people, construct a small block of residences, establish a shop, purchase sewing machines and looms, and begin manufacturing carpets and ceramics. She also established a second site in the countryside, where residents worked in a poultry farm.

A friend, Zsuzsa Olah, who ran a biotech company, provided management advice. Two other friends who worked at a bank, Iván Góra and Nóra Kozma, helped develop the financial systems. Béla Pravda, a sort of jack of all trades who was drawn to working with disabled people, came on as technical supervisor.

Szekeres and Pravda focused on assembling working groups. They broke down work—carpet weaving or ceramic decoration or sewing—into steps suitable for people with different ability levels. They discovered that the formation of these groups was a delicate matter. The groups had to be stable, because Szekeres found that mentally disabled people require a high degree of regularity in their lives.

Conflicts were unavoidable. Some of Alliance's residents had spent years in institutions and had serious social deficits. Others who were deaf and mute had never been taught sign language. But Szekeres discovered that reports from the institutions were unreliable. One deaf and mute resident was said to have "sadistic tendencies." After less than a year, his behavioral problems were gone.

As it turned out, making the groups work was a time-consuming process, but not a mysterious one. Trust had to develop. People had to acquire basic social skills. "They were coming into a totally different environment," Szekeres recalled. "They hadn't been introduced to the world and the world hadn't been introduced to them. In institutions, you can't leave, you can't be in couples. Here you have a lot of freedom. Here you are challenged to become part of a community."

When problems emerged, Szekeres enlisted the residents to solve them as a group. For example, in the case of a man who was abusive to a woman resident, other residents refused to interact with him until he stopped his violent behavior. It worked.

Teaching the community to govern itself took effort. It would have been easier to administer tranquilizers to keep people under control, but Szekeres refused to do so.

* * *

Alliance's first major order was a contract to assemble antennae kits for the Hungarian army. Believing that a reputation for high quality would attract more business and help to shift perceptions about the disabled, Szekeres carefully monitored production.

As Hungary's economy moved toward a free market system after 1989, Alliance's business expanded. The cooperative won contracts to assemble curtain clips and fluorescent light bulb holders; paint decorative plates; separate perforated sheets of post cards and stuff them into envelopes; assemble health kits for schools; weave rugs, sew clothes, and make brooms.

The staff tried to keep residents engaged. "If someone seems bored," explained Szekeres, "we try to make the work easier or more difficult, adjusting to their capabilities and attraction to regularity." But Alliance's residents had incentives to show up for work even when they didn't feel like it. "Just like you and me," Szekeres said, "disabled people know that if they don't work, they don't make money."

One day, while Szekeres was touring a state institution, she observed a disabled person carrying a mug. "Now here, it is immediately understood

Alliance resident learning to assemble curtain clips

105

that someone carrying a mug wants something to drink," she explained. "But there, the disabled person handed the mug to the staff person and the staff person thought it was a game and passed it back to the disabled person. And they passed it back and forth and eventually the disabled person got very upset, and then he got violent. So they gave him a sedative and put him in a restraining bed."

Why didn't it occur to the staff person that the man was thirsty?

Because the staff person saw the disabled person as "fundamentally different" from herself, Szekeres contends. "And when I thought about it," she added, "I realized that the context *requires* that the staff see it that way. Otherwise how can you justify having disabled people locked up with no freedom and no privacy?

"We all have the same needs. However, mentally disabled people often have great difficulty communicating their feelings. They get frustrated, things build up, and then they erupt and everybody says, 'Oh, they're disabled. What can you expect?'"

Disabled people also stir up powerful emotions in others. Szekeres discovered that many people grew embarrassed in Tibor's presence. Others welled up with pity. Others withdrew reflexively, as if his disability were infectious. But Szekeres found that some people took naturally to Tibor's company. They treated him with respect. What these people seemed to have in common were empathy, flexible thinking, and what Szekeres described as "a strong inner core."

For anyone working with the disabled, these were important qualifications. The state institutions paid no attention to them. At Alliance, when Szekeres hired "helpers," the staff who manage work groups and assist residents (the residents chose the name), they were the overriding considerations, more important than academic qualifications, professional credentials, or job experience. In fact, Szekeres avoided hiring people with experience in state institutions because she found it too difficult to change their attitudes about the disabled. She also found that special educators, social workers, and medical professionals were needed to handle specific problems but not day-to-day assisted living.

"We're very happy to have total civilians here," she added. "On a day-to-day basis disabled people don't need professional care. They need love, tenderness, someone to be there, like a motherly, elderly woman; someone who likes to play football with you or help you make things."

Almost any skill, including sign language, could be acquired on the job, she said. But a "strong inner core" could not.

One had only to observe a staffer for a few days to know if he or she was right for the job. Szekeres developed a standard three-week on-the-job training program, followed by a three-month probationary period in which new recruits worked alongside veterans. Each day "helpers" would write free-form reports detailing their activities. Szekeres kept an eye out for trouble.

One day, for example, a helper wrote, "Zoli has spent three afternoons this week watching TV, although he shouldn't be watching so much." It was an offhand remark, precisely the sort of thing Szekeres tried to nip in the bud.

"Think about it," she told the helper. "If no one tells you how to spend your free time, why do you feel you have the right to tell the disabled person how to spend his free time?"

And: "Are you providing entertainment that's better than TV?"

One of her tests was to see how helpers handled their mistakes. "If a helper makes a mistake that affects a disabled person, the helper *must* apologize to the disabled person. You will find that this is something that is very hard for some people to do. But if they can't apologize, they have no place here."

At the end of the three months, the helpers decide if they want to stay and the community decides if it wants to keep them.

"The community is very good at recognizing when someone has a need to exercise power over them," Szekeres says.

At the institution in Göd, Tibor had initially shared a room with three other boys. But over time, the room grew more crowded, until it held nine. The youngsters received little individual attention. Although the institution employed 200 staffers for 200 residents, the majority worked in maintenance, administration, and medical units. The ratio of attendants to residents was 1 to 14 during the day; at night, it dropped to 1 to 70. Morale was low. Sometimes the entire night staff went out to dinner, locking the doors behind them. One staff member often taunted Tibor, telling him that his mother wasn't coming on days when he was expecting her. Szekeres would find Tibor in his room crying.

When Tibor was thirteen, he fell and cut his head. The wound, which took thirty-two stitches, wasn't properly cleaned, and the subsequent infection almost killed him. On another occasion the young man fell and broke his hip. It went unattended for two days.

The accidents, Szekeres contends, were a consequence of Tibor's living in a crowded room in a situation that produced chronic frustration and violent outbursts.

"I will never be able to forgive myself for having put Tibor in the institution at Göd," Szekeres told me. "Compared to others, he was lucky. He got the best treatment that is available in institutions, but it was still terrible."

In 1994 the Hungarian government passed a law permitting private foundations to operate residential care facilities. Szekeres had been housing disabled people since 1990, but she had been doing it discreetly. Now she established a foundation and secured government funds to construct a series of apartment units and two small group homes—one of which Tibor moved into in 1995.

Tibor's house resembles a ski chalet, with a vaulted ceiling and exposed wood beams. He shares it with five other multiply disabled people and two helpers, who live on the second floor. On the ground floor are six private rooms, as well as living and dining areas and a kitchen. There are couches, cabinets, plants, a wall unit, and a TV. Out back is a porch with a swing overlooking flower gardens and an open field.

In the institution, Tibor had developed compulsive behaviors: rocking, kneading his fingers, making sudden random movements. After several months in his new home, the behaviors subsided. "Tibor started doing simple things around the house and then working at the center, and that got rid of the pointless running around that you find with people in institutions," Szekeres said.

"He also developed a sense of his personal space," she added.

How did she know that?

"Once Gabi's mother came over to his house," Szekeres explained. (Gabi is one of Tibor's housemates.) "Tibor was in his room on a beautiful summer's day standing by the window just looking outside and Gabi's mother interrupted him and said: 'Oh, you poor thing. They left you all alone.' And she entered his room and started talking to him. Tibor came over and gently but assertively pushed her out of his room and closed the door."

As word spread about Alliance, Szekeres's waiting list swelled into the hundreds. "Parents would come with a disabled son or daughter in their twenties or thirties," she said. "They had almost spent their last breath looking for something good and we had to turn them down."

In 1993 Szekeres decided to start training others to do this work. She approached people on the waiting list to see if they wanted to set up assisted living and working centers. She invited individuals who appeared highly motivated to visit Alliance. And she and Béla Pravda began traveling around Hungary, helping people raise funds and organize work groups of disabled.

Szekeres established clear guidelines for association with Alliance. Groups seeking Alliance's help could design their centers as they liked and pursue any work they saw fit. But the primary goal of the centers had to be to help disabled people live as independently and as closely integrated with mainstream society as possible. The centers also had to be demonstrably "client-centered," not "staff-centered," meaning that the needs of the disabled people took precedence over the needs of the staff.

The most important qualification for individuals or groups that sought to initiate centers was "heartfelt commitment," Szekeres said. "It must be based in their *need* to do this."

Between 1994 and 1996 Szekeres helped establish seven new assisted living and working centers across Hungary. Beginning in 1994 she also began helping a number of Alliance's moderately disabled adults make the transition to independent living.

This was a new challenge. The first resident to attempt to live in an outside apartment could not adapt and eventually moved back to Alliance. Over time Szekeres developed a model in which one disabled person would live with two nondisabled people, either coworkers or family members or helpers, who, in turn, received training, counseling, and ongoing support from Alliance. Eventually a number of these former residents were placed in jobs outside Alliance, in restaurants, kitchens, bakeries, and laundries.

As Alliance's network grew, Szekeres saw that it would take more than a scattered association of modest-size centers to influence the disability health establishment. Even as support for Alliance's work grew among disability advocates, many health professionals remained unenthusiastic. Szekeres was criticized as an amateur dabbling in areas beyond her expertise. "They didn't attack my ideas with counterarguments," she recalled. "Instead, they would say, 'What do you know? You're not a professional. You're simply a parent.'" Szekeres saw that, to shift perceptions, she would have to demonstrate that it was possible to run a truly client-centered institution on a large scale.

In 1997 Szekeres received a call from Jody Jensen, Ashoka's representative in Hungary. Ashoka had recently begun working in Central Europe, and the organization had identified only a handful of social entrepreneurs in Hungary. When Jensen, who herself has a disabled daughter, visited Szekeres's centers, she was astonished by what had been achieved. "Most people had been waiting for the political changes to come to do this kind of work," recalled Jensen, "but Erzsi had started way before the [post-communism] transition period. She couldn't wait. She *had* to construct a strategy if she wanted to give her son a future.

"To be a social entrepreneur under a communist regime in the field of *disability* in Hungary—I just find that astounding," Jensen added.

Drawing on employment subsidies available for hiring the disabled, a government fund financed by fines on companies that don't employ enough disabled people, and Ashoka's stipend, Szekeres began building her vision of a working and living complex for hundreds of disabled people—complete with apartments, workshops, greenhouses, a restaurant, and a discotheque.

One of the most extraordinary moments I had while researching this book was entering Szekeres's center in Csömör less than an hour after visiting the Pilisvörösvár Social Home. I have a vivid memory of walking into the main building and seeing residents dressed in jeans, slacks, and skirts going about their business with a sense of purpose. Szekeres told me that Alliance's residents were, on average, no more disabled that those in Pilisvörösvár. Here the residents looked and acted like full human beings. Without pajamas and white coats, it was difficult to distinguish residents from staff. There was a feeling of calm and airiness inside the main building. One of the staffers had said to me: "Erzsi's spirit fills this place!" So did sunshine, color, plants, and music—Hungarian pop tunes playing on a radio in one of the workshops. Before the construction of the center, Szekeres had rejected four plans by architects. "I want it to be light," she told them again and again. And it is. Gazing from one end of the spacious hall out the windows at the opposite end, one can see a golden wheat field, and, beyond it in the distance, Csömör village.

While I was absorbed in taking copious notes, two disk jockeys asked me to stand aside so they could wheel their speakers and lights into the disco.

"You have to come to the party tonight," Szekeres said. "Lots of young people come from the village too."

"Nondisabled people come to the disco too?" I asked.

"Of course."

"How do they get along with the residents?"

"Fine," she said. "See for yourself."

* * *

But first we ate lunch in the restaurant. We drank from glasses and ate from ceramic dishes with stainless steel cutlery, rather than from plastic plates, tumblers, and tin forks. We sat in a high-backed wooden booth in what felt like a college pub in a midwestern U.S. town. The bar served soft drinks, juices, and beer. Residents were permitted to consume alcohol provided they abided by the house rules: (1) You can't drink if you take medication. (2) Don't get drunk. (3) If you do get drunk, don't do any damage.

"It's not usually a problem," one staffer told me. "And when it is a problem, it's usually among the staff."

A few tables down, four residents were finishing lunch. My translator, Zoltan, overheard two men discussing their evening plans.

"Are you going straight to the disco from work?"

"No way! I'm not going dressed like this."

Spread out among several buildings were apartments, workshops, a meeting hall, a greenhouse, and two small group homes. Everywhere, doors were open. In the workshops, residents were pouring candles and painting ceramic gift items; others were sewing children's clothes, curtains, and cushions. Those with severe mental and physical disabilities, like Tibor, sat around tables doing assembly work: separating different- shape pieces, arranging them in piles, fitting the pieces together, counting them. Groups were assembling goggles for tanning salons, fluorescent light bulb holders, and curtain clips. Outside, residents also worked in the fields and in a greenhouse.

A stranger was no object of fascination. Most of the residents paid little attention to me, but a few asked what I was doing. When I said I was writing a story about Alliance, two residents noted that they had lived in other institutions, which they had disliked intensely. Alliance was much better, they said. What was most telling was that almost everybody was absorbed in work.

In the hall, I met a resident with mental retardation who worked in the kitchen. She had spent years in institutions, she said.

"I feel more free here," she said.

"How are you more free?" I asked.

She explained that she could listen to music whenever she wanted to. She could visit friends. And when she wanted to go out she didn't have to tell anyone or be back at a certain time. She was saving money to move into an apartment outside Alliance.

Upstairs I visited apartments with Szekeres. She knocked on the first door we came to and asked, "May I come in with guests?" The reply was a gruff: "I don't want any guests." We moved on to the next unit. Before we knocked, however, a staffer who happened to be passing told us that the resident was with his girlfriend. We moved on.

Next door we were welcomed by two men in their twenties. Both had intermediate levels of mental retardation. It was the end of a workday, and they were smoking cigarettes and listening to the Rolling Stones.

We stopped in on a few more rooms. Each had one, two, or three residents living in them, with an average space allotment, according to Szekeres, of twenty-two square meters per resident, almost four times the legal minimum. Much of the furniture had been donated. The apartments were decorated with family photos and posters of movie stars and nature scenes—a far cry from the cartoon duckies and horsies on the walls at Pilisvörösvár.

That night, inside Alliance's disco, the room was dark and the music loud and heavy on the bass. Dancers were illuminated by strobe lights. A man in a wheelchair tilted and twisted to the beat. Around the perimeter, tentative folks watched from a distance. One staffer tried to lure a wallflower onto the dance floor, while another staffer was struggling to escape from the clutches of a man who had monopolized her for several songs. I searched for Tibor, but was told that he had come early and returned to his room.

A few teenagers from the village of Csömör were clustered outside the disco, standing back like gate crashers at a high school prom. They weren't dancing or interacting with the residents, but as far as I could tell they hadn't come to gawk. They were just hanging out on a Friday night. I asked how they liked the disco.

"It's all right," one said, shrugging. "It's cool."

Across the hall, the restaurant was hopping. Residents were packed five and six to a booth. The air was a brown haze of cigarette smoke. Many people were conversing in sign language. I noticed a few beer drinkers, but the barmaid was doing a better business in soda pop and snacks.

Outside the disco, I found Kati Magony, nicknamed "Smiley," hanging out with her two teenage daughters.

Magony was one of the most popular helpers at Alliance. She had worked there for six years. Previously she had worked in a bakery. She heard about Alliance at the unemployment agency. "The first day I came

Dancing at Alliance's disco

here," she said with a grin, "a guy with intermediate disability started talking to me and he didn't stop talking to me for *four* hours. *I felt as if my brain had been sucked out.* As I walked home I thought how lucky my children are that they weren't born disabled. At the same time I know that at anytime anyone can become disabled."

Magony's work ranged from helping people wash and dress, to helping them manage problems of a personal, sexual, and work-related nature, to helping them visit doctors and attend movies, to simply talking with them about life, fears, and dreams.

"Our job is just to help," she said. "Whatever they need help with, we provide, and whatever they don't need help with, we don't provide. We don't degrade people by doing things they can do themselves. Whatever the problem is, personal, sexual, whatever, because of the intimacy of the relationship we can help. But it's all within the parameters of what the disabled person needs. Probably the people who accept this job and enjoy it have an inner sensitivity toward those vibes.

"There are no shortcuts," she added. "You have to be here and get to know everybody. The most important thing is to develop a steady, level relationship. Most of these people have lived for years in institutions, in stimulus-free environments, with their needs and desires totally suppressed. Trust has to develop slowly. You need patience."

Most of the time Magony found the work uplifting. "If I come in here feeling low, it usually goes away by the end of the day. It's the openness here. Disabled people have a great capacity to love and express it. They don't have the inhibitions that ordinary people have."

It wasn't for everybody, she quickly added. "My elder daughter, who is eighteen, accepts the fact that I work here, but she said she would go mad in this environment. My younger daughter is much more comfortable here. She wants to learn sign language."

Between 1997 and 2001 Szekeres established thirteen more centers across Hungary. By 2001 the Csömör complex itself was housing and employing 300 adults. About 50 percent had multiple disabilities. Szekeres maintained the ratio of helpers to residents at 1 to 6.

Alliance no longer had difficulty soliciting contracts. Szekeres spent most of her time building up the middle management layer, training others in the network, and responding to various emergencies, including unexpected changes in government regulations that often complicated or impeded her work.

However, there were larger international forces working in her favor. In December 1999, for example, a committee from the European Commission visited Hungary to assess its psychiatric and care homes. Because Hungary was seeking admittance into the European Union, the country was under pressure to bring its human rights record into compliance with EU standards. One of the committee's demands was that caged beds, like the one in Pilisvörösvár, be removed immediately.[3] The committee also called for the Hungarian government to improve its institutions significantly—and to give patients a variety of freedoms such as the right to wear their own clothes. (Hungary is not the only country with substandard institutions. Many homes for the mentally ill in New York State have "devolved into places of misery and neglect" with a "stunning array of disorder and abuse.")[4]

In May 2000 Árpád Göncz, Hungary's president, honored Szekeres for improving the quality of life of disabled people. Hungary's Ministry of Health now regularly contracts services to Alliance and enlists Szekeres in prelegislative consultations. Institution directors have paid visits to Alliance to learn about its systems. Szekeres has collaborated with disability groups in Austria, Holland, Russia, and the United Kingdom.

In spite of the pressure from the EU and the recognition of Alliance's work from the Hungarian government, Szekeres is doubtful that the state institutions will be reformed anytime soon. She believes that the people who run them are too deeply invested in the ways of the past to change. "The hardest thing for people to accept is that their conceptualization of their role needs to be changed," explains Szekeres. "There is tremendous resistance to this. It's such a huge step to break out of the familiar control paradigm. People view an open institution like Alliance as an enormous risk and responsibility. Many nurses prefer a superior-to-subordinate relationship because it's harder to take care of people who are equal partners. We have to continually prove that our client-centered approach really works. Only when it is taught in universities will people believe it."

Szekeres expects that it will take ten years before mental health professionals give up on institutionalization. The next challenge will be doing away with the assumption that disabled people should be kept apart from mainstream society.

As part of this process, Alliance residents and employees invest portions of their savings to finance their own apartments. Since 1994, 150 people have been set up in independent apartments. "My vision is this." Szekeres explains: "You come to a street and see a row of houses. In every fifth house, or so, there might be a disabled person. They'd be right inside the community."

There are many who do not welcome this vision of full "normalization" and "integration," including many families of disabled people. When mentally disabled people express a desire to marry, for example, their families often oppose the idea. The notion of disabled people having children is even more controversial. When I visited Alliance, there were six children living with parents who were moderately disabled. The state position is that disabled people are unfit to be parents. But the state's determinations come from the state's institutions. "We don't encourage people to have children," Szekeres says. "But if they decide to, we make sure they've consulted with a geneticist and thought about it carefully from all angles."

Every weekday morning Tibor, twenty-seven, gets up and goes to work, as part of a ten-member work group. He dresses himself, except for tying his shoelaces. He knows to take baths, although he needs help soaping his body and has to be supervised because he likes to drink the bathwater.

"He's doing very, very well physically," Szekeres said. "He's relaxed and balanced. We're about to find him a new area of work, because it looks like he's getting bored."

How could she tell?

"On a recent weekend, Tibor was at home with me and I was preparing dinner, cutting stems off parsley. And Tibor began helping me, tearing the leaves and stems apart. It takes quite a lot of dexterity to do that."

Which meant that he was ready for more challenging work. For Szekeres, it was a special moment. She took three photographs of Tibor working with the parsley.

"This is an everyday experience here," she said. "But you have to watch closely to see it."

10.

Are They Possessed, *Really Possessed,* by an Idea?

Peter Goldmark recalled a visit he made to Bangladesh when he was head of the Rockefeller Foundation: "I'm inside a building in one of the back streets of Dhaka where a group of women are taking care of battered young girls. And this organization is not only delivering care, it is approaching intelligently—with attack and with change strategies—the legal system in Bangladesh.

"It turns out at the end of the day the person running it is an Ashoka fellow.

"How did they find her? How did they choose her from all the people who applied? How did she find them? Well, it happened through a network. You've got this whole system of nominators and referrers and opinion givers. That network multiplied throughout the world is one of the most positive and generous anywhere on this planet."

How would one create a system to identify social entrepreneurs before they were well known? How would the system be structured so that it did not depend on a special person to run it? How to do it globally?

These were Drayton's major how-to questions. "In these early decades of the profession it's especially important that we get it right," he explains. "People understand this field by anecdote rather than theory. A fellow we elect becomes a walking anecdote of what we mean by a social entrepreneur. And we have to be very clear about this."

Throughout the mid- and late 1980s, Drayton spent most of his time building Ashoka's network in Asia and Latin America. In addition to searching for nominators and fellows, Drayton looked for people to represent Ashoka within each country. These "country representatives" handled Ashoka's initial lead generation and investigation and managed the nominator network. They needed to be knowledgeable in a variety of areas. They had to be sensitive to potential political threats. And, above all, they had to be able to listen carefully to people from different backgrounds and gain a detailed understanding of their ideas and life histories.

Social entrepreneurs rarely announce themselves when they walk in the door. They don't volunteer their plans. In some cultures it is considered inappropriate to speak in terms of "me" or "I." And social entrepreneurs are often unaware of the patterns in their own lives. "It's our job to mine for this information," explains Joanna Davidson, a former Ashoka staff member. "People don't identify as social entrepreneurs. They don't think about things like 'spread strategies.' They just do them naturally."

It was the rep's job to dig up this gold. It meant talking to lots of people, a job best done face-to-face. Written applications were helpful for background screens, but not for assessing someone's entrepreneurial quality. "Some of the most incoherent things on paper turn out to be a function of the person just not being a good writer," notes Drayton. "Ibrahim Sobhan's writings are horrible, just *terrible*." (Sobhan is a fellow who has restructured rural schools across Bangladesh.) "But he's a brilliant entrepreneur. We would never have worked with him based on any paper we've ever received from him."

Far more important, from Ashoka's standpoint, were the intangibles: the person's vision, passion, determination, and ethics.

But how to develop a process to assess such qualities and produce rational and consistently high-quality decisions?

Drayton the management consultant devised a system that broke the question into four categories: (1) creativity, (2) entrepreneurial quality, (3) social impact of the idea, and (4) ethical fiber. And Drayton the lawyer got the idea to enlist a jury of one's peers who had to come to unanimous decisions.

The selection process began with what Drayton called the "knockout test": Does the candidate have a new and potentially pattern-setting idea?[1]

If the answer was yes, and if the candidate stood up favorably against the criteria, the rep passed the case to a "second opinion reviewer," a senior Ashoka staffer or board member who was based in another geographical region. (One of the functions of the second-opinion reviewer is to insulate the rep from local pressures. This is how Ashoka handled the "loss-of-face" issue in Indonesia; the nos can be blamed on someone from another country.)

If the candidate made it through "second opinion," the case "went to panel"—that is, to the "selection panel," a jury consisting of two to five social entrepreneurs from the candidate's home country, plus an Ashoka board member or senior staff member from a different continent (to bring both local and international perspectives). Panels were usually held over a weekend. Everyone volunteered their time. On the first day, each panelist interviewed each candidate one-on-one. On the second day, the panelists came together to confer. Panel-approved cases went to Ashoka's board of directors, whose main role was to preserve international consistency.

Ashoka would hold a selection panel at least once a year for each country in which it operated.

Everything discussed was confidential. All decisions had to be unanimous. Each actor in the process—rep, second-opinion reviewer, and all the panelists and board members—had to make an independent affirmative judgment that a particular candidate with a particular idea would produce a change in his or her field at the national level or, in the case of a small country, such as Slovakia, at a larger regional level, such as Central Europe.

If one person said no, it was no.

The "knockout test" sets a high bar. How many new ideas are floating around? What *is* a new idea? Did Gloria de Souza have one? Did Fábio Rosa have one? If so, what was new about their ideas?

The knockout test forces everybody involved in the selection process to think long and hard about what distinguishes a candidate's approach from the way the problem has been handled in the past.

To say that something is new, one must know if the idea has been tried before. If so, what happened? If it failed, why did it fail? If it succeeded, what is the candidate doing to improve on it? What combination of ingredients make the candidate's approach more practical, scalable, or cost effective, or better-rooted politically, than prior attempts?

It turns out that the new idea is not one thing; it is a product of "how-tos." A new idea might include these considerations: How to better use local resources to solve a problem? How to overcome cultural obstacles? How to get legislation passed? How to finance an organization? How to train others to do the work? How to motivate clients and staff?

Such an idea does not arrive in a flash of inspiration. It takes shape over years in an iterative process of adjustments and readjustments, with new pieces continually being added and others continually being dropped.

"I don't believe that *conceiving* an idea and *marketing* it are different," Drayton says. "Every day you're modifying the idea. You're seeing new opportunities. You're seeing new nuances of problems. It's a continuous process. But it's hard to talk about it that way because of the way our language is constructed. Because people think about *having* an idea and *implementing* it."

Consider Muhammad Yunus, who has played the leading role in crafting and spreading the idea of micro-credit as a strategy to overcome poverty. Micro-credit has, of course, been around in various forms for centuries.[2] But Yunus was the one who challenged banking theory by showing how to systematically extend collateral-free loans on a cost-effective basis to poor villagers at a scale that seized the world's attention. The Grameen Bank has 2.8 million borrowers scattered in 42,000 villages. Imagine the job of delivering and recovering all those loans. How would such a system work? How would it stay honest?

Yunus came up with dozens of "how-tos": group lending, weekly installments, center meetings, group funds, emergency funds, simplified methods of interest calculation, a six-month training program that weeds out unmotivated staffers, an early retirement option for staffers who've outgrown the job, a five-star branch rating system to spur competition among staff, a reporting mechanism that balances financial and human considerations, and so on.

It took almost a decade for the basics in the Grameen Bank's system to come into place. There were plenty of missteps and corrections along the way. Yunus had to scrap his early systems for organizing groups. His first repayment system proved unmanageable. His initial plan to persuade the government banks to take over the project was a big miscalculation. The first time the Grameen Bank had to deal with the aftermath of a major flood, its managers made mistakes that alienated thousands of villagers and provoked repayment problems that took years to fix. In the mid-1990s the bank aggressively raised loan ceilings, causing repayment troubles that are still being corrected. And the bank, which is famous for its focus on women, only began lending money primarily to women eight years after it opened its doors.

"The voyage of the best ship is a zigzag line of a hundred tacks," wrote Ralph Waldo Emerson.

Given that a new idea is continually being revised, the relevant question is: Does the person pushing the idea have the consistency to stay focused on the big vision, the creativity to solve unforeseen problems, the insistence to make it work, and the toughness to stay the course—no matter how long it takes, no matter how many miscalculations or screw-ups or reversals of fortune are in store, no matter how much opposition or loneliness lies ahead?

That, of course, is the million-dollar question. Major social change—moving from demonstrating a project in one location, to multiple sites, to shifting behavior patterns and perceptions on a national scale—takes a long time, often decades.[3] But how do you predict what someone will achieve over twenty or thirty or even forty years?

I sat in as an observer on one of Ashoka's selection panels in Rio de Janeiro and listened as Drayton briefed the panelists about how to apply Ashoka's four criteria in their interviews.

"The first criterion is creativity," he began. "This has got two parts to it: the goal-setting creativity—the visionary seeing over the horizon to a different pattern in the field; and the problem-solving creativity—to get to that new place, there are a thousand hurdles, a thousand adjustments that these people have to make and they have to be creative about it. They have to find new ways around barriers all the time. So we have to look for both types of creativity. One alone is not enough.

"What are the tests? Well, you have in front of you the idea that this person has developed. Is it a new idea? What's the quality of the problem solving that you see in the work? Very importantly, is the thinking this person's thinking? It's common to find cases where it's a very interesting idea but it may belong to someone else.

"It's really useful to dig down into a person's past. Creativity does not suddenly appear at age thirty-five. What's the candidate's life history? Have they come up with new ideas? Have they created other institutions? How have they dealt with problems?

"The next one—entrepreneurial quality—is by far the toughest. It's the hardest to understand, and it's the criterion that knocks out 98 percent of the people who don't fit. For every one thousand people who are creative and altruistic and energetic, there's probably only one who fits this criterion, or maybe even less than that. By this criterion, we do not mean what the language typically means. We do not mean someone who can get things done. There are millions of people who can get things done. There are very, very few people who will change the pattern in the whole field. We do not mean that this person is a good administrator. It helps. Or a good manager. That certainly helps. But it is not what we're looking for. One has to get beyond those common understandings of the word and really focus in on the heart of what we're about, and because this is hard and because this is the toughest screen, it's the one you need to focus on most.

"Let me see if I can explain the heart of it. What differentiates the entrepreneur who is going to change a pattern at the scale we're looking for from other people? I think the heart of it is that entrepreneurs, for some reason deep in their personality know, from the time they are little, that they are on this world to change it in a fundamental way. They will not be satisfied expressing an idea. Artists are. Scholars are. Entrepreneurs aren't. Similarly, managers, professionals, social workers are not happy just with an idea, but they are happy when they solve the problem of their particular group of people: their clients, their organizations. So they will find solutions that are idiosyncratic to a particular situation and they are delighted about that. They get professional satisfaction; they get interpersonal satisfaction. But none of that satisfies the entrepreneur. Entrepreneurs have in their heads the vision of how society will be different when their idea is at work, and they can't stop until that idea is not only at work in one place, but is at work across the whole society. And in business, this is called marketing—going beyond the invention in the garage. The same thing is true in the social arena. An entrepreneur is not happy solving a problem in one village or two schools.

"And from that need flows a number of characteristics that you can see very early in people's lives and in their professional lives. And that's where most of the tests come in. The first—the most obvious—is are they possessed, *really possessed* by an idea, that they're going to devote ten or twenty years to it if necessary and it doesn't cross their minds not to do that? The idea—and making it happen across the society—is something they are married to in the full sense of the word. One key test of that is: Is this an idea that you see growing out of their whole life? I get very, very suspicious when I see someone who had an idea two years ago. It just doesn't ring true. Because with the typical entrepreneur you can see the roots of the interest when they're very young. There's a real coherence to people's lives.

"Second—and this is very important—are they totally on top of how-to questions? How am I going to get this idea from one villa in São Paulo to change the pattern across Brazil? How is it going to work? How am I going to overcome all the problems? How am I going to take advantage of the opportunities? How am I going to get the trade unions on board?

"The how-to test is one of the most important tests for going after this type of personality. Press them. Take a how-to issue—'How are you going to solve this problem?'—and push them from the first to the second to the third to the fourth level of the challenge. The real entrepreneurs love that. Because that's what they spend their time thinking about in the shower in the morning and they don't have anyone else they can talk to about it. Most people are very bored with all these how-to questions. But these people, they're constantly building and adjusting and they know how the pieces are going to fit together or at least they're thinking about it.

"Now, because we're getting people early, they obviously will not have thought everything through. So if you find that they haven't thought one aspect through, try another aspect. It's the quality and the perceptiveness of the thinking that you're looking for. Is this person really into the how-tos? The idealists, by contrast, when you start pressing them on the how-tos, collapse. They can tell you what Xanadu is going to look like—many pleasure domes, et cetera, et cetera—but they can't tell you how the sewage is going to work in Xanadu once you get there, and they certainly can't tell you how you're going to get there.

"Another key test is: How realistic is this person? A real entrepreneur has to listen to the environment very well. You cannot cause major social change unless you really understand what's going on. You pick up the symptoms early that something is amiss. And you focus on it. Because you need to. And so these folks are not ideologues. They're not captive of some framework that someone has given them. They are wonderfully free of framework. They are happy crossing disciplinary or organizational boundaries and they listen really well. So if you feel that this person is not realistic and is not really understanding their environment, that's a big warning sign.

"The third criterion is unlike the first two. It does not focus on the person; it focuses on the idea. And this is actually a criterion we added relatively late in our organizational evolution. People kept saying to us, 'What happens when this wonderful entrepreneurial person disappears from the scene? You really should think about the idea's inherent value as well.' And so there are two levels of test here. Let's imagine that this entrepreneur demonstrates this idea in one place, one school, one village, whatever, and then is dispatched to Mars for the next twenty years. The question is: Will ordinary people working in that field look at that demonstration and say, 'This is a practical, feasible idea. This will help me do my work better. I'm going to try it'? In other words, is the idea good enough in its own right to spread once it is demonstrated?

"The second test is: How many people will be affected and how importantly?

"Now, the final criterion—ethical fiber—we put last because it requires an appeal to your gut. The mind is not enough. The key question here is: Do you deeply trust this person? If you were in a dangerous situation, would you be totally at ease if this person was with you?

"Now, why do we ask this? There are three reasons. First, the fellowship does not work if there is someone in the room you don't trust. People will not share information, and that is fatal for us.

"The second reason is that to cause fundamental social change, you are asking people to change how they do their work, how they relate to other people. You're asking a lot of them. And if they don't trust you, your probability of success is greatly reduced. The trustworthiness of the social entrepreneur—their integrity—is one of their most important assets. People sense that—and if they don't trust you, they won't follow you. They won't make those leaps in their own lives that are necessary.

"The third reason is that we do not want to add to the ample supply of untrustworthy social leaders. We are in the business of watching people, giving them credibility, giving them the support of our fellowship, and we really don't want to do that unless they're good people.

"So there are three very important reasons to go through the discomfort of applying this criterion. And this is a criterion that requires a jury of several people. It's very hard for one person to trust the faint intuition that they don't trust someone. We do it every day in our own lives, but we're told not to do it. When you walk down the street, you make a decision a thousand times a day about whether or not to be concerned about someone coming. You are using exactly the skill we're trying to put to work here. When you decide to get in a car with someone or not, you make that decision. When you decide to go into a business deal with someone or not, you make that decision. It is a skill that we all have in a very highly developed way. If we don't, we're in big trouble.

"And that's why the judicial system employs juries, because ultimately you have to make a judgment about who you're trusting and who you're not trusting. And that's what we have here, a jury of very sensitive, caring people. And as a jury, if three people out of the four in the panel have a slight inarticulate tickle of concern about this person, then we have to look at it more carefully.

"Now, the test that we've found very useful is to bring primal emotion—fear is a good one—to the surface and mix this person with that emotion. I'm afraid of heights. I do not go near the edge of cliffs. I get uptight even thinking about it. And so what I do is I close my eyes and I imagine myself walking along a cliff edge on a dark and stormy night, and I imagine this person being with me. And if I feel myself grabbing the edge of the chair, the person gets a two [a score that indicates "cause for concern"].

"Gloria de Souza, who is one of our Indian fellows, is afraid of snakes. One of our Indian fellows actually works with snakes, and one day this fellow came to her classroom. And at one point, he turned to her and said, 'Teacher, why don't you hold the nice snake.' And Gloria had to make one of those instant decisions about whether she was going to flee the room or trust this fellow. And she ended up trusting him. So her test is: Would she take the snake? Try claustrophobia. Whatever works for you.

"So those are the four criteria. When you put them together, the ultimate question is 'Do you believe that this person and this idea together will change the pattern in the field?' Environment, health, education—whatever—on an all-Brazil basis. Not in the city of São Paulo, not in the state of Minas Geras; all Brazil. And it doesn't have to happen this year, but it will happen in fifteen or twenty years. Social change takes a long, long time. And if you answer yes to that, you're saying we should elect that person."[4]

Ideally, at what stage in a social entrepreneur's life did it make most sense for Ashoka to elect him or her a fellow?

To answer the question, Drayton broke down the entrepreneur's "life cycle" into four stages: (1) "apprenticeship," a long period in which entrepreneurs acquire the experience, skills, and credentials they need to cause major change; (2) "launch," the early period during which entrepreneurs begin testing and demonstrating their ideas; (3) "take-off," an extended period in which entrepreneurs consolidate their organizations and continue to refine and spread their ideas until they become widely adopted; and (4) "maturity," the point at which entrepreneurs' have had demonstrable impact on their fields.

Ashoka wanted to catch people early, but not too early. Fellows had to have identified a major opportunity in their field and mastered the skills to exploit that opportunity. They also had to be prepared to pursue their ideas full time. Drayton found that the moment of "greatest magic and maximum vulnerability" was the "takeoff" point—the point at which "a small investment of resources and collegial support" could produce maximum gains.

For Ashoka's staff and panelists, the toughest part of this process is turning down a candidate. It is particularly difficult because all of the people who reach the second- opinion stage are at the very least doing impressive work at the local level. "There are hundreds of thousands of people doing wonderful and essential things who don't fit Ashoka's specific criteria," explains Jody Jensen, Ashoka's former rep in Hungary. "Society couldn't function if everybody was a social entrepreneur."

11.

If the World Is to Be Put in Order

Vera Cordeiro, Brazil: Reforming Healthcare

If Florence Nightingale were alive today, she might be doing something along the same lines as Vera Cordeiro, a physician in Rio de Janeiro who is working to redefine healthcare in Brazil. Cordeiro is the founder of Associação Saúde Criança Renascer (Rebirth: Association for Children's Health), the flagship in a network of organizations that extend care to poor children after they are discharged from public hospitals.

Tens of millions of Brazilians live in urban slums that lack decent housing, clean water, and proper sanitation. Millions of children are stunted from chronic malnutrition.[1] Cordeiro founded Renascer in 1991, while she was working in the pediatric ward of Hospital da Lagoa, a public hospital in Rio, because she could not bear to see so many children discharged only to return weeks later, sick again.

From the perspective of a doctor, it makes no sense for a hospital to discharge a poor child back to the slums without following up. But that is the norm today, and Cordeiro intends to change it. To her, health and social conditions are two sides of the same coin. "Hospital treatment as it is conducted today—ignoring poverty and the conditions of the family—is a *false* treatment," she explains.

To date, Cordeiro has extended her work to fourteen public hospitals in Rio de Janeiro, São Paulo, and Recife, bringing direct benefits to 20,000 children and influencing a growing circle of medical practitioners. Her goal is to carry Renascer to every public hospital in Brazil.

There may be no city in which the juxtapositions of wealth and poverty are more stark than Rio de Janeiro, where poor people in hillside *favelas* (urban slums) look out on the rich in beach-side enclaves such as

Vera Cordeiro

Copacabana and Ipanema. Each day Vera Cordeiro made the commute from her leafy suburb, Barra da Tijuca, where she lived with her husband, Paulo, an IBM executive, and their two daughters, Marina and Laura, to Hospital da Lagoa, which served some of Rio's poorest areas, including the Baixada Fluminense, the lowland slums, and Rocinha, the largest *favela* in Latin America.

Rocinha is a massive hillside expanse of cinder block, wood, tin, and cardboard. From afar it is a beautiful sight. At night lights sparkle and sounds of percussion drift down to neighborhoods below. But although they are not exclusively poor, Rocinha and the other *favelas* that are home to millions in Brazil are unhealthy places. Gangs dominate the slums, and the sound of gunfire is commonplace. Families are pressed together in ramshackle houses, in which children often sleep on damp concrete or dirt. The streets are full of vermin, and the stench of sewage rises from narrow alleyways.

At Lagoa, Cordeiro encountered the by-products: children with pneumonia, tuberculosis, rheumatic fever, anemia, birth defects, and other ailments. The kids often had skin lesions. Many suffered from leptospirosis, a disease caused by bathing in or drinking water contaminated with rat urine, with symptoms of fever, jaundice, vomiting, and diarrhea.

Cordeiro found that many of her patients' mothers were single parents, without child support, living in dilapidated shacks. They lacked basic knowledge about health, nutrition, and sanitation and were totally unequipped to manage their children's illnesses or prevent recurrences.

The children would be admitted to the hospital, treated, and discharged—and then they would be readmitted, sometimes within weeks. It was a grim cycle. "I could not stand to go one more day seeing children locked in this cycle of hospitalization, rehospitalization, and death," Cordeiro said.

"We were stuck," Odilon Arantes, the head of Lagoa's pediatric ward, told me. "Here you have a government-run hospital with the best equipment and the best doctors. After making this huge investment in the children, we just let them go. Of course, we had to discharge the children at some point, but how could we discharge them into the same conditions that produced the disease?"

One day a one-year-old boy arrived at Lagoa. His hand required amputation. Cordeiro was often called in to counsel patients in stressful cases, and she tried to prepare the boy's mother, Pedrina, for the amputation. Pedrina told her that she had just lost her job as a maid. She didn't know where she was going to live or how she was going to buy food. She couldn't begin to think about purchasing a prosthesis for her son.

That night, as Cordeiro sat in her living room amid the stereo, sofas, and plush carpet, with her daughters, Marina and Laura, in their rooms talking on the phone, she could not get Pedrina out of her mind. She remembered how shaken she had been when Marina had contracted a serious infection and had been unable to eat for days.

"And I have all this help," she recalled thinking. "I have my mother, two maids, the best pediatricians...." Her thoughts drifted to other mothers she'd met over the years who had had to make what she called "Sophie's Choices": buy medicine for one child or food for them all.

The next morning she canvassed the hospital to solicit contributions for Pedrina. It would help a little, but it was far from a solution.

The following day Cordeiro was asked to counsel another mother whose seven-year-old son had kidney cancer. This woman was thirty-five but looked sixty. She had ten children. She'd come from another state and was staying with relatives in Rio who were extremely poor.

"The mother asked me if I had something to cover her son," recalled Cordeiro. "She said, 'If I don't have something to cover him, he might catch cold and then the doctor will stop the chemotherapy. Do you have a blanket or a sweater to give me?'"

What good was chemotherapy when patients lacked blankets?

Increasingly, Cordeiro found herself dwelling on these contradictions. In 1991 she was forty-one years old. The previous year she and her husband had reunited after a four-year separation. With Marina thirteen years old and Laura ten, Cordeiro found that she was needed less at home. She also began to feel that her life was a little "stagnant."

Some years before a friend had given her a copy of the *I Ching*, the ancient Chinese text known as the *Book of Changes*, which she had gotten into the habit of consulting. One day she tossed the three coins and was directed to hexagram number 12: stagnation. "The lines said that the moment of stagnation was at its end," recalled Cordeiro, "and that many blessings were to come to families involved." The *I Ching* also counseled: "The time of disintegration does not change back automatically to a condition of peace and prosperity; effort must be put forth in order to end it. This shows the creative attitude that man must take if the world is to be put in order."

One Sunday in April 1991, Cordeiro wrote a proposal for a healthcare project to stop the cycle of readmissions among poor children. She presented it to Lagoa's directors and was promptly told: "Vera, this is the government's work." Undeterred, she spent the next six months persuading staff in the pediatric unit to help her.

On Friday, October 25, 1991, at 7:00 P.M., she brought together fifty colleagues in the playground of her apartment building, announced her plan, and raffled off a set of sheets that her mother, Cordelia, had embroidered. The $100 they raised was used to cover the incorporation fees for Associação Saúde Criança Renascer, a new organization that would begin where hospital care ended.

Today Renascer's headquarters are located in a pink house in a forested park five minutes' walk from Hospital da Lagoa. (For six years, an old horse stable had served as the office.) The house looks like the headquarters of an efficient but modest health program. The small rooms are crowded with psychologists, social workers, nutritionists, volunteers, and mothers of sick children. There is a storeroom stocked with food and medicine and a bulletin board by the entrance that lists supplies currently in need. On various visits I noticed that the list included: fans, shoes, mattresses, cradles, blenders, water filters, eyeglasses, clothes, blankets, a wheelchair, a sewing machine, a nebulizer, a safety fence, and a carriage for a child with hydrocephalus.

Along the walls in the hallway are several photographs showing Cordeiro accepting awards. Beside them is a framed quotation from

Discussing treatment plans in Renascer's volunteer room

Goethe, which concludes: "Whatever you can do or dream, you can begin it now. Boldness has genius, power and magic in it. Begin it now."[2]

The most critical work in Renascer's office takes place in the volunteer room, where volunteers interview mothers about their children and help them develop "treatment plans."

On one of my visits, I met a woman named Maria whose seven-year-old son, Daniel, had hydrocephalus, a life-threatening condition characterized by extreme swelling of the head. Maria had grown up in a village and come to Rio as a teenager to support her parents. She had an alcoholic husband and two sons whom she supported by selling sandwiches and juices to police officers at the city morgue.

Daniel had undergone three operations. He needed to have fluid drained regularly from his head. Because it was dangerous for him to move around, he spent most of his time indoors. "He's a very joyful boy," Maria said. "He loves football. He imitates all the radio and TV sports commentators." Renascer's team was keeping a watch on him until he was beyond the danger zone from his last operation. The volunteers were trying to procure a special carriage to support Daniel's head so he could spend more time outside.

At the next table sat Ivonete, a gaunt woman of twenty-five with anxiety lines etched deep into her face. She had been referred to Renascer by a social worker at Hospital da Lagoa after her son Marcos had been hospitalized for dehydration due to diarrhea. At the time, Ivonete had two other children and was pregnant with a fourth; there were "serious troubles" at home that she didn't want to talk about. Renascer had been closely monitoring Marcos's health for a year. Ivonete received nutrition supplements and learned how to improve the family's hygiene and diet. Renascer also helped the family move out of its damp basement dwelling into a healthier living space. Now Ivonete wanted to start a small business selling sweets. The volunteers were helping her get it started.

The most striking thing about the volunteer room was the seriousness of the work. At every table mothers and volunteers were discussing problems, making decisions, and planning actions. It wasn't all smiles. Some mothers became frustrated when they ran into Renascer's limitations, and some volunteers became frustrated when mothers didn't live up to their promises. "I have been trying for six months to help this woman get her government documents together," one volunteer exclaimed. "She hasn't made an effort at all."

But no one seemed bored or resentful. No one was saying: "That's not my department" or "Fill out this form and come back in three weeks." The prevailing attitude seemed to be: "Let's roll up our sleeves and see what we can do about this problem."

The bottom line was clear: Without Renascer, children like Daniel and Marcos would be hospitalized more often. They would suffer more; their families would suffer more; the doctors would suffer more; and society would bear the expense.

In 1999 the director of Lagoa's pediatrics unit, Odilon Arantes, reported that, between 1991 and 1997, Renascer's follow-up had brought a 60 percent drop in readmissions in the unit. The impact, he said, was "stunning." Doctors and nurses were now able to do what they had trained to do: heal. "It has completely changed the motivation in the unit," Arantes told me. "Before Renascer, we used to spend lots of effort and money in the emergency room or ICU [intensive care unit] on treatment knowing that there was a high probability that kids might die afterward from lack of assistance and follow-up at home.

"Now when we discharge a poor child, we can feel at peace. And this makes our work more meaningful and rewarding."

What, then, in the context of poverty, constitutes a *real* treatment? Cordeiro has found that, on average, it takes about eight months of regular contact between mothers and an organization that can address a range of social problems to do the trick. Sometimes it takes twelve or fourteen months, or even longer.

And sometimes even that isn't enough. Cordeiro frequently has to remind herself that Renascer does not exist to solve all of Brazil's woes. Its job is to ensure that vulnerable children treated at Hospital da Lagoa truly benefit from the medical care they receive and, as far as possible, stay healthy outside the hospital.

It's a limited mission, with measurable, time-bound goals. The idea is to do it systematically, showing the way so that, in due time, the real treatment becomes the *standard* treatment.

Vera Cordeiro grew up in an upper-middle-class family in a poor suburb of Rio called Bangu, where her father, Horst, was a senior engineer in a textile factory. Horst was a reserved, disciplined, and honest man. Cordeiro's mother, Cordelia, a psychologist, was warm, outgoing, and charismatic. Compared to their neighbors, the family was rich. They had maids, cooks, a driver, and a guard. As a child Cordeiro was acutely aware of the differences between her family and their neighbors. She often overheard her mother urging her father to give a job to a neighbor's son. At the age of six she was reprimanded by her nanny for giving away too many of her toys.

At ten she won a scholarship to a private school and was sent to live in Copacabana with her uncle Mauricio and aunt Leonor. Mauricio and Leonor socialized with intellectuals and artists, and, at their parties, Cordeiro took part in exciting discussions about philosophy and social justice, and the future of Brazil's government—then a dictatorship.

Cordeiro's decision to study medicine was influenced by her uncle Mauricio, a doctor. In medical school, however, she found the focus too narrow for her interests. She liked the study of anatomy, but she was more intrigued by emotions and the role they play in illness—a question that received almost no attention in her courses.

After graduating from medical school, Cordeiro, twenty-five, landed a position in Hospital da Lagoa. She was immediately assigned to the hospital intake ward, where she had to diagnose as many as twenty patients each morning. At first the days were a blur. But, in time, she learned to steal moments to talk with the patients. Many of them were poor women. And she began to make connections between their physical ailments and the stress in their lives.

Before long Cordeiro was pressing the head of Lagoa's medical clinic to allow her to establish a department of psychosomatic medicine. (Psychosomatic medicine explores the relationship between emotional stress and illness.) After two years of lobbying, Cordeiro finally received permission. The department of psychosomatic medicine she established at Lagoa became the first such unit in a public hospital in Brazil. Cordeiro introduced an array of social and psychological treatments, including art therapies, group therapies, and relaxation techniques to help patients cope with chronic diseases such as asthma, heart disease, and hypertension.

In 1988 Cordeiro requested a transfer to the pediatric ward—a decision that would set her life on a new course. "I had always wanted to work with children," she explained, "but whenever I had to, I felt such pain. I worked with adults for thirteen years and I never thought to start an organization like Renascer. But after I came to the pediatric department, I realized that I had two choices: to give up working with children or to continue working in a different way."

Renascer's initial team was made up of ten people, including Cordeiro, her mother, Cordelia, a few other psychologists and nurses, and some friends. They operated out of a small room in the hospital. They began by scouring their Rolodexes, seeking contributions of milk, medicine, and food. Each night they consulted with one another on the phone: Who knows where we can get a vaporizer? Should we have a bingo night?

"We used to sit around a table and clap hands each time we received a donation of milk or medicine," Cordeiro recalled. "I would think, 'I'm a doctor and here I am clapping for milk.' But I knew that that was the way we would grow stronger."

Cordeiro's objective was to help the mothers of vulnerable children learn how to prevent recurrences of illnesses and minimize crises. She enlisted doctors, nurses, and social workers at Lagoa to identify poor children who were about to be discharged. To entice the mothers to work with Renascer, Cordeiro offered an incentive: free nutritional supplements and medicine for six months. In exchange, mothers had to agree to visit Renascer's office at least twice a month.

On the first visit, Cordeiro or one of her colleagues would interview the mother, inquiring about the family's income, diet, and other social conditions. Does your house have running water? Does it have a solid roof? Is there a toilet? Do the children sleep in beds? Did they have adequate clothing?

Each family was given a baseline score for poverty, education, employment, housing, and health awareness. (In later years it became Renascer's policy to pay home visits to verify the accuracy of information.)

Renata Nascimento Moises at her house in Cidade de Deus, in the outskirts of Rio de Janeiro. Her son, William, has sickle cell anemia

For the next six months Renascer's team would work with mothers one-on-one. In conjunction with social workers and nutritionists, they sketched out treatment plans and set specific, time-bound goals. The goals might include fixing a roof, modifying a child's diet, getting into the habit of boiling water, getting a bed for a child, or acquiring the documentation to be eligible for government assistance.

"The key is that the mothers know exactly where they need to go," explained Cordeiro. "Then, step by step, we help them get there."

From the outset, mothers were informed that Renascer would help them gain control of their family's health, but the organization's support was temporary. "It's important to put this in their minds from the beginning," said Cordeiro.

Each time mothers visited the office to pick up food and medicine, they would discuss the progress of their treatment plans with one of Renascer's volunteers. If necessary, mothers might consult with a psychologist, nutritionist, or social worker. With each visit Renascer recorded changes in the children's health. As problems emerged, the team did whatever it could to try to solve them. This might mean anything from navigating the health system, to procuring a water filter, to helping a mother enroll in a hairdressing course.

In some cases, mothers failed to keep up their ends of the bargain and Renascer "discharged" them. In some cases, the family situations seemed impossibly desperate and Renascer lacked the resources to bring about long-term changes in the family. But most of the time, Renascer's work made a real difference, and after a few months, a child was past the danger zone or at significantly reduced risk of recurrence, and the mothers had adopted healthier habits. These successes occurred most frequently with acute illnesses, such as malnutrition, pneumonia, tuberculosis, leptospirosis, and infectious diseases. "This group are the happiest for us, because the sicknesses come from poverty and we can bring a lot of change to them," Cordeiro said.

With chronic illnesses, such as kidney disease, asthma, sickle cell anemia, rheumatic fever, or neurological problems, the goal was to show the mothers how best to manage the conditions at home. And with terminal cases, such as AIDS or leukemia, the goal was to keep the children comfortable until death.

Early on Cordeiro discovered that she had a gift for attracting helpers. "When Vera first started, she pulled in everyone," recalled Maria Aparacida Carvalho, who oversees Renascer's job training programs. "She would say: 'Come work with me! Come work with me!' 'We need you!' She has no idea how much energy she projects."

Regina Milanez, who sits on Renascer's steering committee, recalled how she got involved: "I saw Vera on the cover of a magazine and called her up. You know that doctors don't know how to deal with money. When Vera heard that I was a retired financial analyst from IBM, she said: 'Please help us!' So I started coming in twice a week. I looked at the accounts. And I realized I really had a lot of knowledge about how to do this and I was very excited to be doing it. And I developed a series of costing structures to figure how many families we could serve."

Martha Scodro, who is the president of Renascer's steering committee, saw an article in a newspaper. "I had small children and I wasn't working. I went to the hospital to donate some toys and I spoke with Vera. When I told her I was a psychologist, she said, 'We need you! Please go into that room to help take care of that child who is dying.'

"So that's how I started."

Cordeiro gets away with this behavior because her focus is clearly not on herself, but on the work that needs to be done. She seems to spend most of her life thinking about the needs of others. She even seems to experience much of life through other people's eyes. When talking about patients, for example, she instinctively switches to the first person. Rather than say "This woman was worried about her child. She didn't know what to do," she will say "This woman said to me, 'Dr. Vera, please help me. I am so worried about my child. I don't have anywhere to turn.'"

Cordeiro also spends a great deal of time reminding people of their importance to Renascer. The first day I visited her office, she introduced four people as "the most important person in Renascer." None appeared to doubt her sincerity. When Luís Carlos Teixeira, a respected physician who is president of Renascer's advisory council, dropped by one afternoon, Cordeiro declared: "Luís Carlos is our King Solomon! The most important person in the history of Renascer!"

At the outset, Cordeiro saw that she would have to rely on volunteers to reach a large number of children. There were not enough professionals to meet demand. Her method of recruiting and motivating people was to get them excited about helping children and to give them considerable latitude to solve problems. She found that most of Renascer's volunteers, middle-class women who had self-selected for the work, were conscientious and respectful. Those who were condescending to poor mothers were quickly asked to leave.

However, Renascer's use of volunteers drew fire from social workers at Lagoa. They told Cordeiro that it was "irresponsible" to have nonprofessionals providing social support to poor women. Cordeiro's response—like Erzsébet Szekeres's response in Hungary—was that professionals were needed for special cases, but not in the front lines. "What people in the front lines have most to give is themselves," Cordeiro said. What was irresponsible was discharging children to the slums and then forgetting about them.

Two questions that Ashoka interviewers commonly pose to candidates during the selection process are: "Who are your enemies?" and "Who are your allies?" "When you have an idea that's going to change how things are done, that means you're changing how people relate to one another," explains Drayton. "You're changing their power positions. You're threatening to obsolete their knowledge, the 'human capital' of their experience. This is not always welcomed with open arms." And social entrepreneurs need to be prepared.

At Lagoa, it was the social workers who initially turned out to be Renascer's "enemies." Why? "Renascer showed clearly what should be done and what wasn't being done," explained Odilon Arantes. Tensions mounted until a group of social workers lodged a complaint with Lagoa's directors. The directors called a meeting. "At the meeting," recalled Arantes, "there was Vera, the group against Vera, the directors, and me. The idea was to put an end to Renascer."

After the social workers aired their grievances, one of Lagoa's directors asked Arantes to offer his opinion on Renascer. Arantes replied: "I had a problem in the pediatrics department, a problem of children returning over and over. Renascer solved my problem. If it goes, I will demand something to replace it." The directors had nothing else to offer.

Afterward, the social workers quieted down, but the directors asked Cordeiro to move Renascer's office outside the hospital. Cordeiro knew she had to stay nearby, but she couldn't afford to rent a space. Then she remembered Parque Lagé, where she had played as a child. There was an abandoned horse stable in the park. Its walls were crumbling, its roof leaked, and a drunk slept on the steps. But it was only a short walk from Lagoa and situated in as tranquil a setting as one could hope for in Rio.

In the summer of 1992, Ashoka's representative in Brazil, Candace Lessa, received a call from an Ashoka nominator suggesting that Lessa pay Cordeiro a visit. "The program was incipient then," Lessa recalled. "The innovative aspect was introducing a new notion of what providing medical care was."

That fall Drayton traveled to Brazil to conduct "selection panel" interviews. As Cordeiro recalled, one of the first questions he asked her was: "What do you expect to have in ten years' time?"

"It's a crazy question," Cordeiro recalls thinking. "I can't even make plans for tomorrow! How can I think about ten years from now?"

But reflecting on that interview almost ten years later, she added: "I'm beginning to see that if you think this way your dreams come true."

Cordeiro found herself moved by Drayton's interest in her idea and her life. He seemed hungry to understand every detail of Renascer's operations. How did they decide when to discharge a child? How did they motivate the mothers? How did Cordeiro plan to spread her idea? How did she plan to engage with the government? No one had ever forced her to think so deeply about the practical obstacles she would face as she attempted to expand beyond one hospital.

Cordeiro outlined her vision: In a government system otherwise characterized by corruption and indifference, the public hospitals remained one of the few doors open to the poor. And a child's illness was a powerful event that could trigger change in a family. It was senseless to provide hospital care to poor children without following up. But this was a new idea, and the health system was not yet prepared to take it on. Citizens had to develop the systems. Renascer had a solid base of volunteers—no small achievement given Brazil's history of dictatorships. It was helping to unleash the civic spirit of Brazilians. It was also connecting people from upper and lower classes. "I don't know who gains more in the exchange," Cordeiro said. "A person who earns less than the minimum wage can transform the life of someone from the elite. Because poverty is not only a lack of money, it's a lack of a sense of meaning.

"This is the best antidepressant we have. It causes a revolution in people. I am sure it will multiply not only in Brazil, but internationally."

In October 1992 Cordeiro was elected an Ashoka fellow. A year had elapsed since Renascer's launch in the playground of her apartment building. She was working out of a stable with a leaky roof. And now an organization with offices around the world was telling her that her work would change healthcare in Brazil. The distinction came with a Brazilian-level social sector salary—about $9,000 a year for three years; no fortune by any means, but the timing was critical. It doubled Renascer's budget.

More important than the money, however, was the encouragement: the vote of confidence and the connection to a network of like-minded people. "I remember very clearly the clothes I was wearing"—blue pants with a flower print and a T-shirt—"and how I cried the afternoon that I was told by Ashoka that I was elected a fellow," Cordeiro said. "One of the fears we had at the time was that what we were doing had no name, that it would die even before it could be born. So, it meant so much to me that other people understood the importance and essence of Renascer.

"And I understood then that my idea would not die."

The Ashoka stipend was a boost, but Cordeiro needed to raise considerably more funding. "I had no access to business at the time," Cordeiro recalled. "But I thought, 'I can put out a newsletter.' And I felt confident that people would read it and give me some money." She began with neighbors, relatives, friends, and doctors at the hospital. Then she started making speeches at schools. "But I could see people's eyes," she recalled. " 'Is she keeping the money? Does she want to be a politician?' "

Brazilians could be forgiven for their skepticism. In the early 1990s, citizen activity of this sort was still fairly unusual. And practically every day the newspapers carried another story of a scandal involving the abuse of public trust. It didn't help that Fernando Collor de Mello, the first president elected in the postmilitary era, had defrauded Brazilians of a billion dollars before he was thrown out of office and forced to flee the country.

"How can I prove to people that I am honest?" Cordeiro asked her friends.

One day, over dinner, she raised the issue with another Ashoka fellow, Valdemar de Oliveira Neto. He suggested that Cordeiro find an accounting firm to do an audit. It had never occurred to her. So she approached Arthur Andersen (this was years before the firm became mired in the Enron scandal) and convinced the firm to help her pro bono. This act made all the difference. Since that day financial transparency has remained an integral part of Renascer's organizational culture. Each quarter a detailed "presentation of accounts" is published in a newsletter and sent to thousands of volunteers and supporters.

At home, every Cordeiro family gathering turned into a discussion about Renascer. It would go on until Laura or Marina would yell: "Mom, are you going crazy? Stop talking about Renascer!" Paulo, Cordeiro's husband, recalled: "This work was brought into the home each day of our lives from 7:00 A.M. until midnight."

"There was no food in the pantry," Cordeiro said. "There was day-to-day confusion in the household. I had no time and no interest to do things at home."

It didn't take long for Laura, who was ten years old in 1991, to come to despise Renascer. "It was like suddenly having a younger brother, and it caused a lot of anger in my sister and me," she recalled.

Marina and Laura volunteered at Renascer, then quit, then volunteered again. Despite their resentment, they found themselves drawn into relationships with Renascer's families and changed by their experiences. Today Laura is studying law and plans to devote herself to social causes. Marina, who is also pursuing a law career, adds: "I plan to use my skills to help build a more inclusive society."

"My contribution on a daily basis was to be a supporter," added Paulo. "To understand that more than anything Vera needed time to devote to this."

"Without Paulo, there would have been no Renascer," Cordeiro says. "He has been my great partner. He was very punished by this revolution. Without him, I don't think I would have had the emotional strength to do this."

By 1994 Renascer had 508 dues-paying members whose fees totaled $4,000 a month. Cordeiro had also received grants from foundations and private sources. While she expanded the membership, she continued to deepen the work. She got transport agencies to provide discounted bus tickets, which Renascer distributed free to mothers. When it became clear that many families required more than six months' assistance, she launched a program to connect middle-class families with Renascer's families to provide nutritional and medical supplements for six-month extensions. She then launched a work program to boost the incomes of mothers who had to stay home full time with children, teaching them to manufacture gift items, which Renascer marketed. Then, seeing that most of Renascer's mothers lacked basic understanding about breastfeeding, family planning, and prevention of gynecological cancers and AIDS, Cordeiro began training mothers to run health workshops in *favelas*.

When a TV producer who had received care at Lagoa got wind of Renascer, Cordeiro was invited to appear on *Fantastico*, a popular variety and talk show. The appearance led to a spate of newspaper and magazine stories and helped double Renascer's paying membership.

Meanwhile, everywhere Cordeiro went, she invited people to visit Renascer. Before long calls were coming in from out of the blue: "We've heard you have a system that can help us. Can we visit?"

"It was funny," she recalled. "We felt we had just started. But already doctors were coming to us to learn how to multiply the experience."

The first successor, Reviver (relive), was established in 1993. Next came Ressurgir (reappear), Reagir (react), and Refazer (redo) in 1995. Cordeiro made sure replicators met four criteria before she agreed to work with them: They had to have: (1) a strong working relationship with their hospital, (2) extensive experience treating poor patients, (3) a willingness to sign an agreement promising to uphold Renascer's standards, and (4) a "genuine need" to do the work.

Ressurgir, for example, was founded by Albenita Barros Correia, a dynamic woman who had worked for years as the chief mental health professional at a small children's hospital in central Rio. Like Cordeiro, Correia couldn't stand that children with preventable or manageable illnesses kept being readmitted to the hospital. She also saw that the solution was to work closely with their mothers.

In 1996 and 1997 Renascer's model began attracting considerable attention. Cordeiro won Brazil's Serviço Social do Comércio (SESC) Medal and the Serviço Social da Indústria (SESI) Fiftieth Anniversary Medal, both major social service honors. In 1997 the model spread to three more hospitals, and more awards followed: the Tiradentes Medal, the Beija-Flor Trophy, the Bem Eficiente (Efficiency) Award, the Rio de Janeiro Government Award, and, from Washington, D.C., the IVY Inter-

American Foundation Award. Since 1997 the model has been adopted in nine more hospitals.

In 1998 Cordeiro sent a letter to the former president of BNDES, Brazil's national development bank, inviting him to visit Renascer. The letter was passed on to the director of BNDES's social development sector, Beatriz Azeredo, who followed up. Azeredo was impressed by the way Renascer's model complemented the public health system and by the fact that it had spread to several other hospitals. "When we look at a program, we immediately look to see if it has a potential to spread nationally," she told me.

However, before expansion was possible, Renascer would have to consolidate its systems and institute professional management procedures. Fortunately, around the same time, Cordeiro received a phone call from Anamaria Schindler, the director of Ashoka's Center for Social Entrepreneurship in São Paulo. Schindler had established a partnership with the São Paulo office of McKinsey & Company, and she wanted to know if Cordeiro was interested in having McKinsey consultants work with her pro bono. Of course, Cordeiro said. They could begin immediately—by helping to prepare a $50,000 expansion plan to submit to BNDES.

McKinsey is considered the Rolls-Royce of management consulting firms. The world's richest corporations pay the firm millions of dollars a year for its advice on strategy and how to achieve "organizational excellence." Drayton had initially established contact with McKinsey, where he had worked for nine years, before Schindler turned the relationship into a full-fledged partnership.

In contacting McKinsey, Drayton wasn't looking just to drum up free consulting work for fellows. He saw it as something bigger: an opportunity to build respect and improve coordination between the business and citizen sectors. What better way than by linking McKinsey, a leader in its field, with leading social entrepreneurs at a point when the entrepreneurs were gearing up for expansion? It would be a two-way learning process: The consultants would learn from the social entrepreneurs' strategic insights and their ability to achieve results in difficult contexts, and the social entrepreneurs would benefit from the consultants' management and organizational expertise.

To convince McKinsey that it was a sound investment—not just an opportunity to "give back" to society—Drayton, in meetings with McKinsey partners, stressed the institutional logic from the firm's perspective. McKinsey's basic mission is to help companies understand their environments and develop strategies and management skills to seize new opportunities. But societies were changing. In many countries the growth of the citizen sector was outpacing overall economic growth by a large margin. At the same time, boundaries among the business, government, and citizen sectors were becoming blurred. These changes were happening, but the understanding had not yet caught up with the reality.

"Most of it is still unforeseen, but it is probably the most important change in the world today and it promises a rapidly growing opportunity over the next decades," Drayton explained. "If McKinsey knows how to make this business-social bridge, everyone will benefit. The firm will be positioned ahead of the curve to understand new dimensions—economic, social, ethical, professional—and its advice will be better and deeper. Its consultants will better understand the whole future environment. Social clients will benefit from business knowledge and business clients will benefit from the social knowledge. And society will benefit as a whole."

It didn't take long for the marriage between Renascer and McKinsey to take. As with corporate clients, the consultants came in and spent weeks inside the organization, interviewing everybody, inquiring about mission, values, opportunities, problems. "These McKinsey consultants—they're so serious," Cordeiro said. "They wear suits and ties every day. But I love them! They're so smart. They think of everything."

"People fell in love with Renascer," explained Frederico Oliveira, a McKinsey partner who became Renascer's champion in his office. "The organization is straightforward and humble, definitely very ethical, and very action oriented. In fact, you have to hold back because Vera jumps on ideas like crazy. That attitude is very exciting for us. They're willing to discuss and listen and they will go for it."

Consultants analyzed how Renascer selected and tracked its cases, how it managed its volunteers, how it decided when to discharge a child, and how it measured impact. They looked at the organizational structure: who was responsible for what, who reported to whom. They broke down service offerings into "core" and "noncore," defined key "competencies," and assessed where Renascer was strong, where it was weak, and what would need to be strengthened if Renascer were to grow by 30 percent within the next two years.

With help from the consultants, Cordeiro upgraded her $50,000 proposal to a $250,000 "strategic plan" and convinced BNDES to fund it. She decided to establish a new position analogous to a chief operating officer to free her from direct management duties. The consultants helped

Cordeiro delineate three divisions: operations, administration, and fundraising. They helped clarify responsibilities and reporting lines. "McKinsey taught me that you need to have a matrix for the guilt," Cordeiro said.

Renascer had records on more than 1,500 families, but the information was not in a form that could be analyzed readily. The consultants helped Renascer develop a database to track cases from admission until a year after discharge. Renascer instituted new documentation systems and produced operations manuals for replicators. BNDES financed a research project to examine postdischarge cases.

Renascer also instituted guidelines for evaluating the health, housing, and employment conditions of families, as well as standard reevaluation cycles for cases. A color-coded system was introduced to segment cases: green (acute but curable, maximum eight-month term of assistance, 40 percent of Renascer's cases); yellow (chronic diseases, maximum fourteen-month term, 50 percent of cases); and white (terminal, extremely poor, need to find a social institution or family to provide long-term support after discharge, maximum twenty-four month term, 10 percent of cases).

The discharge criteria was standardized as follows: After Renascer's intervention, a family must have attained a minimum monthly income (after rent) of R$180 (Brazilian *reais*; in mid 2003, one *real* was equivalent to about 35 cents) or R$250 for families with more than five members. The family must be receiving all available public benefits for seriously ill or disabled children. The house must be a brick structure with a cement floor and no serious damage to the walls or roof, with two rooms, a bathroom, sink, shower, and toilet—either a pit latrine or sewer system—and a water filter. The children's health must be evaluated as "satisfactory" or "good" by Renascer. All children over the age of four must be in day care or receiving special care as needed. All children between five and sixteen years old must be in school. All children under ten must be vaccinated. All family members must have proper government documentation. The mothers must have completed a family planning course.

"What McKinsey did was like a revolution!" Cordeiro exclaimed.

But the revolution was not without complications. What happens, for example, when you apply a business management framework to an organization involved in social change? How do you balance financial and human considerations? How do you professionalize without losing intimacy? How do you standardize without losing flexibility? How do you redraw reporting lines without alienating old friends?

These were some of the questions that came up. One day, for example,

Philip Reade, a consultant, asked Cordeiro: "If there were only ten openings in Renascer and there were twenty poor families who needed assistance, how would you choose?"

Cordeiro replied: "Since the beginning when we had no money and a leaky roof, our rule was to bring in all twenty families. Something has always allowed us to grow."

But what was that something? And how did one plan for it?

For McKinsey, working with Renascer was also a valuable experience. "Nonprofits have a different way of thinking than we're used to," explained Frederico Oliveira, from McKinsey. "They look much more like family-owned companies, with many soft aspects being taken into account in the management. We have to find a way to work in these situations, not just apply our pragmatic, logical frameworks. I think McKinsey as a whole will learn a lot."

In addition to the "sheer personal satisfaction" gained by consultants, Oliveira noted that McKinsey benefited by having its junior and foreign consultants exposed to real-world difficulties rooted in local context. "Any barriers are magnified in nonprofits—lack of resources, infrastructure, management ability," he added. "But they are more savvy at finding constructive solutions and alternatives. They have no information technology department to come and solve their problems."

In 2001 Cordeiro was selected as one of Brazil's ten "women of the year" and one of the country's twenty top social leaders. She was also honored as a leading innovator by the Schwab Foundation for Social Entrepreneurship. And in early 2003 Renascer was awarded the $100,000 "Most Innovative Development Project Award" from the World Bank's Global Development Network.[3]

By 2002 Renascer had assisted 6,000 children and 4,000 other family members in 1,740 families. The replications had assisted another 10,000 people. A 2002 study of families discharged from Renascer reported that the percentage of children whose lives were "at risk" dropped from 42 to 10 percent, while the average monthly incomes for their families had increased 58 percent.[4]

Three paid staff members and seven volunteers now handled fundraising. The organization had opened a second office. The crafts-making program, which had long been a marginal undertaking with revenues of about $20,000 a year, was fast becoming a professional operation turning out quality bed, bath, and kitchen gift items. McKinsey consultants believe it will develop into an important source of earned income.

Renascer had also added formal job training. By 2003 more than 600 mothers had completed courses in manicuring, hairdressing, embroidery, seamstress work, and computer operation. Renascer provided loans for business tools, such as car wash equipment, freezers, marble saws, and carpentry gear. Cordeiro had also established a U.S.-based Friends of Renascer to advance international replication of the model.

In their first meeting, Drayton had asked Cordeiro, "What do you expect to have in ten years' time?" On October 25, 2001, Renascer celebrated its tenth anniversary. Cordeiro, fifty-one, recalled the raffle in the playground, the conflict with the social workers, the day she was elected an Ashoka fellow, the years in the stable, the *Fantastico* TV show, the spread to other hospitals, the awards, the McKinsey "revolution," the launch of U.S. Friends of Renascer, hundreds of volunteers, thousands of children. They had certainly come a long way since the days of clapping for milk.

And yet, to fulfill her vision of carrying Renascer to every hospital in Brazil, the next ten years will require even a steeper climb. It will take salesmanship, savvy, and stamina to effect change within the health system. Cordeiro will have to spend a great deal of time persuading doctors, hospital administrators, health officials, and funders.

Looking ahead, I can imagine two possibilities: (1) Renascer continues to be influential, but its replications are sporadic and they fail to match the strength of the original; or (2) Renascer transforms itself into a reference and training center that successfully spawns and supports cells across Brazil. Every major decision Cordeiro has taken since 1998 foretells the second result.

When I try to envision what the next decade may hold, I am reminded of a comment made by Odilon Arantes when I asked him what the key factor had been in Renascer's success. "Here I can say with absolute assurance that the main element for Renascer's success was Vera," he replied. "Without her, we would still be living in the past. She is perhaps the strongest person I have ever met in my life. She is so persistent; she insists and insists until she wins."

When I mentioned Arantes's comment to Cordeiro, she insisted that everyone in Renascer had been a "co-creator." She acknowledged that she had been the one to bring people together, but it was their collective energy that made it all happen. "Nobody is more important than any other person," she said. "But sometimes a person has success because that person continues fighting. I think if I have some value it is that I continue fighting."

In Search of Social Excellence

By the late 1980s, Ashoka had supported close to 200 fellows in India, Indonesia, and Brazil, and its approach was beginning to attract attention in funding circles and among international aid organizations. "Donors were beginning to realize that if you wanted to build an institution you needed an entrepreneur," recalled Susan Davis, who was then the Ford Foundation's representative in Bangladesh. "You couldn't design one and just go out and hire somebody to run it."

At the same time, the world's leading international development funders, including the World Bank, the United Nations, and the United States Agency for International Development were coming under fire from critics who charged that foreign aid had degenerated into a wasteful and unaccountable $60-billion-a-year industry dominated by high-priced consultants who parachuted into Third World countries, pressed their advice on beleaguered and often-corrupt governments, and then returned home.

Against this backdrop, Ashoka's approach appeared fresh and promising. The problem wasn't with foreign aid per se or, for that matter, with government spending. The problem was with the *distribution channels* of foreign aid and government spending. As long as money continued to be channeled through large bureaucracies, subject to the dictates of far-flung experts, aid would remain mired in poor performance. To be effective, Ashoka argued, resources had to be placed in the hands of people who would really use them well.

Who were those people? Local entrepreneurial change agents who recognized the problems; who understood the political and cultural environment; who had a special talent for spotting opportunities, crafting solutions, and building organizations; and who were determined to pursue their work over decades.

To produce real change and accelerate social innovation, far more resources would have to be channeled systematically to social entrepreneurs. They were out there. Ashoka could point to hundreds. It could explain what they were doing and why their work was significant. Perhaps more important, the organization was beginning to understand *how* the social entrepreneurs were succeeding.

By the late 1980s Drayton had personally interviewed hundreds of social entrepreneurs, and he had begun spotting common strategies in their work. "I started seeing patterns in the way the entrepreneurs solved problems," he recalled. "And I began thinking: 'How do we draw out the principles?'"

In 1990 Ashoka invited ten social entrepreneurs from South Asia who were working with youths to its first "mosaic meeting"—"mosaic" in the sense of assembling the pieces. The purpose was to see how the fellows' ideas fit together and to look for patterns. At the meeting, which was held in Dhaka, Bangladesh, Gloria de Souza detailed how she was making experiential education feasible in different parts of India.

Another fellow, Ibrahim Sobhan, from Bangladesh, explained how he was improving the quality of rural schools where student dropout rates were 70 percent and the student-teacher ratio was 60 to 1. To provide better instruction, Sobhan placed his students in ten-member groups and assigned quick learners in each group responsibility for co-teaching their peers. He introduced a program in which young girls taught their mothers to read. And he found that he could cut the dropout rate dramatically by doing away with homework and incorporating income-generating activities such as fish cultivation and livestock rearing in the school curriculum.[1]

Another social entrepreneur, Anil Chitrakar, an engineer from Nepal, had devised a scalable program to train eleven- to fourteen-year-old children in rural areas to maintain solar electric pumps. He soon found that the youngsters were not only quick studies, they were eager to help older villagers adopt new technologies to improve rural life. He created a network of technology and environmental camps to show them how.[2]

Putting Children in Charge

The key insight that emerged from the mosaic meeting was that each entrepreneur had found ways to put children and youths in charge of problem-solving and decision making. Not only did this strategy create

147

enthusiasm and help the youths develop skills and confidence, it solved a major resource problem for the entrepreneurs. Ibrahim Sobhan wanted to reduce the student-teacher ratio, but he had no money to hire more teachers. In his own classroom, however, he discovered an underutilized teaching resource: the students themselves.

Following the meeting, Drayton continued to interview fellows in other parts of the world, and he began to see that wherever social entrepreneurs were working with youths, they were struggling with similar challenges and applying similar strategies. And in essence, the fellows were all trying to do one big thing: help children succeed in a world that was fundamentally different from the one in which their parents and grandparents had grown up.

In less than two generations, population growth and structural changes in the global economy had transformed the patterns of life everywhere. The most obvious indication of the changes was massive population displacement. The urban population in the developing countries soared from 300 million in 1950 to 1.5 billion in 1990. It is projected to reach 4.4 billion by 2025.[3]

No longer could the majority of the world's inhabitants count on living out their lives in small towns and villages where change came slowly, families remained intact, people didn't move far, and the skills needed for survival could be acquired close to home. In the modern world, youths had to acquire the confidence to adapt to new situations, the ability to manage information, and the sensitivity to work in mixed groups.

Consequentially, the systems and worth-affirming rituals that societies everywhere relied on to educate, guide, protect, and motivate young people had to be redesigned. That was the challenge that many fellows—independent of one another—had taken up. It was why Gloria de Souza had shifted from rote learning to problem-solving education in India. It was why Jeroo Billimoria had established a system to protect millions of children living as adults in India's cities. And, as we will later see, it was why J. B. Schramm, a social entrepreneur based in Washington, D.C., founded the college-access program College Summit.

Enlisting "Barefoot" Professionals

Another pattern emerged from the social entrepreneurs' efforts to devise cost-effective ways to deliver basic services. Many of the social and medical advances of the twentieth century have bypassed vast numbers of the world's population. The bottleneck is distribution. Relative to global need, the professionals who deliver services—doctors, nurses, teachers, lawyers, psychologists, bankers, social workers, and the like—are both scarce and expensive. Intuitively, the social entrepreneurs have turned away from professionally intensive models in favor of models that mobilize ordinary citizens to reach underserved markets at scale.

The most famous organization to make use of this strategy is the Grameen Bank, the so-called barefoot bank, which delegates its loan oversight to borrowing groups and village-based "center chiefs," making it possible to administer millions of tiny loans cost effectively. In the field of education, BRAC, another of the world's largest and most successful citizen organizations, founded by Fazle Abed, has trained women villagers to run schools that have educated more than 3 million children across Bangladesh.[4]

In the field of health, social entrepreneurs like Vera Cordeiro have demonstrated that nonprofessionals can assist families in a variety of health-related matters. In India, the Comprehensive Rural Health Project, founded by Raj Arole in the state of Maharashtra, trains "village health workers" to provide prenatal care to hundreds of thousands of villagers, significantly reducing infant and maternal mortality rates.[5]

In the field of human rights, Nemzeti és Etnikai Kisebbségi Jogvédő Iroda (Legal Defense Bureau for National and Ethnic Minorities), Hungary's leading legal defense organization for Roma (Gypsies), founded by Imre Furmann, teaches Roma in rural areas to collect evidence immediately after a human rights abuse has occurred.[6] In Burkina Faso, the Burkinab Movement for Human and People's Rights, established by Halidou Ouédraogo, places the primary responsibility for human rights monitoring not in international organizations, but in thousands of dues-paying local citizens.[7]

An important application of this strategy is in the field of disability. Seven to 10 percent of the world's population is disabled, and most of these people remain in the care of their families.[8] Yet in many parts of the world a disability—mental illness, deafness, paraplegia—is still seen as a curse or punishment from God. The disabled person is hidden away and the family is stigmatized.

In the case of mental illness—the most common form of disability—the professionally intensive treatment model prevalent in wealthy countries is almost totally irrelevant for developing countries. India has a population of 1 billion people and, as recently as the late 1990s, it had only 6,000 trained psychiatrists and psychologists. Using a professionally intensive approach, the problem will never be solved. Left to their own devices,

Indians often lock mentally disabled relatives inside their homes or take them to "holy men," where they are subject to various modes of "treatment" in the name of "driving out the evil." Some of these "treatments" involve physical abuse, such as beating and whipping.

Again, the social entrepreneurs have arrived at a common insight: The key is to put the problem-solving knowledge directly into the hands of family and community members.

This insight remains central to the work of Thara Srinivasan, a psychiatrist in Madras who cofounded India's ground-breaking Schizophrenia Research Foundation.[9] Working for years with schizophrenics in the slums of Madras, Thara found that the best approach to the problem was to train the "primary caregiver" in each family and use mental health professionals, if available, on an emergency basis. Families that were given basic training to manage the illness were far better equipped to anticipate and avert crises than others. And by educating neighbors about mental illness, Thara was able to further reduce the shame, stress, and stigmatization that families experienced. A similar approach is being applied today in Kosovo, where small teams of psychiatrists and psychologists are using a family-based mental healthcare model in an effort to manage the war-related stress disorders that have afflicted tens of thousands of families.[10]

Designing New Legal Frameworks for Environmental Reform

How do we strike a balance between human economic needs and sustainable environmental practices? Many social entrepreneurs addressing this challenge focus initially on creating new legal frameworks that align economic interests with environmentally responsible behavior.

One such example is Drayton's "bubble," a regulatory framework that moves away from a government-led "command and control" approach to one that harnesses market forces to promote pollution-control innovations on a decentralized basis.

Another example is the "extractive reserves" idea pioneered by the late Chico Mendes and Mary Allegretti in the Amazon rain forest in the mid- and late 1980s. Mendes and Allegretti sought to solve two problems at once: protect the rain forest and protect the livelihoods of hundreds of thousands of indigenous people. While Mendes organized the rubber tappers, Allegretti lobbied the Brazilian government to have areas of the rain forest rezoned as "extractive reserves." The strategy was to shift from an exclusive ownership framework, in which ownership is vested in an asset itself, to a nonexclusive ownership framework, in which ownership is vested in the right to use an asset in reasonable fashion (similar to that of an apartment co-op). The owner of an apartment co-op can sell his rights to live in the apartment, but he cannot destroy or substantially change it. A similar approach was applied to the rain forest, with transferable usage rights granted to locals whose livelihoods depended on the continued health of the whole "asset." Currently 9 million acres in the Amazon are protected under this law.[11]

Helping Small Producers Capture Greater Profits

Much of the criticism of economic globalization has centered on factory labor abuses. But the majority of the world's poor are not employed in factories; they are self-employed—as peasant farmers, rural peddlers, urban hawkers, and small producers, usually involved in agriculture and small trade in the world's vast "informal" economy ("informal" because economists have difficulty measuring it).[12]

Social entrepreneurs seeking to alleviate poverty among this target group usually begin by asking: How can we help these small producers benefit more from their trade and productive activities? And the solution they usually come up with is to change market conditions or redesign the "value-added chain" for whole classes of small producers.

Social entrepreneurs have attacked this challenge from many different angles. Some, like Muhammad Yunus of the Grameen Bank, focus on access to capital. With small amounts of working capital, villagers can purchase assets, increase their productive capacity, and capture profits that historically have accrued to moneylenders and land owners.

Some focus on market relations. In Ahmedabad, India, the Self-Employed Women's Association (SEWA) founded by Ela Bhatt, has helped 318,000 self-employed women, including paper pickers, cigarette rollers, kite makers, and vegetable vendors, organize themselves into a powerful trade union.[13] SEWA not only protects its members from exploitation and promotes government policies favorable to the informal sector, it offers a range of services—collective purchasing, credit and savings, legal representation, health and child care, and insurance—that enable poor women to work for themselves more profitably while reducing their exposure to business and personal risks.

Some focus on market access. The Association pour le Soutien et l'Appui a la Femme Entrepreneur (Women Entrepreneurs Support Association), founded by Gisèle Yitamben, in Douala, Cameroon, helps small businesswomen in West Africa—fruit growers, craftswomen, French-

English translators—market their products and services to European buyers via the Internet.[14] Similarly, TransFair USA, based in Oakland, California, founded by Paul Rice, links small coffee growers in Latin America to major U.S. coffee retailers, such as Starbucks, Safeway, and Green Mountain Coffee Roasters.[15] The farmers gain access to credit, information and farming supplies, enabling them to grow high-quality, often organic coffee for which they receive a decent price. In exchange, consumers get to savor the unbitter taste of coffee that has been "Fair Trade Certified."

Some social entrepreneurs focus on adding value to productive processes. A remarkable example is the Associação dos Pequenos Agricultores do Município de Valente (Small Farmers Association of the City of Valente), a cooperative of sisal farmers known today as APAEB located in the drought-plagued interior of the Brazilian state of Bahia.[16] (Sisal is an agave plant with lance-shape leaves whose fibers are used to make ropes, rugs, and brushes.)

In the early 1980s a soft-spoken man named Ismael Ferreira decided that the economics of sisal farming needed to be changed. The son of a sisal farmer, Ferreira had spent his childhood working in sun-scorched fields in a region where most families lived in shacks without electricity or running water.

But Ferreira had the opportunity to study accounting and engineering. And when he returned from school, he no longer would accept an economic arrangement that kept sisal growers dirt poor while intermediaries and manufacturers reaped big profits. Ferreira saw that farmers needed to pool their output and add value to the sisal before selling it. That meant working together. It took countless meetings to organize the farmers—cooperatives had a bad reputation in Brazil—and four years of fighting to receive a government export permit. Eventually, however, the farmers built a brushing and threshing plant.

Today APAEB operates a multimillion-dollar factory that sells export-quality ropes and rugs to buyers for large U.S. and European retailers. From 1997 to 2002, according to Ferreira, annual factory revenues increased 400 percent, reaching $6 million, with three-quarters of sales coming from finished products. The local price for sisal has tripled, bringing direct economic benefits to thousands of families and creating a powerful economic multiplier effect in a poor region where a million people earn part of their livelihood from sisal. In recent years dozens of researchers have visited APAEB to learn how an organization in an isolated rural area has managed to compete in the global economy.

Linking Economic Development and Environmental Protection

Fábio Rosa is another social entrepreneur helping small producers to capture greater profits. But Rosa's approach also illustrates another principle: Rosa is helping farmers and grazers add value to milk and beef through organic farming. In so doing, he is helping them protect their land *and* gain access to lucrative markets for organic produce.

Vera Cordeiro has noted that health and social problems are "two sides of the same coin"; the same holds for economic development and environmental protection. Social entrepreneurs typically find that they cannot address one problem without addressing the other.

Another social entrepreneur who has made this linkage is Jadwiga Łopata, the founder of the European Centre for Ecological Agriculture and Tourism (ECEAT), based in Poland.[17] Because Poland's farmers resisted the communist government's efforts to collectivize their land, there are still 2 million small farms in the country. However, many are struggling to survive in the face of competition from corporate farms in Western Europe.

Łopata has identified two competitive advantages that Polish farmers enjoy. First, having relied far less on chemically intensive agriculture than their European counterparts, they are well positioned to become Europe's

Jadwiga Lopata

leading producers of organic produce. Second, the farms are ecologically diverse and picturesque.

In 1993 Łopata founded ECEAT to encourage small farmers to pursue ecologically sensitive farming. She offered a deal: If a farmer went organic, ECEAT would help supplement the farm income by arranging visits from tourists.

ECEAT now works with 130 farms and has arranged vacations for 15,000 tourists, boosting its farmers' incomes by 25 percent. Łopata's objective is to use ECEAT as a lever to influence the government's farm policy by demonstrating the market opportunities for small-scale, organic farming. In 2000, Łopata cofounded the International Coalition to Protect the Polish Countryside (for which she won a $125,000 Goldman Environmental Prize in 2002), pulling together 450 organizations in a campaign to pressure the Polish government to support organic family farming. The coalition draws on the success stories of ECEAT's farmers.

Unleashing Resources in the Community You Are Serving

It takes a real flash of insight to attack a large-scale problem when you have very little money to spend. That, however, is the position in which many social entrepreneurs find themselves. One solution is to look for new ways to unleash and redirect the creative energies of people within the communities being served. This strategy has worked beautifully for the Comitê para Democratização da Informática (CDI; Committee for the Democratization of Information Technology), based in Rio de Janeiro, which has extended access to computer education in hundreds of slums in Brazil and other countries.[18]

CDI was founded by Rodrigo Baggio, an impassioned businessman, teacher, and technology buff who has been assisting underprivileged youths since he was twelve. In 1995 Baggio, concerned about the growing "digital divide" in Brazil, established his first computer school inside one of Rio's *favelas*. At the time he had the idea to set up five, or perhaps ten, computer schools in slum communities.

Baggio's strategy was not to run the schools himself, but to market a simple computer-school franchise model—the start-up manual reads like a comic book—that could be picked up by modest social service organizations almost anywhere there was electricity. The process had to begin with community leaders initiating a request for a CDI franchise. To demonstrate commitment, the leaders had to find a secure building, identify potential teachers, recruit students, and produce a school-management plan and budget, with the teachers supported by local fees. If the plan seemed viable, CDI would then provide hardware and software (donated by companies) and train local teachers to run the schools and maintain the equipment.

By 2002, using this simple franchise model, CDI had established 376 schools in Brazil, Japan, Colombia, Chile, Mexico, and Uruguay, providing access to computers to thousands of youths. In 2002 the organization's budget was about $300,000.

Two other organizations that have found ways to address large problems by unleashing the creative energies of people within communities being served are:

- Fé y Alegría (Faith and Happiness), an international federation of community-supported schools headquartered in Caracas, Venezuela, that has used this strategy to deliver low-cost, quality education to "where the asphalt ends"—reaching more than a million students in 2,500 impoverished and isolated communities in fifteen Latin American countries;[19]
- Gram Vikas (Village Development), founded by Joe Madiath in Orissa, India, which has helped thousands of *dalits* (untouchables) and *adivasis* (tribal people) initiate new village-based organizations to construct bio-gas stoves, drainage systems, latrines, fresh water pumps and community halls.[20]

Linking the Citizen, Government, and Business Sectors for Comprehensive Solutions

Many social needs can be addressed effectively only through a cross-sectoral strategy. One such need is access to books. In South Africa, for example, most citizens still lack access to books in their mother tongues that are both affordable and tailored to their reading abilities. It was this market gap that led Beulah Thumbadoo, a book lover since age eight, to quit her job at Penguin Books in Johannesburg to establish Easy Reading for Adults (ERA) in 1991. Thumbadoo's goal was to make suitable books available to the millions of South African adults who, under apartheid, had been systematically denied access to education. (ERA has since expanded its mission; it now stands for "Everyone's Reading in Africa.")

Thumbadoo began ERA's work by compiling South Africa's first catalog of "easy readers." She then toured the country, persuading librarians to allocate prominent shelf space to these books. She created "ERA

Book Boxes," portable adult literacy collections in attractive display cases, which she marketed to libraries, adult literacy programs, and companies with in-house libraries. "If you're a miner and you're lying in bed at 9:00 P.M.," says Thumbadoo, "you should have a book that's right for you."

The problem with easy readers was the selection. Most of the books had been produced by "do-gooders on shoestring budgets," and they were not terribly attractive or well written. Moreover, only a few were available in African languages. Thumbadoo launched the "ERA African Language Series," commissioning forty new, attractive easy readers by South African writers in the languages Tsonga, Sotho, Xhosa, Venda, Ndebele, Afrikaans, Pedi, Tswana, Swati, and Zulu. She raised a half million rand and negotiated with five publishers to produce 120,000 books. But she ran into a Catch-22. The publishers weren't interested in promoting the books or exploring alternative distribution channels because there was no ready market. And there was no ready market because apartheid had prevented it from being built.

Thumbadoo saw then that South Africa needed a national book development program. It was the government's job to create one. Adult literacy education was a national priority, and research showed that people learned to read most easily in their mother tongue. But the government did little to encourage African language writers or to push publishers to market books in rural areas and former townships. These were not minor omissions. "We must not forget the intimate relationship between oppression and efforts at preventing people from reading," notes Thumbadoo.

Thumbadoo studied the problem. Working with South Africa's Book Development Council, of which she was a member, and the national Department of Education, she tracked where and how low-income people bought and borrowed books. Then she outlined the steps needed to promote wider access to books. These steps included extending libraries into poor communities, encouraging African language translators and black women writers, establishing a national book trust to stimulate publishing, promoting reading through special campaigns, and encouraging book distribution through grocery stores and hawker stands in bus stations.

In 1999, taking a lead from her own recommendations, Thumbadoo pressed the government to sponsor a ten-year campaign to promote reading. She found an ally in South Africa's education minister, Kader Asmal, and after eighteen months of phone calls and e-mails, her efforts led the South African government to declare 2001 the National Year of the Reader, or, in Zulu and Sotho, languages spoken by almost half the country, Masifunde Sonke 2001 (Let's All Read Together).[21] The campaign involved library pushes, writing competitions, special events, and promotions in newspapers and on radio and TV. It has since been extended to 2004.

"I will eventually get my decade of reading," declares Thumbadoo, "even if it's one or two years at a time."

Another vitally important cross-sectoral strategy is currently being pursued by the International AIDS Vaccine Initiative (IAVI), headquartered in New York.[22] Founded by Seth Berkley in 1996, IAVI is working with pharmaceutical and biotech companies, academic labs, governments, multilateral agencies, scientific research bodies, media organizations, and nongovernmental organizations to spearhead a range of AIDS vaccine candidates and to prepare the ground for fast global access if an AIDS vaccine becomes available. Berkley, who helped the Ugandan government craft its response to AIDS in the mid-1980s, supervised health programs for the Rockefeller Foundation before he founded IAVI at a time when AIDS vaccine research was, in his words, "dead in the water." Since then Berkley has raised about $300 million for IAVI's work, including more than $125 million from the Bill & Melinda Gates Foundation.[23]

"When we originally figured out that HIV was a virus," Berkley told me, "everybody said 'vaccine'—it's the only proven technology to deal with a virus." As pressure for a cure mounted, however, the budget for treatment swelled and the budget for vaccine development dwindled. Moreover, big pharmaceutical companies found vaccine research to be an unattractive investment—both because the disease was spreading fastest in poor countries and because it is more profitable to market drugs to treat diseases than vaccines to prevent them.

IAVI acts like a nonprofit venture capital firm. It invests millions of dollars in companies or academic labs anywhere in the world that have promising AIDS vaccine candidates. It also provides logistical and scientific support to help the companies move quickly to clinical trials. If the companies succeed, they will be free to sell their vaccines at market rates in industrialized countries, but they will be contractually obligated to make the vaccines available at low cost in developing countries. To create market incentives for industrial research, IAVI is also lobbying governments and international agencies to create a multibillion-dollar global AIDS vaccine purchase fund.

IAVI's approach is unique both for its public-private partnerships and its global approach to vaccine development. Historically, it has taken ten to twenty years for vaccines developed in wealthy countries to become widely available in poor countries.[24] IAVI is focusing simultaneously on viral strains in Africa, India, and China, so that successful vaccines will be developed where they are most needed. "We've gone from having very little in the pipeline to a half-dozen approaches moving forward all fast-tracked, all for the developing world, all state-of-the-art science," explains Berkley. "Everybody agrees that the AIDS vaccine has got to be made available to everyone. And this is the model."

The Talent Is Out There

J. B. Schramm, United States: College Access

In the late 1980s, while attending Harvard Divinity School, Jacob ("J.B.") Schramm first recognized the college "market gap." To pay his way through graduate school, Schramm had taken a job as an academic advisor to freshmen. Each year he had to review the admissions files of thirty newly enrolled students. Reading through the applications from low-income students, he frequently came across handwritten notes in the margins: "Wish we could find ten more like him!"

After graduating from divinity school, Schramm, then twenty-eight, moved to Washington, D.C. He opted not to become ordained. He joined the Good Shepherd Ministries, a nonprofit organization that runs after-school programs for teenagers, including a teen center located in the Jubilee Housing Development, a low-income housing complex. In 1991 Schramm became the director of Jubilee's teen center. One of his first initiatives was creating the "Flyers Tutoring Program." The deal was if a student showed up at the teen center three nights a week to do homework for an hour with a tutor, at the end of the school year the student would get to take a trip on an airplane, typically to an outdoor youth program in Colorado or Florida.

The Flyers program allowed Schramm to establish his credibility. "I could never pull off being a cool inner-city youth leader," he says. "I am a square, thoroughly white, not street. But I was a straight shooter. The kids knew if they stuck with Flyers, they'd get on a plane."

Flyers helped the students succeed in high school, but what next? At Jubilee, Schramm saw the "college market gap" from the other end of the pipe. Students with top grades and test scores were zipping off to college. Ivy League schools sought them out. But the vast majority of the kids had average grades and test scores, and colleges paid little attention to them.

Schramm (in beard) with youths from the Jubilee Teen Center

There was a reason. Colleges have systems to identify low-income "stars." They buy lists from the College Board and compete for the top students.[1] All communities launch their academic stars, but only the middle- and upper-income brackets regularly launch their "mid-tier" performers.

The seniors in the teen center all told Schramm, "Yeah, sure, I'm going to college." But two months after high school ended, he would find many of them hanging out on the street. "A year later, their eyes were dulled," he said.

What went wrong?

"Absolutely mundane things," recalls Schramm. "I'd hear: 'I sent the application incomplete and never heard back. I only applied to two schools and didn't get in.'" Schramm discovered that most of these students' parents had not attended college themselves. They had difficulty guiding their children through the application process. And many of the students didn't really believe that they were "college material."

But Schramm saw them differently. "The kids who had middling scores had other things going on," he recalled. "One had written a screenplay. Others took care of brothers and sisters. Some were outstanding artists. Or one day there would be a fight, and I'd see a kid do something wise and courageous. Then I'd see the application and know there's no way the college is going to know about this kid's grit and moxie. But if you saw the kid handle challenges in the teen center, it was crystal clear. For me that was the 'aha!' moment. The challenge was to get the colleges to see these kids as *I* saw them. Because many were *better* than their numbers suggested."

In 1993 four students—Theresa, Desmond, Yonday, and Alimamy—approached Schramm asking for help getting into college. They were smart kids with lots of ability, but their grades and Scholastic Aptitude Test (SAT) scores were average. How to convey their potential? Schramm believed that a heartfelt essay could make a difference. "I had faith that if people told a part of their story that was important to them, it would convey their strengths to another human being in a way that nothing else could," he said.

He called Keith Frome, his closest friend from divinity school, who had taught expository writing to freshmen at Harvard, and asked him to come down from New York to Washington for a weekend to help the students write essays that would "jump off the desk." "Keith was the best writing teacher I had ever seen," recalled Schramm.

On the Amtrak train, Frome designed a curriculum based on writing theories he'd studied at Harvard. It would begin with ten minutes of unstructured "free writing," in which students would be encouraged to scribble random thoughts without editing themselves. Afterward, they would read the pieces aloud while the other students took note of images and phrases that stuck in their minds. Frome called this process "gold mining." Everyone's comments would be written on charts taped to the walls, a process that would both validate the students' thoughts and help them identify guiding ideas for their essays. Then the main job would be to remind the students to *show* what they mean, not just to *tell* it.

When Frome arrived in Washington, he and Schramm ran out to buy pencils, markers, butcher block paper, and masking tape. By late Sunday the students had first drafts of their college admission essays.

Then Schramm called up Derek Canty, a youth motivator whom he had met on a Flyers' excursion to Colorado, and invited him to Washington to conduct a motivational "rap session" for the students. Schramm wanted to help them identify personal obstacles that might derail their college plans. "Derek was without question the best youth facilitator I'd ever seen," he recalled.

Canty had a gift for getting teenagers to see themselves as one another's coaches, rather than one another's critics. One of his exercises was to ask each student to write on a flip chart at least one major obstacle he or she was facing, or had overcome, vis-à-vis college. "What comes up often is 'Family,'" Canty explained. "'*My father says I'm not smart enough for college.*' Or 'Money.' '*We can't afford it.*' 'Self-esteem.' They never believed they were good enough. 'Schoolwork.' They messed up in the first two years of high school and one year of doing well is not going to make a difference.

"When it's all up, you hear kids say: '*I have that one too.*' The sheet gets filled up and they see that other kids are struggling with the same things. The kids coach each other—which is so much more powerful than when it comes from an adult. The walls come down."

In the months that followed, one student enrolled in Brown University, one went to Montgomery County Community College, and the other two received full scholarships to Connecticut College, a liberal arts school in New London. Lee Coffin, who was then dean of admissions at Connecticut College, recalled: "Most college applications from low-income students fail to provide a good picture of the kid. The essays are flat. The recommendation letters consist of a single paragraph or even just a sentence. We're asking ourselves: 'If we accept the kid, can he succeed?' We're looking to predict the future. So when the kid doesn't have the numbers, you need something else to hang on to. And these kids told evocative stories that gave a vivid sense that they were succeeding against the odds. And J. B.'s recommendations came alive. That's what tipped the scales in their favor."

In 1994 four more students—Habibatu, Abass, Jenice, and Zainab—went through the same process. All four were also admitted to colleges. One decided to join the air force and another ran into personal problems during senior year in high school and failed to graduate.

"The difference between someone who is an entrepreneur and someone who isn't," explained Frome, "is that *I* went back to my job, but J. B. knew that we had invented something unique. He *saw* it. And he refined it and bottled it."

J. B. Schramm grew up in a middle-class family in Denver. Schramm's mother, Nancy, a sixth-grade teacher, was a book lover who placed great emphasis on academic achievement. "My mother insisted that I perform well in everything that I did," Schramm says. Schramm's father, Ray, had built a business from scratch selling used oil field equipment. "I thought my dad was one of the smartest people I knew," recalled Schramm. "But he'd always gotten Cs. It's not surprising. He grew up on a farm in North

Dakota. He had ten siblings. There was no English spoken at home. They all had jobs on the farm. But he still got himself to college. And it caused me to become very skeptical about taking numerical evaluations as the only indicator of someone's promise."

Schramm was an only child. With nobody to play with at home, school became his playground. It was where he felt happiest. In high school, he played soccer, acted in plays, joined the speech team, played trumpet in the jazz band, and headed the student council. Due to forced busing, Schramm had attended inner-city schools throughout his childhood. His friends came from a variety of ethnic and economic backgrounds. "I went from elementary to junior high and from junior high to high school with the same group of guys," he recalls. "We all had our strengths. And I just assumed that we'd all go on to the next stage in life together. College was a given." (Schramm had gotten accepted to Yale.) "When I found out that a lot of them weren't going, it was a jolt. It lodged in me. It profoundly didn't make sense. And the difference was not that they were less college capable than I was."

Schramm is articulate and fervent, with an agile mind and a streak of the performer in him. At Yale University, he helped create an a cappella comedy singing group called Mixed Company. "J. B. has always attracted all sorts of folks to him," explains his friend Keith Frome. "When we were in divinity school together, he was very charismatic in a traditional way—gregarious, a great actor, a great singer, always lots of fun to be around."

After graduating from Yale, Schramm had enrolled in Harvard Divinity School with the intention of becoming a Baptist minister. However, in 1988 he volunteered for the summer at a camp run by an African American Episcopal church for adjudicated youth in South Carolina. There he encountered the harsh reality of young people, mostly African Americans and Latinos, who had grown up without opportunity. "J. B. had a hard experience in South Carolina," recalled Frome. "The kids had had brutal lives. They did not readily accept him. He had always been well liked, but he couldn't charm *them*. And I think he saw that his charm wasn't going to be enough to do the kind of spiritual work he wanted to do. After that summer, his charisma became more internal, quieter. And his active commitment to helping inner city kids deepened."

By the time Schramm arrived at the Jubilee teen center, he had seen talented high school buddies fail to enroll in college for no good reason. He also had seen that colleges were hungry for low-income talent. But supply and demand weren't meeting. In fact, Schramm's organization,

College Summit, estimates that, out of the 900,000 low-income students who graduate from high school each year in the United States, at least 180,000 could succeed in college but fail to enroll.[2]

The problem with college access, as Schramm sees it, isn't that low-income students lack ambition. It isn't primarily that they lack money. (In many cases, financial aid is available.) And it's not just a function of the deficiency of public schools. "There is no question that K–12 education needs to be reformed," says Schramm. "But it isn't as simple as that." Why do A students from low-income backgrounds enroll in college at the same rate as D students from high-income backgrounds?[3] The answer is that many low-income students who could succeed in college don't grow up in a college-going culture: They don't know how to advocate effectively for themselves, and they don't get the step-by-step guidance that others do. Moreover, colleges don't know how to identify promising students beyond the limited measures of grades and test scores. "I don't believe that every low-income student is ready for college," says Schramm. "But the only way you can tell who is capable of going to college and who isn't is by looking at the whole student. It's not rocket science. The talent is out there, but the systems are blind to it."

By the summer of 1995, Schramm's first four students had completed their freshmen year. When Schramm called up Lee Coffin from Connecticut College to follow up, he was told: "Whatever you are doing is working. Please keep working with us."

By then Schramm had a new idea. For two years, after Frome's and Canty's workshops, students had continued coming to the teen center every Saturday for six months to work with mentors on their essays and applications. But often the students failed to show up, or they showed up without their essays. And, over time, mentors got burned out. Schramm recalled: "It was heartbreaking seeing a student at the end of a Saturday who had the sparkle in her eye because she'd just beautifully articulated something she felt—six days later, after homework, and brothers and sisters, and all the distractions, the recollection was gone."

That's what gave him the idea to compress everything into four days. That summer he wrote up a one-page concept paper for a "college summit." The plan was to bring thirty-five or forty students to a college campus from Thursday afternoon until Sunday, throw them together with writing coaches, college counselors, and a youth facilitator (a "rap director"), and, by Sunday noon, come out with each student having completed a college essay and a universal college application and having met individually with a counselor to decide where to apply to college. If the students were kept busy enough over the weekend, Schramm reasoned, they wouldn't have time to dwell on college fears.

Schramm put out a call to youth agencies, asking for students with "more college promise than their scores suggested." Then he set out to recruit writing coaches, college counselors, and a rap director. Initially no one believed that what he was proposing could be done in four days. But Schramm is a gifted salesman. And he pulled in thirty-five students from seven states, eight writing coaches, three college counselors, and a rap director. He persuaded Lee Coffin to host the summit at Connecticut College. Keith Frome agreed to teach his writing curriculum to others. Derek Canty agreed to act as the rap director. Schramm's wife, Lauren, had met a young college admissions officer named Tim'm West, who had grown up in a low-income family in rural Arkansas and gotten himself into Duke University. West agreed to be a writing coach. Schramm had heard high praise for a college counselor named Kpakpundu Ezeze. He enlisted his help, too.

"I recruited everybody, registered everybody, got a drop-dead date one month before the workshop to get good airfares. And then I went to friends, to churches. I talked to twenty-five people. I needed $13,800 to cover everything. I didn't get a *cent*. I was two days away from canceling the program. But my backbone stiffened. I said, 'I'm going to talk to twenty-five *more* people. Why aren't they *getting* it?'"

Finally a friend put him in touch with Carolyn Stremlau from the Banyan Tree Foundation. They met at a Mexican restaurant in Washington, D.C. By the end of the conversation, Schramm had his money.

Then, a week before the summit, he received a call from Canty.

"I have good news and bad news," Canty said. "What do you want to hear first?"

"What's the bad news?" Schramm asked.

"I broke my jaw. It's wired shut."

There was silence on the other end of the line.

"The good news is I'm learning how to talk with my jaw wired shut and I'll be there."

By Sunday noon every student had written a 500-word personal essay, completed a universal college application, and compiled a short list of colleges, as well as leads for financial aid. One of them, PinPoquin Theresa Downey, a Native American student from Tesuque Pueblo, New Mexico, wrote an essay about her grandfather and her adobe house. It began:

Theytay. That means "grandfather" in my traditional Tewa language. It's more than just a definition, though. He's my culture, my language, my songs, and my dances. He's a respected elder in my community. When I look at Theytay I see 85 years into my past—85 years still standing strong. He might need to use a cane now, but his spirit will never need one . . .

Three-quarters of the students who attended that summit were accepted to college, according to Schramm. Downey, who had envisioned herself going to a local community college, enrolled in Stanford University.

By then Schramm knew he was on to something, and his instinct was to grow it. A college friend put him in touch with Peter Goldmark at the Rockefeller Foundation. Although College Summit didn't fit into Rockefeller's funding priorities, Goldmark loved the idea and made use of the foundation's Special Initiatives fund. "He was the first major foundation person to see the promise in the idea," said Schramm.

In 1996 Schramm ran three summits for ninety-seven students at Connecticut College, Georgetown University, and Colorado College. Several months later, he quit Good Shepherd and opened a College Summit office out of his bedroom. For his board, he recruited Theresa Atta, one of the first four students he'd assisted in 1993, as well as two Flyers' tutors: Maurice Foley, a federal judge, and Dean Furbush, who was then the chief economist and head of strategic planning at Nasdaq.

The following year Schramm organized six workshops in Connecticut, Washington, D.C., Denver, and Chicago for 195 kids. He received funding from the New York–based Echoing Green Foundation, an organization modeled after Ashoka, which supports social entrepreneurs during the launch stage of their ideas.[4] He persuaded Cynthia Cheadle, an elementary school teacher, and sister of his best friend from high school, to move to Washington to help build the organization. (Schramm's friend, actor Don Cheadle, is a member of College Summit's board and has provided assistance with fundraising.) Schramm asked colleges to cover the room and board for the four-day summits, roughly $10,000, and asked schools to pay $100 per student, suggesting that the students pay half.

In January 1998 he moved his office to a donated basement space in Washington. That year the program doubled again, to twelve workshops in six states, reaching close to 400 students. Schramm delegated the direction of workshops to Cynthia Cheadle and Jaime Harrison, a recent Yale graduate who had grown up in a low-income community in South

Carolina. He also recruited College Summit alumni, now college freshmen and sophomores, to handle much of the logistical work. The organization received a big boost when the John S. and James L. Knight Foundation provided a get-to-know-you grant of $30,000 and, later, a $480,000 infrastructure grant. By 2000 the program had doubled again, reaching close to 800 students.

During the summer of 2001, I served as a volunteer writing coach for a College Summit workshop held at the University of Colorado at Boulder. As the manual instructed, my job was to manage a creative process that would help five students compose authentic, "heartbeat" essays. On Thursday night I received a crash training in Frome's curriculum. On Friday morning I met with my students in a college lecture room. After introductions, we went over a few ground rules—full confidentiality, no making fun—then dove into the free writing.

Free-writes begin like this: "I'm sitting in College Summit. My writing coach is telling me I have to write something, but all I can think about is lunch..." And they evolve in two days into engaging personal essays—not essays free of grammatical errors, but honest and frequently moving pieces of writing.

Students participating in Colorado College workshop.
Schramm is kneeling at far left; Derek Canty stands second from left.

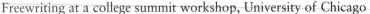
Freewriting at a college summit workshop, University of Chicago

One of my students, a young African American woman, wrote about the experience of discovering that she was gay. "When I was eleven years old," she began, "my cousin and I were walking down the street in sunny southern California when a guy, half naked, passed us smiling because of my cousin's mesmerized eyes. 'Look at that,' she said. 'He is cute, right?' I replied shyly, 'I don't know.' I was confused because I didn't find him attractive. . . ."

The student went on to describe what it was like living with a "dark secret" around a mother who expressed scorn for homosexuals and a grandmother who was fond of declaring that "God made Adam and Eve, not Paul and Paul." As the essay continued, the writer explained: "I found my own little world—a world of writing and designing. In this world I could free my mind and my thoughts. My writing and designing gave me wings; wings to fly above the raging storm." Her "wings," she concluded, would fly her to "college, and to becoming a fashion designer, and beyond...."

On Saturday night the students donned suits, silk shirts, and festive dresses for the banquet. At the event, the writing coaches read aloud short (carefully selected) paragraphs from the still-to-be-completed essays. Many of the students, even the coolest ones, could not conceal their delight at hearing their words applauded. After listening to portions of forty-nine personal essays—the struggles, the humor, the diversity of voices, and the common urge for achievement—I felt as if I had been given a glimpse into an alternate future that is available to the United States. I was amazed by what the students had produced, amazed by how much potential could be unleashed in two days. And it made me think about the thousands of talented low-income youngsters across the country who end up with their "eyes dulled" each year for lack of guidance during the most critical transition in modern life.

During the summer of 2003 College Summit completed its 124th workshop. By August 2003 nearly 5,000 students had passed through the program. Ninety-five percent were minorities: 50 percent African American, 35 percent Latino, and 10 percent Native American. The average grade point average (GPA) was 2.8. College Summit reports that, between 1993 and 2002, the college enrollment rate for high school graduates who attended its workshops was 79 percent; retention was 80 percent. According to the U.S. Census, the national enrollment figure for high school graduates at similar income levels is 46 percent.[5] (There are no national data on college retention rates.)

Of course, students who are willing to attend four-day college preparatory workshops are not fully representative of the total low-income student population. Indeed, College Summit specifically looks for students who have demonstrated potential beyond what their test scores reveal. Even so, all of College Summit's participants are referred by teachers or youth counselors who believe that, without extra guidance, the students are at risk of failing to reach college or enrolling in institutions poorly suited to their needs where their chances of success would be diminished.

One might ask why society does not do more to facilitate college access for college-capable low-income students. College Summit's board chair, Dean Furbush, says the problem can be understood as a failure of markets. One such failure has to do with "market coordination." Although the benefits that accrue from college education are considerable, they are broadly distributed and, without an organization like College Summit, there is no way to bring them together.

"Imagine that it costs $1,000 to provide the guidance for a kid to get into college who currently has a 2.5 GPA and would otherwise become a parking lot attendant, which is fine, but does not fulfill her potential," explains Furbush. "Say the kid goes to college and that $1,000 investment yields a $500 net benefit for the firm which, five years from now, she's going to end up working for; but, of course, we don't know which firm that will be. Say $100 accrues to the high school which can brag about getting kids into college. Say $400 accrues to the city that wouldn't have to pay to assist her and another $200 accrues to the college that's paying people to find her, and so on, including tax collections, indirect effects on her peers, and most of all, the benefit to her wealth and well-being.

"What if it turns out that all those smaller amounts add up to a return to society well in excess of the $1,000 that changed her life, but any single one of them wouldn't be enough to economically justify paying to change her path? It's hard for markets to arise when that coordination is difficult. There is fascinating economic work which says that firms arise where markets and one-on-one transactions don't coordinate well enough. What College Summit says is: Let's create a 'firm' that can coordinate across all of these stakeholders so that each one can make a rational decision that will end up with this kid going to college—and with so many people benefiting."

In addition to the intangible gains, college graduates can expect to earn $1 million more during their working years than high school graduates and contribute $300,000 more in taxes.[6] In first-generation college families, graduates generally establish new patterns of achievement that carry forward in siblings, cousins, and children. "That young man who is the first in his family to get a college degree has basically ended poverty in his family line forever," says Schramm. The effect also spreads to their high schools, neighborhoods, college campuses, and workplaces.

In 1997 and 1998 Schramm was presented with two opportunities to transform College Summit's model into a vehicle for bringing systemic changes in high schools. In the fall of 1997 he was contacted by Nancy Sutton and Patricia Ludwig, the principal and college counselor from Manual High School, a public school in Denver in which 80 percent of the students are poor enough to qualify for federally subsidized lunches.

In 1997 five Manual students had attended a summit. When the students came back boasting about their essays, Sutton and Ludwig called

Schramm to see if he would run a workshop the following summer exclusively for Manual students. Schramm agreed. The following year Manual sent one-fifth of its returning senior class to College Summit. That fall Sutton and Ludwig were pleased to discover that the workshop had not only had a positive effect on the college motivation and preparedness of the students who attended it, but also had a positive effect on those who had *not* attended it.

When 20 percent of the students in a senior class return to school in September with college essays already written, applications already completed, and colleges already selected, Sutton and Ludwig discovered that the effect is to make the other 80 percent think more seriously about their college plans too. That's when Sutton and Ludwig began to see College Summit's program as something that had the potential to "transform the school's college-going culture."

Each year since 1998, Manual has enrolled one-fifth of its returning senior class in College Summit. "Kids are most influenced by the successes of their older peers," explains Patricia Ludwig, today Manual's operations principal. "In a school like this, the only achievement models kids have to identify with are the varsity athletes. The charismatic, respected leaders in school need to be the kids who are going to college."

In 1998 another opportunity presented itself when Schramm was contacted by Tim Schwertfeger, chairman and chief executive officer of Nuveen Investments, an investment company based in Chicago. Schwertfeger, who had grown up on the South Side of Chicago and attended college on a scholarship, had recently established the Chicago Scholars Foundation, a scholarship program to assist students who were struggling to get ahead in Chicago's public schools. Schwertfeger soon saw that the students needed more than money to make the transition to college. His team did an Internet search and discovered College Summit.

In 1998 Chicago Scholars sent six students to the program. "They came back raving," Schwertfeger recalled. He followed up and asked Schramm if he would run a workshop the following summer exclusively for Chicago Scholars. Schramm agreed. Again the students came back raving. "So then," recalled Schwertfeger, "we said, 'Let's take it to another stage.'" Schwertfeger helped Schramm make inroads into the Chicago public school system, which paid for 200 of its students to attend College Summit workshops the following year. "Again the schools were positive," recalled Schwertfeger. The next question was: Could College Summit develop a model to strengthen college guidance within the Chicago public school system?

* * *

As these new opportunities and challenges presented themselves, Schramm began rethinking his expansion strategy. The organization had spread to eight states, but its growth had been scattershot. Furbush put Schramm in touch with two management consultants, Charlotte Hogg and Steve Sacks, who offered to help think through strategy. When they asked Schramm where high schools and colleges were responding most enthusiastically, and where it was easiest to raise money, they found a pattern. In cities or states where there was a concentration of partner high schools, colleges, and businesses, such as in Colorado and Chicago, the program was taking off. "With concentration, the program achieved a kind of critical mass," recalled Schramm. "Scale was magical." Schramm also saw that the key to success was to work with "local champions"—people like Tim Schwertfeger in Chicago—who were resourceful, influential, and committed.

The following summer Schramm pushed deeper into Colorado, Chicago, Washington, D.C., and Florida, and pulled out of sites where there wasn't a concentration of interest. Withdrawal was "painful and scary," he recalls. "I loved these partner institutions and the deans at them. And it was a real shift in the kind of thinking you get used to in the nonprofit world, where you can't say no to anyone. Someone gives you a twelve-year-old computer, it's 'Wow, thanks!' That is not the way to scale."

The work in Manual High School, in Denver, was an experiment to see if College Summit could develop a model to transform the college-going culture in a whole school. To accomplish that, the organization had to find a way to reach out to all of the school's seniors and make sure that they didn't derail halfway to their college destination.

So, in 1999, College Summit introduced a new product—a "Senior Year Curriculum"—and tested it out in Manual High School. Designed to complement the summits, the curriculum would help teachers guide all the school's seniors through the eight-month college-application process. It was based on the recognition that getting into college requires two very different kinds of guidance. "There is a fundamental misunderstanding in high schools across America about what it takes to move students to college," says Schramm. Everybody focuses on the role of the experts: the college counselors, he says. Equally important is the role of the nonexperts: the college-experienced parents who keep their children on track through a complicated and intimidating process. This role involves a lot of encouragement, a lot of suggesting, a lot of nagging. *Dear, did you mail the application? It's due next week.... Honey, did you pick up the financial aid form?*

In low-income schools, where college counselors are responsible for hundreds of students, the experts have limited opportunities to follow up with students. And in low-income families, where parents have not been to college, the nonexpert role is often missing.

College Summit's Senior Year Curriculum addresses this problem by training teachers to play the nonexpert, management role. Beginning in September 1999, several Manual teachers began acting as college mentors for seniors. That summer, at a College Summit workshop, the teachers had received training in College Summit's application curriculum. They learned how to use online tools to complete student aid forms and find sources of financial aid, as well as how to employ free writing and gold mining to enliven their recommendation letters. Then, when school got under way, College Summit began sending them weekly faxes, reminding them about test registration dates, application deadlines, when to collect letters of recommendation, and so forth—all the potential derailers. The work was handled during advisement periods, which Manual seniors were already required to attend twice a week. Each college mentor had fifteen to twenty seniors in advisement. And within each advisement group were three or four seniors who had attended a summit, who were enlisted as peer leaders.

None of this was easy to implement.

"It took an enormous amount of energy initially to convince teachers to buy in to the process and to convince parents to let their kids go to the summits," recalls Patricia Ludwig. But the skepticism dropped off quickly once teachers came back from the summits and parents began hearing about neighborhood kids who'd gotten into college. Of the sixty-two Manual seniors who attended summits in 2000, sixty-one graduated from high school and forty-seven enrolled in college in 2001, a rate of 76 percent. In 2002 Manual reported that its 2001 graduates received $1 million in scholarships.[7] Today bulletin boards in the school hallways feature photo displays from the summits; coaches encourage athletes to enroll as a strategy to lure others; and College Summit alumni regularly return to the school to talk about their experiences as college freshmen and sophomores.

While College Summit was developing a model to tip one school's "college-going culture," Schramm got the idea to tinker with the "student-admitting" culture on the other end of the pipe. In 1999 he introduced a third product: a "portfolio reviewing and matching" system to help college admissions officers find what they were looking for among College Summit graduates.

Schramm found that college guidebooks often failed to capture the nuances in admissions decisions. He thought: Why not interview admissions officers from partner colleges and inquire about the real internal criteria they used? If the college guidebook said that the median SAT score was 1,000, was it rigid? What was the low range the school was willing to consider? What were the characteristics of students without high scores who succeeded? How important was athletic or artistic ability? Did the school distinguish between in-state and out-of-state applicants? Did it want more students from a particular part of the city?

In the fall of 1999 College Summit delivered 370 prescreened "preview portfolios"—including essays, applications, and recommendation letters—to its partner colleges months before their application deadlines. Since then it has done the same every year. In late 2001 College Summit made 800 telephone calls to graduates of the 2000 summits and found that the college enrollment rate for that year was 81 percent.

In the summer of 1999 Schramm persuaded a college friend, Kinney Zalesne, to volunteer as a writing coach. Zalesne had served as a White House fellow focusing on domestic policy and education technology, and worked as counsel to Attorney General Janet Reno. "I had traveled with Reno around the country and seen a lot of community revitalization programs," Zalesne explained. "When I saw the workshop, I said this is not only the best community intervention I've ever seen, but it has the seeds for scale." Zalesne left the Justice Department to become College Summit's deputy director.

In 2000, when Ashoka launched its North American program, Schramm was one of the first four U.S.-based fellows elected. The same year College Summit received a grant from the U.S. Department of Education to expand its model in the Chicago public schools and evaluate its impact on college enrollment and retention. The organization opened a Chicago office. In 2001, with the support of the Chicago Community Trust, College Summit ran workshops for 420 Chicago students from twenty-five Chicago public schools. Elsewhere it served 600 students in Florida, Washington, D.C., and Colorado. In Denver the public school system also agreed to pay for students to attend the summits. That year the National Association for College Admission Counseling (NACAC) gave Schramm its annual award for "making postsecondary education opportunities available to historically underrepresented students."[8]

In 2002 College Summit moved forward with a strategy of working in partnership with cities to improve the college guidance system in public schools. College Summit expanded its work in Chicago and opened new offices in Denver and Oakland. In Chicago the superintendent of the Chicago Public Schools, Arne Duncan, committed to implement and pay for the "whole-school" model in five Chicago high schools. In California, with support from the Irvine Foundation, College Summit did the same in five schools in Fresno and the Central Valley, with the Irvine Foundation evaluating the impact on the schools' "college-going cultures." College Summit also began work in West Virginia, where it had established partnerships with the Energy Corporation of America and the Kanawha County Public Schools and begun implementing its whole-school model in two high schools in Charleston. Negotiations were under way with the Oakland and Los Angeles unified school districts.

To manage College Summit's aggressive growth, Schramm hired Bo Menkiti, a former management consultant who had run youth programs in Boston to centralize processes, clarify responsibilities, and strengthen the organizational structure. "Some of the challenges we're facing as we open up offices around the country are similar to multisite businesses," explains Menkiti, who is now College Summit's chief operating officer. With leadership from board member Rick Cohler, College Summit also launched CSNet in 2002, a web-based system that allows students to manage their college applications and essay-writing through the Internet; helps alumni maintain contact with one another; and will be used to help colleges do more holistic applications screening of College Summit students.

As part of the strategy of creating a "product" that schools want and are willing to pay for, College Summit continues to "codevelop" its model in partnership with school systems the way computer companies codevelop new software releases with their clients. College Summit has increased the fees that it charges schools. One benefit is that school principals and administrators are more likely to complain if they are not receiving value for their money. (It's hard to complain about something that comes free.)

By 2002 College Summit's budget had climbed to close to $4 million. The organization plans to expand to fourteen cities by 2009 and is looking to raise $17 million in new funds by 2006. In 2002 the organization received a $3 million five-year matching grant from the Samberg Family Foundation. Currently College Summit receives 15 percent of its revenues from fee-for-service arrangements with schools, school systems, and colleges; Schramm expects that figure to exceed 50 percent as the model reaches scale. At a time when U.S. colleges are moving toward more holistic decision-making in admissions, Schramm envisions colleges competing to host summits and paying fees to gain access to College Summit's "preview portfolios," just as they pay the College Board to receive standardized test scores.

In recent decades college education—like the computer—has gone from being a narrow-market good to a mass-market good. It can no longer be considered a luxury. This means that the distribution channels for college guidance need to be redesigned. That is a challenge College Summit has taken up.

Schramm believes that improving college access, especially for the 180,000 "college-capable" low-income high school graduates who fail to enroll each year, will not only motivate students and teachers in underperforming schools, but will catalyze positive changes in low-income neighborhoods across the country. "Teenagers are the single most influential group in a low-income community," he says. "If the teens are well engaged, it shifts the dynamic in that neighborhood. You are never going

Bo Menkiti, J. B. Schramm, and Kinney Zalesne

to see lasting transformations in low-income communities until there is a critical mass of college-educated youth in those communities."

In the years to come, College Summit will have to work hard to persuade teachers, school administrators, college counselors, and political leaders to buy in to its model. "Teachers have heard all about magic bullets," notes Deputy Director Kinney Zalesne. "They are skeptical before they even know what the program is." In the meantime, Schramm is gearing up for 2006, when the data from the Chicago and California evaluations will be in. "By 2006 we'll have a couple of school superintendents and mayors in a couple of highly referable cities who can stand up and say this model works community-wide," he says. "We're building up the infrastructure and testing our sites and franchise model, so we'll be ready to *move* when all that attention comes."

14.

New Opportunities, New Challenges

In the late 1980s, as its budget increased and its young staff gained experience, Ashoka was able to respond to social and political changes occurring around the world. In Asia, Africa, and Latin America, authoritarian governments were on the defensive. Social controls were being loosened and social entrepreneurs were seizing the new opportunities.

In 1987, after launching Ashoka in Brazil, Drayton and Michael Gallagher carried the work to Mexico, where citizens had been galvanized into action after the government failed to mount an adequate response to the earthquake that devastated Mexico City in September 1985. In 1988 Ashoka staffer Michael Northrop launched the program in Nepal, which was experiencing a period of political liberalization under King Birendra. Drayton then spread the work to Bangladesh, where martial law had recently been lifted and the military dictatorship of Hussain Mohammad Ershad was on its last legs.

In 1989 Drayton recruited David Bonbright, a program officer with the U.K.-based Oak Foundation, one of Ashoka's funders, to help launch the program in Zimbabwe, which was then embarking on an experiment with multiparty rule. Bonbright, formerly the Ford Foundation's point person for South Africa, then carried the work to South Africa as the formal dismantling of apartheid got under way. Staffer Michael Gallagher then launched the program in Nigeria, which appeared to be moving toward civil rule.

During the late 1980s and early 1990s, Ashoka also began working in Pakistan, where military rule had ended in 1988 (for a while); Uruguay, where military rule had ended in 1985; the Côte d'Ivoire, where opposition parties had recently been legalized; Cameroon, Mali, and Ghana, where multiparty systems were being established; and Senegal, which had recently reformed its electoral laws. By 1993 Ashoka had supported 463 social entrepreneurs in eighteen countries.

Ashoka expanded without fanfare. It didn't begin by renting office space or setting up legal entities. The strategy was to fly in under the radar and just begin electing fellows. Representatives frequently worked out of home offices and conducted interviews at their kitchen tables. It was Ashoka's policy to spend as little money on itself as possible. In 1993 the organization's annual budget was $2 million. Ashoka staffers hunted for cheap airfares and found lodgings through the Lonely Planet backpacker guidebooks. Reps typically signed on out of a personal commitment to Ashoka's mission. Their salaries were pegged to local social service rates, a fraction of the six-figure incomes earned by development consultants.

In the mid-1990s, after five years of widespread, opportunistic expansion, Ashoka began feeling the strains of its growth. "Establishing ourselves and sustaining high-quality operations in each country really stretched our organization, possibly beyond the limits of its capacity at that time," explained board member Julien Phillips. "We decided that we needed to take a more disciplined, region-wide approach to further expansion, one that included an explicit organization-building element."

Ashoka's board, seeking to ensure that the organization would be able to train and support staff who could identify high-quality fellows, as well as support existing ones, established a policy that Ashoka would not expand into a new region until it had raised sufficient funds to cover all costs in that region for three years.

A big break came in 1993, when the Avina Foundation, which had been established by the Swiss billionaire Stephan Schmidheiny, contacted Ashoka, seeking to form a partnership. Avina's mission is to promote sustainable development, particularly in Latin America, and its strategy is to "invest" in individual leaders.[1] "Avina challenged us to expand Ashoka systematically throughout Latin America and build institutional capacity as we did so," explained Phillips. "And it assured us of sufficient funding for the first five years to feel confident we could set out on this road."

To oversee the Latin American expansion, Drayton hired Susan Stevenson, a thirty-year-old McKinsey consultant who had worked for Save the Children in Bolivia and had spent her teenage summers doing volunteer work in villages in Mexico and Honduras. Stevenson had left McKinsey because she was looking for work she could feel passionate about. Everybody she met took one look at her résumé and said: "Talk to Bill Drayton."

Not long after their first meeting, Stevenson found herself back in Latin America, traveling nonstop for fifteen months. "It was absolutely fascinating," she recalled. "I had a license to talk to the most interesting people in every country in all the different fields." By the end of 1995 Ashoka had elected new fellows in Argentina, Bolivia, Chile, Colombia, Ecuador, Peru, and Paraguay. Not long after, it elected fellows in Costa Rica, Venezuela, and El Salvador.

After the fall of the Berlin Wall, Ashoka began exploring the feasibility of expanding into the postcommunist countries of Central Europe. Its major concerns were: Had the governments relaxed social restrictions enough to let social entrepreneurs function freely? Would Ashoka be able to find sufficient numbers of entrepreneurs, given the dampening effects of five decades of communism on human initiative? Finally, would Ashoka be able to avoid inadvertently electing ex-communists who might damage the organization's reputation and undermine confidence in the citizen sector?

The expansion into Central Europe was led by Shawn MacDonald, an activist in the labor, environmental, and educational fields who had worked in Africa and Asia and, after 1989, assisted the government of Poland in its efforts to reform the education system. Ashoka raised funds from the Open Society Institute, the Jurzykowski Foundation, and the Pew Charitable Trusts.

Whatever doubts people had about the feasibility of finding fellows in Central Europe were quickly put to rest. Almost immediately the organization encountered a backlog of social entrepreneurs. In 1994 and 1995 it elected fellows in the Czech Republic, Hungary, Poland, and Slovakia. "The whole concept of entrepreneurship was at the forefront of people's minds as the economies were changing," recalled MacDonald. "And people understood the importance of reinventing things, seeding new ideas, and spreading them."

Ashoka's practice of conducting detailed interviews and delving into personal histories did, however, raise some eyebrows. "A few early candidates mentioned that they'd never been so deeply probed except by the secret police," recalled MacDonald.

In a variety of ways, social entrepreneurs were already responding to the challenges involved in moving from a top-down, communist system to a decentralized, open society. They were building organizations to help citizens adjust to political pluralism and free market economics. They were working to repair strands of trust that had been severed by four decades of governments encouraging citizens to inform on one another.

They were at work devolving the old command-and-control structures—decentralizing healthcare, education, environmental management, political decision-making. They were aggressively attacking problems that had festered for decades: authoritarian school systems, environmental catastrophes, rampant alcoholism, homelessness, disabled people herded into institutions, lack of trust in government and media, medical systems that had never given women the option to have a natural childbirth.

While Ashoka's work flourished in Latin America and Central Europe, the organization stumbled badly in Africa. Africa presented an array of challenges: vast distances, political upheavals, poor infrastructure, lower levels of urbanization and education, and a perennial lack of development money. Africans also tended to be skeptical about Western-based organizations, and many social leaders still favored a statist approach to development. But Ashoka's big mistake was rushing into ten African countries before it had raised sufficient resources to ensure that its staff would receive the support necessary to succeed in their context. "The things we were willing to do and follow through on in South America and Asia we didn't do in Africa," explained board member Bill Carter. "And we fell flat on our face. We didn't stop to realize that it was going to be a much bigger problem with a different set of issues. As a result we've had to start there all over again."

The most serious problems occurred in Nigeria, where a combination of government interference—Ashoka's rep had to carry cash into the country from Ghana to pay fellows—and management oversights led to a temporary collapse of the program; and in South Africa, where the rep had established an independent South African board to oversee the program. The conflict, which revolved around the issue of whether the South African program would be controlled locally or by Ashoka's international board, touched on sensitivities about race.

One of the characteristics of Ashoka fellows in newly democratizing countries is that the first ones usually spring from the middle and upper classes, largely because they enjoy access to resources and information. In South Africa, where nonwhites had been deprived of life and liberty, to say nothing of education and economic opportunity, Ashoka encountered an uncomfortable problem: A preponderance of its early fellows were white. As a result, the local office sought greater flexibility in applying Ashoka's selection criteria.

Ashoka had a policy of making special efforts to identify social entrepreneurs in communities that were underrepresented in public leadership.

In India, for example, the organization had worked to elect women, untouchables, and people from tribal communities as fellows. However, while Drayton believed that reps should search harder for fellows from underrepresented communities, he did not believe that Ashoka should modify its standards to do so. He worried that if Ashoka modified its rules to satisfy the concerns of every country—no matter how legitimate those concerns were—there would soon be a dozen different standards and the designation "Ashoka fellow" would become meaningless. "From the very beginning, I knew there were two things that could destroy us," Drayton told me. "One was for us to lose our focus on being of and for leading social entrepreneurs. The other was losing our global operating unity."

For three years Ashoka's international board struggled to retain control of its South African program. During that time Ashoka's program in South Africa stalled. The situation finally turned a corner in 1999 after the legal problems were resolved to Ashoka's satisfaction and the organization hired a spirited new rep, Anu Pillay, a forty-one year old psychologist based in Johannesburg who had extensive experience in South Africa's women's rights movement. Setting out on a tear looking for social entrepreneurs, Pillay found thirty-two fellows in her first three years—including Veronica Khosa, whose story is detailed in the next chapter. Today the majority of Ashoka's South African fellows are nonwhite.

Ashoka still struggles to raise funding for its Africa region at levels commensurate with other regions. However, it has since rebuilt its Nigeria program, redoubled efforts in West Africa, and initiated new country programs in Uganda and Kenya.

15

Something Needed to Be Done

Veronica Khosa, South Africa: Care for AIDS Patients

In 1991, while Vera Cordeiro was launching Renascer in Brazil, Veronica Khosa, a fifty-four-year-old nurse working in Pretoria's main AIDS testing center, was getting a view of South Africa's future. Khosa had been a nurse for thirty-seven years. She thought she had seen everything in her day, but that year 21 percent of the babies in the Pretoria AIDS center tested positive for HIV. At the time, South Africa was still celebrating Nelson Mandela's release from prison. The government was talking about repealing the apartheid laws. It was a time for jubilation. But how could one rejoice when so many were testing positive for HIV and when AIDS patients could not even get basic care?

"People came to us when they were already showing symptoms," Khosa recalled. "We would send them to the hospital and they would return and tell us, 'The hospital said, "There is nothing we can do for you. Go home."'" Patients were being sent away without dressings or ointments for open sores, without so much as aspirin for pain.

"We weren't prepared for this," Khosa said.

Within a half dozen years, South Africa had the highest HIV infection rate in the world, by some estimates as high as 25 percent. By 2001 more than 4 million South Africans had AIDS or were HIV positive. The United Nations was calling AIDS in Africa the "worst infectious disease catastrophe since the Bubonic Plague" and projecting that AIDS would leave 40 million children orphaned by 2010.[1]

Veronica Khosa is a dignified woman, large-boned and imposing, at once grave and serene. She has a wide, earnest brow, warm eyes and a big-toothed smile, and a tendency to burst into laughter then settle into heavy

Veronica Khosa on a home visit

silence. She lives in Mamelodi, a sprawling, dusty former "township" about ten miles east of Pretoria, where she is well known as Mama Khosa.

Under apartheid, South Africa's townships, of which Mamelodi is one of the oldest, served as containment areas for blacks who were needed to work in the cities but required to be gone by dark. Today about one and a half million people are pressed into Mamelodi's houses, hostel rooms, tin shanties, and cardboard boxes.

Unlike Pretoria, where spectacular jacaranda trees shower purple blossoms each spring, Mamelodi has few trees to shade its tin-topped shacks, parched sandlots, and cracked roads. In addition to its racialism, apartheid was a for-profit enterprise, and the townships were designed to be cheap. For decades the government invested little in infrastructure, job creation, education, or health services. Unemployment rates in former townships today run as high as 70 percent. High unemployment, high population density, and low education levels, combined with a socio-economic order that systematically tore apart black families, have proven to be ideal fuel for the conflagration of AIDS. In addition, Pretoria, the administrative capital of South Africa, a bastion of Afrikaner nationalism, was one of the last areas in the country to mobilize a response to AIDS. Mamelodi did not have its own AIDS center until Khosa's efforts led to its establishment in 1994.

In the early 1990s Khosa saw that hospitals and clinics were unable to meet the need for AIDS information and care. In Mamelodi, few people understood how to prevent HIV infection or avert the opportunistic illnesses that kill people with AIDS. Instead of information, the airways were full of terrifying warnings. "The way AIDS was introduced was that black South Africans were all going to die of AIDS," Khosa recalled. "And that led people to think, 'Okay, if we are all going to die then why should we try to prevent it?'" The fear led people to recoil from HIV-positive family members. It forced people with the disease to conceal the fact or lose their jobs.

A belief grew that AIDS was brought on by evil spirits. Another myth maintained that AIDS was a disease of homosexuals and only whites were homosexuals. As a rule, black South Africans are uncomfortable talking about sex. Health workers avoided the topic, and the government pamphlets were mostly in English and Afrikaans, languages that many blacks couldn't read. These were some of the obstacles that Khosa would have to contend with.

One day a man walked into the AIDS center in Mamelodi, where Khosa was working, and collapsed. "We rushed and applied CPR and he revived," Khosa recalled. "We gave him a little bit of water. His mouth was full of sores. We looked for food for him. We bought a pint of milk.

"When he recovered, I said, 'Who are you?'

"He said, 'I'm Zakaria. I've been taking my treatment at Pretoria hospital but now the doctors say there is nothing they can do for me anymore. And my mother has not got her pension for the last three months.'

"For almost four days he had had nothing to eat. I rushed out to the social workers to say, 'Could we quickly purchase some food for him to take home?' I asked the social workers if they would apply for a bursary [government subsidy] for him, and that went through."

Thereafter, Khosa began visiting Zakaria at home after hours. Seeing him so alone, she thought, "My God, where are all the other people? What is going on inside those homes?"

On weekends, she started visiting squatter settlements to counsel poor patients who could not come to the AIDS center. She recruited retired nurses to help and ferried them around in her car. But Mamelodi is spread out and gasoline was expensive; visits had to be curtailed whenever Khosa ran out of fuel.

Khosa has many vivid memories of the patients she worked with during her early days doing home care. But the one that never leaves her is of the day she received a telephone call from a social worker in Mamelodi, informing her that one of her patients was trapped inside his house. Khosa rushed over and found that the man's family had padlocked the door from the outside and gone to work. "I was standing outside with the social worker," she recalls. "We couldn't get inside. The windows were closed. We could only see him through the window where the curtain was open a little. He was crying and asking for water and then he fell and dropped dead."

Not long afterward Khosa was in the Mamelodi AIDS center when a group of young prostitutes approached her. Khosa had often counseled the girls about the risks of AIDS. "We have been looking for you," one girl said. "Our friends are getting infected with AIDS. We don't know whether we're infected yet, but we want to stop.'"

Khosa recalls: "The youngest of them said to me, 'If you say I must stop standing there and getting this guy who's going to give me 15 rand, what are you going to give me instead?'

"Like what?" asked Khosa.

"'Something that I can do to earn money and get food.'

"I said to these children, 'Look, I'm not a company. I don't know the skills out there. I can't even sew.'

"But at the end of the day, a very sick man came into the AIDS center, and he had sores all over his legs and I immediately said to these girls, 'Put him into the next room. We can start now—helping these people who are sick at home.'

"And they said, 'Will it pay us?'

"And I said, 'I don't know. But I can teach you skills and those skills will help you to help your own families and maybe somebody will say to you, 'Look after my grandmother' or 'Look after my child.' And if you're able to do that the person will pay you.'"

The incident got Khosa thinking: There were so many young people in South Africa who were unemployed and so many people who needed to be cared for at home. Someone had to train the young people to do the caring.

* * *

Veronica Khosa was born in 1937 and grew up on a farm in the province now called Kwa-Zulu Natal. Her mother died when she was four. After her father abandoned her, Khosa was raised by her widowed grandmother, Nicholine Sibiya.

Each morning Nicholine would shake Khosa and her sisters awake before the sun was up, before the girls had to weed the fields and wash for school, and command: "Wake up and read for me!"

Drowsily, Khosa would go through verses from the Bible with her grandmother correcting every slip. Many decades later Khosa took her grandmother to the hospital and, asking her to review a consent form, was shocked to learn that Nicholine could not read.

Nicholine had been too poor to attend school. But she was a sharp-minded woman. She was also the person village women called on when they were giving birth. Sometimes, when Nicholine would leave for a delivery, Khosa would follow quietly behind. Zulu huts have small doors that admit little sunlight. Inside, in the dim glow of paraffin lamps, Khosa would hide. "I used to observe a lot of procedures which I would not discuss with anybody because as a child I was not supposed to see them. This had a lot of bearing on me when I grew up because I had this desire to help people especially when they could not help themselves. To be honest, I'm not a very jolly or friendly person. But I tolerate somebody who is sick. I don't know why that is."

As a teenager, Khosa was intent on becoming a nurse. After completing eighth grade, however, she was told by her grandmother that the family could no longer afford the school fees. Because Khosa was an excellent student, the principal offered her a scholarship—provided that she agreed to become a teacher.

"I want to become a nurse," she told him.

"No," the principal said, "I would like you to be a teacher."

"No," Khosa recalls replying. "I'm not going to be a teacher. I told you I want to be a nurse."

The scholarship offer was withdrawn, and Khosa left school and returned to her village. At the bus stop, she bumped into a local resident named Gannett Mhlongo. Khosa had often done odd jobs for Mhlongo in exchange for firewood. After learning why Khosa was home from school, Mhlongo asked her to stop by his house the following morning. When she arrived, Mhlongo handed her a letter and bus fare. She was to return to school immediately. The letter, addressed to her principal, said that he would be paying her tuition.

After high school, a minister helped Khosa find work at a rural missionary hospital in Kwa-Zulu Natal, where the one doctor on staff frequently traveled a hundred miles to visit patients. Khosa began training as an "auxiliary" nurse. On typical days she and the doctor would drive as far as local dirt roads would take them, then walk along mountain paths carrying medical supplies on their backs. Khosa not only learned how to dress wounds, relieve pain, and give bed baths, but because so many patients were isolated, she learned how to teach family members to care for each other.

"There was a lot of improvising," she recalled. "Things would run out, but you could not fail to dress or wash the patient because there was no linen. You always had to do something—even if you had to use a sack—as long as that sack was clean. I think that was when this knowledge of actually using anything to comfort the client came in."

She spent four years at the missionary hospital. After repaying Mhlongo, she moved to a town called Wittbank, not far from Pretoria, to work at a tuberculosis hospital. She then worked as a midwife, before joining the Pretoria City Council as an assistant nurse. Because she had not completed formal nursing training, on clinic days she was ordered to wash dishes. At that time black nurses were not permitted to continue their education while working, so Khosa resigned and returned to school, earning a diploma in general nursing with a concentration in community health. Later she returned to the Pretoria City Council and taught community health to medical students and nurses, many of whom had never visited homes without electricity or running water. In between, Khosa married and had two sons and a daughter.

I accompanied Khosa on several visits to AIDS patients. I noticed that she didn't offer people reassurances or invoke God. Instead, she meticulously examined swollen calves and bedsores and inquired about medication, income, food, children, relatives—looking for any possible opportunity to ease the patient's discomfort or burden. In the midst of so much unspoken fear and shame, her direct, purposeful manner seemed to have a calming effect.

Khosa does not lack courage. In November 1985 her teenage son, Samuel, was arrested along with hundreds of other black youngsters during a time of political unrest. Khosa spent two days searching for him. When she learned where he was being held, she walked into the police station past a group of officers, up a flight of stairs, and began shouting the name of the officer in charge: "Mr. Smith! Mr. Smith!"

"Oh, my, I shouted," she recalled. "And when he came out he yelled, 'Stop!' And you heard the silence. Because they had been busy hitting these children. The blood was on the floor. This guy he said, 'Who are you?' I was in my nurse's uniform. And I said, 'I'm here just to talk to you. I want to know why are you doing this? Because if you are fighting with us, you should fight only with *adults*.'"

That afternoon dozens of youngsters, including Samuel, were released. "We had to take him straight to the hospital," Khosa said. "He didn't look like himself for a long time."

When I asked Khosa why she thought she could get away with talking to a police chief that way, she replied, "Why did I think that I would not be killed? If I tell you, death did not matter to me. I am this type of person. If I'm alone I can have a way of moving a thing that many think would never move. If I can crack a person's eye, he's going to give me my way. I really don't know why."

After getting the idea to train young people as home care attendants, Khosa met with doctors, nurses, and social workers to generate support. Then she began looking for an organization to provide instruction in home care, but none existed. So she decided to adapt the teaching syllabus of the South African Nursing Council to the needs of people in Mamelodi. She designed a six-month course teaching such things as how to identify symptoms, give sponge baths, give pressure-point massages, dress wounds, care for mouth and bedsores, maintain catheters and urine bags, and, with the medications available, manage pain. She also met with administrators from old-age homes, tuberculosis clinics, and day care centers, seeking to arrange internships for her students.

She recruited twenty-seven students, including the sex workers, as well as nursing students and assistant nurses who wanted to learn new skills. She got permission to teach in an abandoned tin shed in a vacant lot in Mamelodi. Those who could afford it paid small fees to cover her expenses.

Early into the process, Khosa sought to answer a basic question: How big is this problem?

Nobody knew.

"We have to go to the houses," Khosa told her team.

She prepared a questionnaire and got the students, nurses, and social workers in Mamelodi to administer it. Beginning in March 1994, over the course of a year, they visited 2,000 houses in an area known as Mamelodi West and found 1,000 people who were chronically ill, 427 of whom were bedridden or in wheelchairs. The majority had chronic conditions due to strokes, disability, or an unspecified disease. The word "AIDS" was never spoken.

One of the survey's questions was: "Who remains with you during the day?"

Some of the patients replied: "I'm locked in the bedroom five days a week because everybody works," or "The first person who opens the door is the child coming from school at two o'clock."

Khosa planned to focus initially on those who were completely neglected and needed to be regularly bathed, turned, bandaged, fed, massaged, and assisted for pain. In her target group, seven people had AIDS; all were young. The number was less than Khosa had anticipated, but the situation did not last long. In her province, Gauteng, which has a population of between 8 and 10 million people, the HIV infection rate jumped from 6 to 20 percent between 1994 and 1996.[2]

As the full gravity of the situation in Mamelodi was revealed, Khosa began to wonder what she was doing working for the Pretoria City Council. "I said to myself, 'Am I here for myself or am I here for my patients?' Because at the end of the day, we continued testing people and they continued to be positive and on the other side, the hospitals were just rejecting them. I couldn't stand these people dying, locked in houses, rejected by their relatives or loved ones because people did not understand what was going on. I decided I had to throw myself from my job even if it was to stand on top of the roofs and shout, 'This is the problem!'"

In March 1995 Khosa, a divorced grandmother living in a country with mass unemployment, relinquished her coveted job with the Pretoria City Council, accepted a reduced pension, set aside one-half of her 30,000 rand (about $8,300) retirement package for her old age, and reserved the other half to do home care in Mamelodi. She would end up spending all of her savings. One month later Tateni Home Care Services—"Tateni" is a Nguni word of affection for a child who is beginning to walk—opened its doors out of the tin shed in the vacant lot in Mamelodi.

"There wasn't any planning," Khosa recalls. "It was an emotional response to seeing problems and just reacting and saying, 'I can do something. I can help. People cannot just be left to die like dogs.' Something needed to be done."

Five years later Tateni's office had moved to a flat, cement building in an isolated corner of Mamelodi. Its rooms were divided by corrugated tin partitions and decorated with health posters. There were desks and phones but no computers. The rent was cheap because security was a problem. Khosa discovered that practically anything of value—fans, sewing machines, the kettle and hot plate, vegetables from the garden—quickly disappeared. "People don't steal," Khosa said, laughing. "They just take."

One afternoon, I accompanied Eva Shibambo, a young home care attendant, and Ephodia Ngwako, a retired nurse, on a visit to several patients. It was a beautiful spring day in October, the sky an uninterrupted expanse of blue. With its dwellings set in grids against a backdrop of barbed wire and empty hills, Mamelodi looked like a military base in Nevada.

The first patient we visited, Peter, lived with his wife and son in a tiny corrugated-tin shack not much larger than a newsstand. Inside, it was stifling and the air was heavy with the oily smell of paraffin. Clothes, furniture, and cooking utensils were piled six feet high around a bed on which a man with an emaciated body lay prostrate in the dark. Eva quickly brewed tea and helped Peter lift his head to drink. He groaned and said that he had had nothing to eat since the previous day.

"When I'm hungry," he exhaled, swallowing hard, "it's worse."

Eva didn't bother to explain my presence and Peter didn't seem to care, but I felt like a voyeur of death and stepped outside as Eva attended to Peter's bedsores.

Outside, Eva disclosed: "His wife left for work without giving him food. She's rejecting him."

In a low tone she confided that Peter's wife had "the same diagnosis."

Eva went to search for Peter's teenage son. She discovered him a few doors down. He had no money for food. Eva gave him 1.5 rand (about 20 cents), and he returned shortly with a half loaf of bread. Eva said she would return in the morning, to give Peter a bath and massage, change his linens, and feed him porridge and tea. She made a note to confer with one of Tateni's social workers to apply for special assistance for him and to contact the clinic to see if he could get stronger medication for pain.

"He is suffering greatly," she said. "He cannot be left this way."

The afternoon was a succession of visits with people who were suffering at home. In a larger gray cement house lived Godfrey and Julia, a married couple, and Julia's mother, Martha, all three with AIDS, plus four children, two boys and two girls. Godfrey was a dignified-looking man who, despite being extremely weak, stood up when I entered and escorted me to a chair. Ephodia explained that I was writing about Tateni. Godfrey nodded thoughtfully. He coughed and rocked himself on his sunken couch. His stomach hurt, he said.

While Eva inquired about Godfrey's tuberculosis medication and examined him, Ephodia explained quietly to me that Julia was still able to bathe him, but her strength would soon give out. Ephodia informed Godfrey that James Chauke, his usual attendant, would be by the following morning and would take him to the clinic if the pain got worse. Godfrey thanked her quietly and looked at the ground. I asked how he felt about Tateni and he said, weakly, "It's good." He said he liked when James visited. After a few minutes of quiet, we said good-bye. Godfrey seemed to apologize with his eyes for not having the strength to stand.

In the car Ephodia said sadly: "Those four children are going to be orphans."

Tateni's first six-month training began in May 1995. Khosa enlisted retired nurses to help teach it. Word of mouth spread rapidly, and by July Tateni had fifty-six students. The major attraction was the opportunity to acquire marketable skills. But many also came to learn how to help their relatives. And others, like Eva Shibambo and James Chauke, were strongly motivated by the desire to help people in the community.

Besides acquiring caregiving skills, Tateni's students were taught how to assess their patients' illnesses and develop, in accordance with the patients' wishes, a care plan. They were assisted by nurses, social workers, and doctors, as well as physical or occupational therapists. The students learned to care for patients directly, as well as to teach their family members to provide care.

Tateni's strategy was grounded in four principles: (1) complement the formal healthcare system; (2) seek partnerships with all organizations in the community; (3) enhance the home care skills of family members and neighbors, including schoolchildren; and (4) involve the community in all major decisions concerning Tateni's activities.

Khosa's objective was for every student to graduate from the program knowing how to provide basic home care, apply for disability and child care, help families prepare for death (gather legal documents, decide on child custody, make funeral arrangements, etc.), and communicate effectively with local church groups, counseling agencies, food pantries, and hospices.

After three months of training, the students began making home visits. They began with fifteen patients. In October 1995, when the first class graduated, ten of Khosa's students immediately found jobs. Some had dropped out of the course due to family illness. A few had developed AIDS themselves.

A serious problem soon arose. Because Khosa was known for her AIDS work, families were reluctant to receive help from Tateni. They didn't want their neighbors to know that AIDS had struck them.

Khosa prepared another survey and had her students administer it to 500 families. The main question was: What should Tateni's approach be?

The consensus from 369 respondents was: Take a general approach; don't focus just on AIDS.

In November 1995 Tateni organized a gathering in Mamelodi. Khosa announced to the 1,200 people who turned out that Tateni's mission was to assist anybody in the area who was chronically ill who needed care at home regardless of age, gender, race, religion, sexual orientation, or disease.

It was a deft positioning. Tateni would be known as a general home care agency—even if the majority of its clients had AIDS.

In early 1996 thirty more students enrolled, and the number of families served increased to sixty-five. Khosa applied to the South African Nursing Council for accreditation as a home care training agency. Then she approached the provincial government's department of community health services to learn from their experiences in home care. She discovered that, in terms of practical systems, she was way ahead of them. So she suggested that they pay a visit to Tateni. She still hadn't received one rand of public funding.

Initially Khosa had hoped that hospitals would support Tateni by donating medical supplies. But they proved unwilling to do so. Instead, her staff improvised, creating homemade petroleum jelly and gauze dressings for bedsores and recycling sheets as bandages. Khosa dreamed of being able to afford latex gloves, catheters, and urine bags. For such things as antibacterial ointments, gasoline, furniture, and note pads, Khosa approached businesses, church groups, and individuals. Many contributed, but the amounts were small. Unlike many social entrepreneurs, Khosa's contacts did not extend into elite and wealthy circles.

Each month Khosa dipped deeper into her retirement fund. Each month she sent out more letters and grant applications. Donor funding, which had been abundant for grassroots organizations during apartheid, was now in short supply because donor agencies had redirected most of their support to the government.

When Khosa did manage to get in a funder's door, she heard the same criticisms, mainly that Tateni wasn't "focused." Funders were looking for AIDS programs, not general home care. Khosa maintained: "It is difficult to go into a home and assist only a twenty-four-year-old boy who is terminally ill because of AIDS when the mother or father is groaning with bedsores and arthritis. If you are a health worker, you have to help them both."

Donors also questioned Khosa's ability to run an organization. "They kept saying to me, 'You're just some community women. Who's going to control the money?' People tell you, 'We are international. You are just too tiny for us.'"

In late 1996 the World Health Organization (WHO) contacted the Gauteng Department of Health. The WHO and UNAIDS (the Joint United Nations Program on HIV/AIDS) were convening an international conference on home and community care for AIDS, and they wanted to know who in Gauteng was doing this work. When provincial health officials made inquiries, they kept hearing about one program: Tateni.

As a result of the international interest, in early 1997, almost two years after it opened its doors, Tateni received its first major government grant: 20,000 rand, equivalent to about $4,500 at the time. Sometime later the provincial health department provided additional funding of 45,000 rand. Khosa used some of the money to start paying home care workers small stipends. However, without sufficient funding to offer competitive salaries, Tateni had trouble holding on to its students after they graduated. Most found higher-paying work as caregivers elsewhere.

Later that year the South African government sent a representative to Geneva to present Tateni's work to the WHO and UNAIDS. After evaluating projects from forty-eight countries, UNAIDS selected Tateni as one of six best global practices in the field of community-based AIDS care.[3]

That caused the provincial government to take a closer look at Tateni's model. At the time, in Gauteng Province, with 1.6 to 2 million people infected with HIV/AIDS, there was virtually no palliative care beyond a few cancer units and hospice beds. It was clear to many in the government that a new kind of health response was needed to cope with AIDS. The health system could no longer remain self-contained and inaccessible to poor communities, as it had long been under apartheid. Across South Africa, hospitals and clinics would have to forge partnerships with community groups. It was the only way to reach millions of people suffering in their homes.[4]

In 1998 the Gauteng Health Department announced a plan to launch pilot home care projects in five locations. The government turned to

Khosa for guidance. Elizabeth Floyd, the director of the Gauteng Province AIDS program, explained: "Tateni could show in practice what we were thinking about. They were the group we could really build on. Veronica was the pacesetter and an inspiration to everyone. [Tateni] demonstrated an extraordinary level of humanism. That's a key leadership role."

After studying Tateni's systems, provincial health officials identified four components to successful home care:

1. The work had to be run by people from the community to be both cost-effective and locally accepted.
2. It had to be professional. In Tateni, retired nurses oversaw the training and monitored the caregivers.
3. The training had to be practice-based; students had to acquire skills by working directly with patients.
4. The program had to demonstrate that it could bring in young, unskilled people and turn out graduates with the ability and the credentials to pursue careers in healthcare. To attract sufficient numbers of trainees, it was essential that programs offer economic opportunities.

Khosa found her spirits buoyed by the health department's response. For a brief spell she even allowed herself to think: "Maybe I have shouted enough." She anticipated an easier time with fundraising, but, in 1998, she still had to dig into her personal savings to cover Tateni's expenses. Nevertheless, she continued to expand program offerings. She extended the training course to twelve months to conform to standards set by South Africa's national policy for health workers. To boost training capacity, she began enlisting her best graduates, supervised by nurses, to train new recruits. She also instituted a training program aimed at youth and children who were the primary caregivers for chronically ill family members. Like so many other social entrepreneurs, Khosa found that youth tended to be overlooked when problems needed to be solved. She found them to be competent, less judgmental than adults, and always eager to help.

From July 1998 to March 1999, Tateni's annual report documented 396 new admissions and 220 patient deaths. A footnote explained: "Many of the clients died dignified deaths because our home carers had been able to be with them when they passed away." The report detailed a variety of obstacles the organization faced: "High staff turnover, transport expense, family members' non-cooperation, ill patients living alone faced with burial expenses, hungry clients, poor referral systems, burglary, thieves destroying records and medication, trainees exposed to physically and emotionally stressful situations and high numbers of orphans increasing. . . ."

It was noted that Khosa's car had been broken into.

There were positive points as well: "We have satisfied clients who look forward to our next knock everyday. Trained personnel are prepared to develop, motivate and support junior members."

UNAIDS reported that between 1995 and 1999, Tateni's staff made 224,000 home visits, trained 2,100 family members to care for a sick person at home, and provided home care orientation to 980 nurses, 176 teachers, and 66 social workers. Its AIDS workshops had reached thousands of youth in Mamelodi.[5]

By 1999 the Gauteng Department of Health was supporting seventeen home care programs; by 2000 it was supporting thirty-six. That year Khosa was elected an Ashoka fellow. Shortly thereafter the health department approached Tateni to oversee the training of home care organizations in the Pretoria-Tshwane district of Gauteng Province. Khosa's goal was to establish uniform standards for home care delivery. By late 2001, according to Khosa, 1,050 students had graduated from Tateni's training program and 76 percent had found employment. Within Mamelodi, three other organizations had replicated its home care model.

Meanwhile, Khosa continued to add new programs to help Tateni's patients stay economically and physically active. Khosa found that patients who were healthy enough to cook could supplement their incomes by preparing meals for those who were too ill. Patients could also prepare dried vegetables, which did not spoil, for people living in squatter camps who were without refrigeration—so they could eat nutritious food during the winter. Tateni got others involved in beadwork and sewing. Khosa established a program to teach orphans how to cook and bake.

"Life is not just pain management," Khosa explained. "People are not dying tomorrow. While they're still able, they should do things that give them satisfaction and a purpose."

In 2001 Khosa was selected as South Africa's Woman of the Year in the health category in a national award program sponsored by the South African Broadcasting Company and Shoprite Checkers, a supermarket chain. "The telephone calls and congratulations were overwhelming," she recalled. Local doctors organized a surprise party in her honor. "This was the most happy day of my life—to know that people in my profession appreciated what we were doing."

By the end of 2001 Gauteng Province had fifty-seven home care programs.[6] Early in 2002 Elizabeth Floyd, the Gauteng AIDS Program director, affirmed that home care had become the "core business" of the provincial health department. Twenty million rand (equal to 40 percent of the provincial AIDS budget) had been allocated to home care and hospice beds.[7] Khosa's two principal recommendations—that home care programs be coordinated by trained nurses and adhere to uniform standards—had become government policy.

By 2002 Khosa was anticipating a move to a new office in a more central and secure location in Mamelodi. Funds for the new office—about 90,000 rand—had been raised from local individuals. "We'd been collecting bits and pieces—10 and 20 rand—for a long time," Khosa said. Additionally, Tateni had joined forces with two other organizations in Mamelodi to form a "care consortium," a one-stop shop for home care, hospice services, and income-generating opportunities. One of Khosa's best students, a young man named Kleinbooi Mogashoa, had launched a home care service in Mpumalanga, a neighboring province, in a town where the nearest hospital was almost forty miles away. "That one makes me quite happy," Khosa said. "Because it has been my dream to train these children that they should be independent and work for their own communities."

Looking ahead, Khosa has two main goals: increasing Tateni's management and planning capacity and developing a community-based model for orphan care for South Africa. For the first challenge, she is trying to convince donors to finance management training for her staff, but many are reluctant to support "nonprogram" expenditures. For the second, she has joined a provincial task force to explore how Gauteng's growing network of home care programs can be employed to better assist orphans. Home care attendants are often the first to learn when a child is to become an orphan.

The challenge is to turn caregivers into quasi social workers who can help grandparents adapt to caring for youngsters, advise families on the placement of orphans, and recognize signs that a child is in emotional distress. Again, the need is immense; again, there is little experience in bringing the requisite skills to market. "My plan is for Tateni to fill in the gap between the community and the family where there are no parents,"

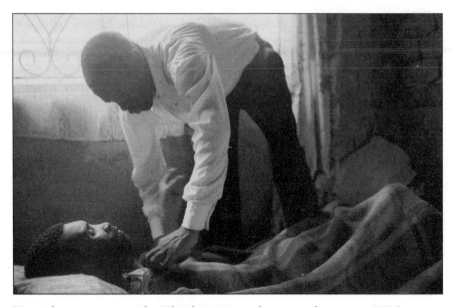

Tateni home care provider Kleinbooi Mogashoa attending to an AIDS patient

Khosa explains. "I know that the moment our model is well established, people will flock to it again. And I'm quite happy if they do that, because I think we have got more orphans than we know."

One subject that Khosa rarely discusses is the fact that, in countries where antiretroviral drugs are widely available, AIDS has become a chronic disease not necessarily a death sentence. Although political pressures and competition from generic drug manufacturers have brought the price of AIDS drugs down to $350 per year, this figure is still beyond what most people in Africa (and the rest of the developing world) can afford. To complicate matters, President Thabo Mbeki has questioned the link between HIV and AIDS and refused to support the distribution of even cut-price antiretroviral medicines. [8] The United Nations has estimated that it would cost $10 billion a year over an extended period to mount an adequate response to the global AIDS crisis.[9]

If, in the years ahead, AIDS drugs do become more widely available in the developing world, the major challenge will likely be effective distribution and care management. At present, there is a dearth of trained health personnel available to monitor and counsel patients in poor and remote areas. In years ahead, organizations like Tateni may prove to be critical linkages between the formal health systems and low-income communities.

Beyond AIDS care, Khosa contends that organizations like Tateni also have the potential to confer lasting social and psychological benefits on low-income communities. "An effective health response organized at the community level, will help black South Africans overcome the lack of confidence caused by ignorance which leads to self-destruction," she says. At essence, Tateni's care is about strengthening the capacity of families and communities while preserving the dignity of human life.

16.

Four Practices of Innovative Organizations

Institutionalize Listening

One of the most important qualities of innovative organizations, I have found, is a strong commitment to listening. Innovative organizations institute systems and guidelines for listening to their clients; they don't leave this aspect of their work to chance. In Childline, for example, every key decision, including the choice of the name and logo, the responsibilities of team members, and the Childline credo—"Every Call Is Important"—has emerged from regularly scheduled meetings and "open houses" with street children. Childline also provides explicit instructions to partner agencies explaining how to listen to children. "The child should know why the study is being conducted," its training manual instructs. "The child should not be prompted with options. If his response does not fit into any option, then it should be listed out verbatim."[1]

At Erzsébet Szekeres's center in Csömör, "helpers" regularly write narrative reports detailing their failures and successes. They are encouraged to be blunt. Similarly, residents are welcome to drop by the administrative offices to voice complaints. "People from traditional institutions have told me that it's not a good idea that disabled people can wander into the administration area," Szekeres said. "I thought about it and then I said, 'Why not?'

"One thing is for sure: We're never going to make decisions that are out of touch with the needs of these people."

Another young organization that excels in this area is Sharing the Things We Have.[2] It grew out of a food bank cofounded in Warsaw, Poland, in the early 1990s by a dissident named Wojciech Onyszkiewicz. The process began when Onyszkiewicz approached farmers seeking donations of food. After five decades of communism, the farmers had no patience for welfare programs. Onyszkiewicz was told: "We don't work for parasites."

But Onyszkiewicz continued meeting with the farmers and listening to their problems. He learned that they were fearful of falling behind the rest of Poland. Onyszkiewicz got the idea to propose an exchange: If the farmers would donate food, the food bank would take their children on educational trips to Warsaw and Krakow—show them the Parliament and the Royal Palace, take them to museums, universities, and amusement parks. They would have the opportunity to befriend city kids and meet the people who ate the food they grew.

Many villagers were too poor to take their kids to Warsaw or Krakow. The idea generated excitement.

The so-called potato trips began in late 1994. That autumn Onyszkiewicz arranged trips to cities for 2,650 rural children in exchange for 106 tons of food.[3] He recruited high school volunteers from Warsaw to manage itineraries and staff buses. He got companies to donate services. By 2001, according to Onyszkiewicz, more than 36,000 children had been taken on trips in exchange for 3,400 tons of food, equivalent to 6.7 million meals.

As the idea took off, Onyszkiewicz passed on management of the food bank and set up Sharing the Things We Have to identify other mutually beneficial rural-urban exchanges.

Each week his team visits villages to listen to locals. In one such session they discovered that young villagers were embarrassed about their ignorance of computers. In Warsaw they discovered that many physically disabled people were skilled computer users. The disabled people, it turned out, were eager to vacation in the countryside, but accessibility was a problem. So another idea emerged: Enlist disabled people to teach computer courses to rural youth in exchange for villagers building wheelchair ramps and facilitating pleasant, fresh-air experiences.

Once you started listening to people, there was no limit to the opportunities, explained Onyszkiewicz. He added: "We have so many ideas like these, and they are all feasible."

Pay Attention to the Exceptional

From the standpoint of innovation, the most important insights gained from listening or observing seem to come from *exceptional* or unexpected information, particularly unexpected successes. For example, when J. B.

Schramm helped his first four students make it to college, he recognized that he was on to something big. It was possible to provide a little extra guidance at the right moment and dramatically alter a student's life for the better. When Muhammad Yunus, of the Grameen Bank, made his first loans to forty-two villagers and was promptly repaid, he also recognized something new: Poor people were not "unbankable," as he had been taught. In fact, they were quite reliable.

Another social entrepreneur who has met with the kind of unexpected success that overturns assumptions is Tomasz Sadowski. Sadowski is a bear of a man who lives near Poznan, in western Poland. In the early 1990s, when the Polish government stopped subsidizing the *kolkholz* (collective farms) and thousands of people suddenly found themselves homeless, Sadowski and his wife, Basha, both psychologists, purchased an abandoned schoolhouse and moved in with their daughter and twenty homeless people, some of whom had been living in the woods, as well as in state shelters and detention homes. Together they renovated the house and started a farm, which grew into the Barka Foundation for the Promotion of Mutual Help.[4]

When I read about Sadowski's work, my first thought was that Ashoka had made a mistake. If ever there was an idea that was destined to remain local, this was it. How many stable, self-managed, partially self-supporting homes made up of former prison inmates, alcoholics, and homeless people can you have?

Tomasz Sadowski

The answer, as of early 2003, was twenty and counting. About 650 people live in Barka's houses, and thousands more benefit from its vocational and training programs. What makes Barka so intriguing is its improbability. Globally, the history of communal living is strewn with failure. Perhaps it is the collapse of communism that has allowed this idea to succeed unencumbered by ideology.

Barka's residents do not aspire to lofty motives. They are not easy people to live with and they know it. "We are all people with a lot of problems," Ela, a resident, told me. "We are in the habit of drinking and stealing, and sometimes these habits prevail. But everybody here is here because of their free will and their need. The reality outside is cruel. Jobs don't provide enough money for rent. I have been here for five years. This is no paradise. We argue, we cry, but we don't beat each other up. We have birthdays, we have holidays. We try, within our abilities, to be friends. The biggest miracle is that we sit at one table and talk with each other. And at the end of the day, I feel needed."

Barka's system is informed by a good-humored acceptance of human imperfection. The rules are few. Drinking and violence are prohibited, and all alcoholics or addicts must attend detox programs before they move into a house. If they still drink or do drugs, they must leave—not because they are unreformable evildoers, but because it is just too tempting for others. If a resident leaves and asks to return the following year, it's up to the residents to decide whether to accept the person back. Residents manage the homes with assistance from Barka's staff. Senior residents supervise junior ones. Everybody keeps busy, doing mostly agricultural, building, and small manufacturing work.

Barka's model has continued to expand for a decade. Its spread has become routinized, with mature "mother" houses hatching new ones. "When we began, people told us that it wasn't possible to create such an inclusive feeling," Sadowski explained. "Then they said it's possible on a limited basis. Now they say it's completely possible. But there is nothing mysterious about it. The worst criminal doesn't believe things can be this way only because he has never come across these kinds of relationships. But we can take on beautiful and fantastic things as easily as we can take on stupid things."

Design Real Solutions for Real People

One of the hallmarks of social entrepreneurs is that they are realistic about human behavior. They spend a great deal of time thinking about how to get their clients actually to use their products. Harley Henriques do Nacimento is a good example. The founder of Gapa-Bahia, an organization that has helped to curtail the spread of HIV/AIDS in poor areas of northeastern Brazil, do Nacimento has spent years fine-tuning his message to ensure that it has the desired impact on his audience.[5]

"We used to arrive the first day in a slum and tell people: 'AIDS is very important to know about. You must take care of your health, and so on,'" he told me. "It would go in one ear and out the other. Now, when we go into a community, we don't mention AIDS for six months. We have learned that people first have to gain knowledge about their bodies and living conditions. So we begin by talking about what it means to be black in our society. We talk about gender. We build up commitment and confidence. When they start the AIDS workshops, they are aware of their rights, bodies, blackness, and situation as women—and how all these can be *threatened* by AIDS. Otherwise, they can just say, 'Why be healthy? What for?'"

A big problem in India is managing hospital waste safely. The solution long advocated by large international development organizations has been for the Indian government to take huge loans and build incinerators across the country. Ravi Agarwal, a social entrepreneur who founded Toxics Link, India's leading network for toxic and solid waste management, has fought to advance a more realistic solution.[6]

Harley Henriques do Nacimento

"There are over 22,000 primary healthcare units in India," explains Agarwal. "They don't have money for incinerators. And even if they did, if you put an oil-fired incinerator in a primary healthcare unit, the locals will sell the oil. *Forget* about incinerators. You need to teach people to cut the tip off needles and disinfect them on site with a basic hypochlorite solution. You need to segregate your waste and deep-bury disinfected waste. It's safe and it's *cheap*. It's all based on low-cost management-based initiatives rather than technology-based initiatives. But low cost doesn't mean low quality."

Jadwiga Łopata, the social entrepreneur who arranges visits for tourists to organic farms in Poland, distributes a booklet for farmers, helping them to prepare for the experience. It is a splendid example of how to communicate clearly and with sensitivity to a select audience. Here are a few excerpts:

> Tourists will notice things that you don't think about and/or you think are worthless: e.g. wood, outdoor toilet, cow shed, old furniture. In your eyes it's rubbish, or impractical, but in the eyes of tourists it's beautiful folk things.
>
> The toilet should be open 24 hours without having to go into the farmer's house. It doesn't make sense to get rid of old ones and replace them with running water toilets. For many foreign tourists, they are an attractive curiosity. If well built they don't pollute and one can handle the smell by putting in nettle every few days. Most important, it must be clean.
>
> Offer interesting, tasty food they won't get at home. If they like it, they will certainly come back. For many people from polluted cities, this will be like medicine. Many guests fall in love with Polish cottage cheese and cream.
>
> Remember: Be yourself. Don't change your behavior for the tourists. You have the right to be busy. If you don't have time to do something because hay has to be collected, simply explain. They'll understand. Tourists will come and go. Your farm work is the most important priority.
>
> Foreign tourists usually need to feel that they have seen a lot and done a lot. They'll want to wake up at 5:00 A.M. to go to see how to milk the cows, collect hay, make cheese and butter. They like to video it and photograph it.
>
> Foreign guests can surprise you by their interest and knowledge about Poland. They want to listen and meet people. They are

interested in agriculture and ecology. Some will follow you around and watch everything you do. Not all farmers have the time for this, but for some it's an opportunity for an authentic human connection.

I attended a health workshop organized by two women who had been assisted by Renascer. The workshop was held in a school room in Rocinha, the *favela* in Rio de Janeiro. Thirty women and two men attended. The topic was "Cheap and Easy Ways to Improve Your Family's Nutrition."

Maria de Lourdes began by explaining that most people throw away nutritious food every day without realizing it. "We can use the leftovers that we normally waste in order to improve the quality of our food," she told the group. Then she got into specifics: The dark green leaves and peels discarded from cauliflower, broccoli, beets, carrots, and sweet potatoes are full of vitamins, she said. "You can make a powder from them easily. Wrap them in groups, dry them, blend into powder, sieve, and eat one teaspoon a day."

She passed around jars containing powders and sample recipes. "Keep the powders in clean glasses with a lid. You can add them to cream sauces, thicken stews, and make soups for your baby. Or add it to salt cakes, like cornstarch."

Fabiana Rodrigues focused on seeds and soy, and passed around more tasters. "It's all cheap and easy," she said. "I've adopted a lot of these changes at home."

I scanned the room. Everybody was engaged. People were discussing recipes and tasting the free samples. The leftovers were raffled off. Lourdes and Fabiana received a hearty round of applause. The workshop was over in an hour.

Focus on the Human Qualities

Organizations whose success hinges on high-quality human interaction generally pay close attention to soft qualities when recruiting, hiring, and managing staff. As we have seen, Erzsébet Szekeres is less interested in the formal credentials of a potential recruit than whether the person demonstrates empathy, flexible thinking, and a "strong inner core"—qualifications that a résumé does not reveal. Ashoka looks to hire people who are intrapreneurial, have strong ethical fiber, and consider themselves "innovators for the public."

In Brazil, Dora Andrade, founder of Edisca, a ballet school that works exclusively with low-income girls, says: "You can't teach someone to work with these kids. We see abuse, alcohol problems, poverty. So many dance teachers have quit. We've gone through four psychologists. We need people who believe it's possible to make a difference. The people who stay, stay because it is in their *nature*."

How do you find people who "believe it is possible to make a differ- ence"? It's often hard to tell where this kind of talent really lies. Erzsébet Szekeres's popular helper, Kati Magony, previously worked in a bakery. Many social entrepreneurs rely heavily on word-of-mouth referrals. That is how College Summit recruits writing coaches for its workshops. Another common solution is to recruit people from a broad range of backgrounds and then watch how they perform on the job.

The Grameen Bank does not screen its recruits by their academic majors. In fact, one of the most important qualifications the bank looks for in new recruits is *no previous banking experience*. Once hired, bank workers are dispatched to villages to train for six months. Their status remains "probationary" for close to a year. Szekeres's staff go through a three-month probationary period. In a similar fashion, College Summit uses its workshops to audition potential staff members.

Keeping people satisfied is another challenge. Because most citizen organizations cannot match private sector salaries, they need to offer greater psychological "remuneration." Above all, they need to give people the freedom to be effective and the sense that they are contributing to something bigger than themselves.[7]

Marcos Po, the technical coordinator of the Instituto Brasileiro de Defesa do Consumidor (IDEC), Brazil's leading private consumer protec- tion agency, keeps an old light bulb socket on a shelf above his desk.[8] When I asked Po about it, he showed me where the contacts were exposed and how the socket was held together by a single screw. This socket was "extremely hazardous," he said gravely. It had been in widespread use in Brazil for thirty years. When Po joined IDEC, he was given the opportunity to choose his battles. He decided to produce a consumer report on the socket. As a result, he said, the government took the socket off the market in 1996 and banned similarly dangerous electrical devices. "I keep this socket nearby because it reminds me that I *can* make a difference," said Po.

Many jobs offer little opportunity for direct or immediate feedback. In such cases, organizations must design processes that help the staff recharge their batteries. Two social entrepreneurs who have instituted such processes are Andrzej Korbel and Jacek Bozek, both leading figures in the Polish environmental movement. Korbel, founder of the Center for Deep Ecology, has created a "magical circle" process, in which people spend three days in a forest. "People begin in a circle talking about themselves," he explained, referring to one aspect of the process. "Many have never been in the forest at night. It's silent. You can't see much. You hear animals. You smell nature. Then we put four stones in the middle. Each is meant to express a different feeling: joy, sorrow, anger and fear. And we ask everyone: 'What do you bring to this place?' And they use the stones to show their feelings.

"Somehow, from this process, we draw increased energy and power to work for nature."

Bozek, founder of the Gaja Club, which has mobilized a national campaign in Poland to protect the Vistula River, periodically organizes silent pilgrimages to the source of the Vistula for staff and volunteers. "We do this to discover the deep reason—the nonintellectual reason—for doing this work," Bozek told me. "For twenty-four hours, we walk, sleep, and eat, but without talking. Why do we do this? You work for the forest or the river. But what does it mean to work for the forest? Most of the time you are on the phone or sending a fax. So you need contact with the earth that is strong."

This Country Has to Change

Javed Abidi, India: Disability Rights

J aved Abidi turned off the TV news. The political situation remained unchanged. The opposition, after clashing with the government over accusations of a scandal, had stormed out of Parliament and was still refusing to return. While this game playing was nothing unusual in India, the parliamentarians were scheduled to vote on a bill that had consumed Abidi's every waking breath for two years: India's first-ever civil rights legislation for people with disabilities.

Abidi had been disheartened when the Disability Bill failed to come up for debate during the Monsoon Session. Now the Winter Session was winding down. It was Tuesday night, December 19, 1995. In a few weeks, the politicians would be preoccupied with the upcoming election. If the bill failed to reach the floor by Friday, the session's last day, Abidi feared that it would go into "political limbo." All the momentum that he and his colleagues had worked so hard to build would be lost.

In 1995, after almost a half century of independence, India still did not have a disability policy. India's disabled population, estimated variously at 60 to 100 million people, enjoyed almost no protections against discrimination and received almost no consideration in government decision-making.[1]

Disability is a problem that cuts across all countries, all cultures, and all social strata. But in poor countries, the problems are more severe. Unlike Americans, the vast majority of disabled Indians lack basic assistive devices, such as wheelchairs or communication aids. For those who can afford wheelchairs, like Javed Abidi, obstacles are everywhere—buildings, buses, streets, parks. One exception to the rule are train stations, where ramps are required for baggage and freight trolleys, a situation Abidi calls "accessibility by accident."

But the physical barriers are mild compared with the social barriers. Millions of Indians view disability as retribution for past sins and a cause for shame. "There are hundreds of thousands of households where the kids are actually hidden away," Abidi says. Even privileged Indians often fail to understand that a person with a disability can lead an independent life. "A disability is not a curse in and of itself," explains Abidi. "A disability becomes a curse in India because it leads to a million other handicaps. Tomorrow if the thinking changed, disability would at most be a setback."

It is said that chance only favors the prepared mind. That may explain why it seems to favor Javed Abidi so strongly. He has been preparing all his life—thirty-eight years—for the role he has assigned himself as the executive director of the National Center for the Promotion of Employment for Disabled People (NCPEDP) in Delhi.

The first time I met Abidi, I was struck by the contrast between his upper and lower halves. While his shoulders and chest were robust, his lower half was shrunken. His legs hung lifelessly. He sported a rather severe mustache, calculated to add a few years to his youthful appearance. His manner was purposeful and sober, his apartment gray and spartan. I noticed that the wheel and rim of his wheelchair were held together with strips of cloth. Abidi explained that he did a lot of traveling and his chairs tended to get banged up. A new one would cost 70,000 rupees, about $1,500, or four months' salary. He'd been postponing the decision to buy one for a year.

Over tea, biscuits, and Pringles, Abidi told me his story. He spoke slowly and with precision. "I have learned to be friends with my disability in a nice, slow, systematic manner," he began. "I honestly don't remember any kind of a sadness or anger associated with my disability. I have never felt handicapped. There must be something wrong with me. I must be missing a gene or something."

Abidi was born in 1965 in a clinic in Aligarh, Uttar Pradesh. As the doctors were washing him, they noticed a strange swelling on his lower back. The story he was told is that the nurse took one look at him and declared: "This child will not live twenty days."

His parents took him to the All India Institute of Medical Sciences in Delhi, where a neurosurgeon diagnosed spina bifida, a congenital birth defect in which vertebrae, meninges, or skin fail to form over the base of the spinal cord, leaving nerve tissue unprotected. Spina bifida can lead to paralysis in parts of the body; however, surgery performed early in life often is a successful treatment.

In Abidi's case, doctors mistakenly told his parents that there was no need to intervene immediately. The family went home to Aligarh, returning to Delhi every six months the next eight years for Javed to receive a checkup.

At eight, Javed's right leg began to drag and his doctors concluded that the time had come for surgery. When the surgeon emerged from the operating room, however, he was not smiling. They had waited too long. Nerve damage had occurred.

Javed continued to walk with a limp. Then, when he was ten, he fell and had to undergo another operation. Thereafter, he walked with crutches.

Following the first operation, Javed's father, Syed Ishtiaque Abidi, had written letters to doctors around the world about his son's condition. After receiving a mildly encouraging reply from the Children's Hospital in Boston, Ishtiaque cashed in his retirement savings, borrowed money from friends, and took Javed there. "People said he was mad to spend all that money on one son," Abidi recalled.

But Ishtiaque had never been one to heed convention. As a teenager growing up in a wealthy landowning family, he had run away from home to join the then-outlawed Communist Party. Although he was a Muslim, he elected to remain in India after the 1947 partition with Pakistan. He enrolled in Aligarh Muslim University, a hotbed of Muslim politics, where he became a student leader. At the insistence of his wife, Zeba, Ishtiaque quit politics and became a lecturer of English, but he remained influential on campus.

In 1960, five years before Javed was born, India's prime minister, Jawaharlal Nehru, visited Aligarh Muslim University to dedicate a new library. At the ceremony Ishtiaque publicly renounced communism and joined the Congress Party. Two decades later, in part owing to that gesture, Prime Minister Indira Gandhi, Nehru's daughter, recruited Ishtiaque to serve as a joint secretary of the Congress Party.

In the unknowable way that events unfold, Ishtiaque's 1960 speech would translate, through his son, into a formidable political asset for India's disabled.

In Boston there were no miracles to be had. The doctors referred Abidi and his father to Cook County Hospital in Chicago, where the diagnosis was reiterated: The spinal cord damage could not be corrected. But, the doctors added, Javed could still live an independent life. The key was *rehabilitation*.

It was the first time that Javed, then ten, had heard the word, and it took on an almost magical quality. Javed was referred to the Rehabilitation Institute of Chicago, where he remained for two months, receiving physical and occupational therapy and learning how to manage basic tasks by himself.

The trip to the United States had a profound impact on him. One incident in particular left a lasting impression. "I was standing outside the Rehabilitation Institute of Chicago on my little crutches," recalled Abidi. "My father had gone to get a cab and I saw this van coming in. I saw a lady in a wheelchair get out. She was a quadriplegic and she had these three pipes in front of her and by blowing into these pipes she controlled the wheelchair. It was an amazing sight—most amazing—for a ten-year-old. And then I came to learn that she was the director of the institute."

Until he was fifteen, Abidi used crutches to walk. He got around well, but occasionally he would fall. The doctors in Aligarh concluded that he should stop walking. "So one fine day, a wheelchair was procured," Abidi recalls. He sat in it and never walked again.

"Any true medical professional would have . . ." Abidi began heatedly, then caught himself and continued in a measured tone: "To say to a person who is walking that he should be in a wheelchair for safety—any sane medical person who has heard this has told me, 'You should be walking today.' People have *shrieked* at this. Had I been in another country with the correct kind of care and advice, I would not have faced these difficulties.

"I am not angry or bitter about what happened," he added to make sure that his point was not misconstrued. "I try to look at my own experiences only to learn about this country: how things were and are and, most important, how things should be. If this kind of thing has happened to me—and I am one *hundred* times more privileged than the vast majority of disabled in this country—what is happening to hundreds of thousands of other people? The point is: *This country has to change.*"

With the encouragement of an American friend, Abidi enrolled in Wright State University, in Dayton, Ohio, where he planned to major in mass communications. In the United States, before heading to Dayton, Abidi paid a visit to the Rehabilitation Institute to say hello to old friends and get a pair of orthopedic shoes. When the doctors took a look at his wheelchair, they were horrified. It was far too large for Abidi. On examination, the doctors found that, because of the way he had been sitting, the young man had severe curvature of the spine, which would require surgical correction within three years.

Abidi put off the decision and immersed himself in school. He got involved in student government, wrote for the university newspaper, and became president of both the International Students Association and the Indian Club.

After his junior year, his doctors insisted that he undergo the spinal operation. It would mean opening up his back and inserting a metal rod. Recovery would take three months. The doctors suggested that Abidi return to India after the operation to rest for the summer.

On the flight, Abidi read about a drought in the northern part of India. Back home, he contacted some college classmates and decided to establish a fund to assist in the relief effort. The doctors had advised him to keep pressure off his spine, but he felt good and spent the better part of the summer fundraising.

One evening, shortly after his return to the United States, he started vomiting and had to be rushed by ambulance to the hospital. Pressure sores close to his backbone had gotten infected.

The doctors in Chicago were apoplectic. "They told me that my whole back could have come apart," he recalled. "They said it would take six months to heal."

Abidi was placed on an air bed and ordered to do nothing.

The hospital bill came to $40,000. Dozens of Abidi's classmates and teachers from Wright State University made donations to help pay the bill. "Only God knows how many individuals have actually contributed to my life," Abidi said.

Returning to India in 1989, Abidi was eager to begin his journalism career. He wasn't worried about landing a job. He had a degree from a U.S. college, a 4.0 GPA, lots of newspaper clips. It took two months of rejections before it occurred to him that perhaps people didn't want to hire a journalist in a wheelchair. Prospective employers always inquired: "How are you going to get around?" Abidi had a stock reply: "How I get around is my problem. Give me an assignment, give me a deadline, and if I don't deliver on time, then you can fire me." And he assumed that editors would give him a chance.

But he was mistaken.

"It was the first time in my life that my disability hit me in the face," he told me. "When I realized sitting in New Delhi—the capital of the country, not some small town—and the managers at the leading newspapers were saying this."

Still, he kept proposing stories to editors. And one day, while speaking with the editor of a magazine that was having difficulty gaining access to three politicians for a preelection report, he was told: "If you can get the interviews, you can do the story."

Abidi managed to land the first two interviews. But the third, India's defense minister, was a problem. Calls to his office yielded nothing. Then one morning Abidi came across a news brief that said the defense minister's son had just returned from college in the United States and was getting married. He got the idea to pretend to be one of the son's college friends. He still had his Wright State I.D. card. That and a little fast talk might get him past the guards.

The following day Abidi found himself face to face with the defense minister. "I am a struggling journalist," he said. "I just need to ask you three questions." In ten minutes he had his interview. Suddenly he was a star reporter. "People stopped looking at my wheelchair," he recalled. "The question 'How will you do it?' wasn't asked anymore. It didn't take long to be writing for *The Times of India*."

In 1988 Prime Minister Rajiv Gandhi had appointed a committee to look into disability. The committee recommended that any serious attempt to deal with the problem had to begin with comprehensive legislation. Before the recommendations could be acted on, however, Rajiv Gandhi's Congress Party lost power. Then, in 1991, while campaigning in southern India, Gandhi was assassinated by a terrorist. Riding on a wave of sympathy, Congress returned to power under Prime Minister P. V. Narasimha Rao. Shortly thereafter Sonia Gandhi, Rajiv Gandhi's Italian-born widow (and future leader of the Congress Party), established the Rajiv Gandhi Foundation and chose disability as one of its five focus areas.

Sonia Gandhi had made it known that she was looking for rare photos of her husband to include in a book memorializing his life. Abidi's father, Ishtiaque, who had worked with Rajiv Gandhi, offered his personal collection and asked if his family could pay a visit to offer their condolences.

Abidi had once written a letter to Rajiv Gandhi, urging the government to pay more attention to disability. When Abidi met with Sonia Gandhi, he mentioned the letter. A week later Mrs. Gandhi invited him back to interview him about the problems facing disabled people. "All I know is based on my life experience," Abidi explained, and he described the surgeon's mistakes, the lack of rehabilitation in India, the problems of access, the difficulty in landing a job.

When he was finished, Mrs. Gandhi asked if he would be interested in running the foundation's disability unit. Abidi's first thought was: "Oh, boy. I shouldn't have shot off my mouth." It would mean an end to his journalism career. But then he reasoned: What difference will one less journalist make? One more advocate for the disabled—that could be significant.

Abidi joined the Rajiv Gandhi Foundation in May 1992 and soon found himself flooded with proposals. People walked into his office requesting money for wheelchairs, surgeries, hearing aids, jobs, medicine, legal aid,

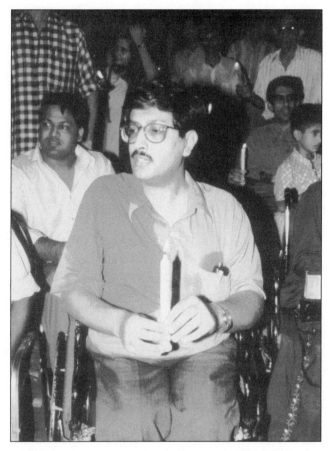

Javed Abidi at a midnight vigil to promote disability awareness, 1998

employment advice. Needs seemed endless. Abidi decided that his strategy would be to support innovative work in education, transportation, surgery, assistive devices, and rehabilitation.

One project that caught his attention was the Lifeline Express, a hospital housed in a train that could reach even the most backwater areas to perform corrective surgery for polio, cataracts, and deafness. Through his work with the Lifeline Express, Abidi traveled to parts of India where the nearest airport was a ten-hour journey by car. "My whole view of the country changed," he recalled. He saw that outside the cities, there were virtually no services or accommodations for disabled people—not in the schools, healthcare units, or workplaces that served hundreds of million of people. He learned that only 1 percent of disabled children in India had access to education.

The Lifeline Express was wonderful, but it reached only 1,500 people a year. "You can go on conducting hospital camps for the rest of your life and you will have only touched the tip of the iceberg," Abidi said. "I saw that service delivery was not the way to overcome the problem of disability in India." Fundamental change had to begin with a coherent, national policy.

In March 1994 the American Center in Delhi hosted a teleconference, bringing together disability activists in India and the United States via satellite transmission. The conference was pegged to the 1993 publication of journalist Joseph P. Shapiro's book *No Pity*, a chronicle of the U.S. disability movement.[2] The American participants included Shapiro, as well as Judy Heumann and Justin Dart Jr., two leaders in the American disability movement. The Indians prepared by reading *No Pity*, in which Shapiro had written eloquently about the struggles of Heumann and Dart, among many others.

Judy Heumann was born in Brooklyn, New York, the eldest of three children in a German-Jewish immigrant family. At eighteen months of age, she contracted polio, which left her a quadriplegic. A doctor advised that Judy be placed in an institution. Relatives whispered that Judy's parents must have committed a terrible sin to have been struck with such misfortune.

As a young girl, Heumann was refused admittance to her local elementary school because the principal deemed her a "fire hazard." In 1961 her mother fought for and won the right for Heumann to attend high school, reversing a New York City policy that required high school age children in wheelchairs to be home-schooled.

Heumann graduated from college. Having studied speech therapy, she hoped to work with elementary school children. After passing her oral and written exams, however, she was denied a teaching certificate because the New York City Board of Education argued that her disability would prevent her from helping kids evacuate the school in the event of emergency. Heumann sued the board, which settled out of court, and awarded her a teaching certificate. But she still couldn't find a job until the principal of her old elementary school in Brooklyn hired her.

In 1970 Heumann was one of the founders of Disability in Action, an early disability rights group. In 1977 she led a San Francisco sit-in in which disabled people occupied a floor of the government's regional office for the Department of Health, Education and Welfare for twenty-five days. The sit-in, a remarkable feat of stamina, sparked, in Shapiro's words, the "political coming of age of the disability rights movement." It led the U.S. government to enact the first regulations that, among other things, made it illegal for a federal agency or contractor or federally funded institution to discriminate against anyone solely because of a handicap.[3]

Justin Dart had contracted polio in 1948, when he was eighteen years old. He too had been denied a teaching certificate because he used a wheelchair. But Dart, who attended university in the early 1950s, "accepted it as a fact that he would have fewer choices," wrote Shapiro.

In 1967, while visiting South Vietnam, Dart was taken to a facility in war-torn Saigon for children with polio. Dart was unprepared for the "vision of hell" inside: a hundred young children with "bloated bellies and matchstick arms and legs" like in "pictures from Dachau and Auschwitz, with their eyes bugging out, lying in their own feces and urine and their bodies covered with flies." The children had been left to die and to be buried in unmarked graves. The experience was "branded" into Dart's soul.

At the time, Dart ran a division of his family's business in Japan. He quit his job and moved with his wife to an abandoned farmhouse on a snowy mountaintop in Japan, without running water, electricity, or a telephone, a quarter mile up a dirt road. When it rained and the road turned muddy, Dart made the journey into town by crawling on his hands to the end of the mud road, where he would catch a ride on a wagon.

The decision to live this way stemmed from Dart's and his wife's need to empathize with the children in Vietnam and to have time to reflect on life. When Dart returned to the United States, he became a spokesman for disability rights, touring the country and conducting town meetings in all fifty states at his own expense.

A Texas Republican, Dart became a member of the National Council on the Handicapped during the presidency of Ronald Reagan. He worked to advance the first version of the Americans with Disabilities Act. In 1990, as chairman of the President's Committee on Employment of People with Disabilities, he fought to achieve the law's passage.[4]

During the teleconference with the Indian activists, Heumann stressed the importance of legislation. It was essential for the government to acknowledge that discrimination against the disabled existed and that it was the government's responsibility to stop it, she said. Dart added that the government could not implement equality. That could be enforced only by the "eternal vigilance" of the people who sought it. He noted that his own activism had been sparked by reading Gandhi's book, *My Experiments With Truth*, reminding the Indians of their contribution to the U.S. civil rights movement, which had, in turn, laid the foundation for the U.S. disability movement.[5]

When the teleconference ended, the Indians conferred. "Why the hell don't we have a similar kind of movement? Why aren't we having sit-ins? Getting out in the streets?" Abidi recalled saying. "Let's do something!"

Not everyone agreed. However, two weeks later, a small group met and formed the Disabled Rights Group (DRG)—the first cross-disability advocacy group in India. DRG was inspired by the Disability Rights Education and Defense Fund, which, under the direction of U.S. disability activist Patrisha Wright, brought self-representation of the disabled to Washington, D.C., and transformed the debate from one that focused on medical care and charity to one that focused on human rights.[6]

Abidi and the other activists recognized that what was missing in India was the sustained, coordinated, cross-disability advocacy that had worked in the United States. DRG would lead the way. It would be nonpartisan. It was to remain broadly focused and loosely knit. And it would not get involved in fundraising. For too long, India's disability groups, hungry for grants, had refrained from challenging the government. No longer.

Over the next year and a half, through vigorous activism, DRG sparked a disability movement in India. The group began by initiating relationships with political parties, individual ministers, and journalists. Abidi found the politicians surprisingly receptive. "It was the first time people at this level of government had met groups of disabled people," he recalled, "and they were genuinely trying to understand and appreciate our difficulties."

Sonia Gandhi was a staunch ally. She personally urged Prime Minister Rao to expedite the Disability Bill. In December 1994, 500 disabled activists held a march along Sansad Marg (Parliament Street) in Delhi that generated national media coverage.[7] The march sparked more rallies, seminars, articles, TV interviews. Advocacy groups sprang up around the country and formed alliances. Momentum built. By August 1995 the Welfare Ministry had produced a draft of a comprehensive Disability Bill.

After all that work, on Tuesday, December 19, 1995, with three days left in the Winter Session and the government and opposition still at an impasse, Abidi thought: We have to do something *now*. He picked up the phone and called a colleague in the DRG. "We have to come out into the open," he said. "We should organize a protest rally."

"What can we do with this protest?" came the reply. "It's politics."

"We have to make our presence felt," Abidi insisted. "If you built a house brick by brick and you saw it catch on fire, would you sit back and watch it burn to the ground?

"At least let us register a protest," Abidi said. "There is no harm in trying."

"What difference could it possibly make?"

"It could make a difference," Abidi said.

He made more calls. "It *could* make a difference," he kept saying. "Who knows? Let us not go down without a fight."

Before the night was over, word had traveled through the network. The following morning a few hundred disabled people gathered before Parliament. Seasoned demonstrators, they had alerted the press; they had a plan of attack.

What nobody anticipated was the media response. By midmorning, it seemed as if there were as many journalists as disabled people at the demonstration. With the election coming up, the journalists were itching for a good political story. The demonstrators handed them one.

As planned, at the end of their march, the demonstrators sat down on the ground and refused to budge until the leader of the opposition, Atal Behari Vajpayee (who would later become India's prime minister), agreed to meet with them. Three hours passed. And then, astonishingly, Vajpayee called. He would meet the demonstrators.

"Why is it so important to pass this bill now?" Vajpayee asked during the meeting.

Rally to demand passage of the Disability Act, 1995
(Abidi is in the center, arm raised)

The activists spoke of tens of millions of disabled Indians and the conditions they faced. They spoke of how much work had gone into the Disability Bill. "This is a nonpolitical bill," Abidi stressed. "It is for all Indians."

Vajpayee said he would think it over. The demonstrators thanked him and left.

The next morning Abidi returned to his office at the Rajiv Gandhi Foundation and tried to put the matter out of his mind. At about three o'clock a reporter called: "Have you heard the rumors? The opposition is talking to the government." In the evening the television news reported that the opposition parties had agreed to reenter Parliament on Friday, the final day of the Winter Session, to cooperate with the government on the disability issue.

On Friday, December 22, the two houses of the Indian Parliament passed the Persons With Disabilities (Equal Opportunities, Protection of Rights and Full Participation) Bill of 1995. Ten days later the president signed the law and, the following month, it was notified in the *Gazette of India*, the final step in the process of a bill becoming an act of law.

"It was nothing less than a miracle," Abidi recalled. "India is a country where rallies of hundreds of thousands of people are not uncommon. Here was just a handful of people. But because they didn't stay home, it happened."

The Persons With Disabilities Act was full of good intentions. But how to press for the law's implementation? How to move forward? Abidi asked himself: Where is the leverage point?

As he considered the questions, he began to narrow in on employment. Prior to the disability act, the history of employment and disability in India had two landmarks. The first was in 1959, when the Indian

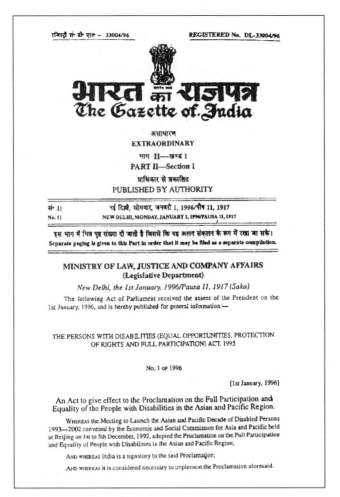

Notification of the passage of the Disability Act
as published in *The Gazette of India*

government initiated its first job placement program for disabled people. The second was in 1977, when the government of Indira Gandhi reserved 3 percent of low-level government jobs for the disabled.[8]

In almost forty years, the government had placed about 100,000 disabled people in jobs.[9] "If you're placing 3,000 to 3,500 people a year," said Abidi, "it will take centuries to set the picture right." The 3 percent reservation raised another question: Was the government saying that if you're disabled, you're qualified only to be a clerk? In the private sector, with the exception of a few executives who hired the disabled out of kindness, there was no activity in this area.

After the push for a comprehensive law, Abidi felt the movement could achieve maximum impact by concentrating on employment. "Working people have money," he said. "They pay taxes. They become visible. They can overturn stereotypes. Ultimately it's the green bucks that matter. Then you don't need all the philanthropy. How else do people become self-reliant?"

In late 1995 Abidi was talking with Maya Thomas, the head of the disability unit of ActionAID, an international development organization headquartered in London. The two decided that India needed an independent organization whose primary focus was to promote the employment of disabled people. To test the waters, they organized a meeting at the Rajiv Gandhi Foundation, inviting government officials, disability activists, and top business executives. The response was encouraging.

Abidi took the next step, establishing the National Center for the Promotion of Employment for Disabled People, which was to be financed initially by the Rajiv Gandhi Foundation and ActionAID. He registered the organization, found an office, hired an executive director, helped recruit staff, and then watched, with mounting frustration, as the organization coasted for a year until the executive director resigned.

Afterward, a consensus formed at the Rajiv Gandhi Foundation that if anybody could make NCPEDP a success, it was Abidi. At the time, however, Abidi didn't relish the thought of relinquishing his position of influence to take over a fledgling organization located in a back-alley office. But he thought: "I'm going to be damned either way. If I say yes, I'm going to have to revive a sinking ship. If I say no, people will think I don't want a challenge."

In May 1997, a few months before Abidi was scheduled to take over NCPEDP, he happened to be sitting in an Indian Airlines plane bound from Bangalore to Delhi waiting to take off when a flight attendant asked him to change seats. Abidi was a regular flier. To accommodate his wheelchair, the airline usually placed him next to the airplane door, even though it is a violation of international air transport guidelines for a disabled person to be seated in an exit row. This time, however, a flight attendant noticed the infraction and decided to enforce the rule.

Abidi knew the aviation regulations, but he also knew the full text of the Persons With Disabilities Act.

"That's fine," he told the flight attendant. "Please get me an aisle chair [a wheelchair narrow enough to navigate an airplane aisle]."

"We don't have aisle chairs," the flight attendant replied.

"Then how can I switch?" Abidi said.

"Someone will lift you."

"I refuse," Abidi said. "If you don't have the proper systems then don't talk about laws. I'm not going to allow any of your people to bodily move me."

"I can't allow this," the flight attendant said, and went to speak to the captain.

Abidi waited. He was annoyed. But he also sensed that he was being handed an opportunity to test the law that he had helped create. The disability act stated clearly that public transport systems were required to be accessible.

The flight attendant returned and told Abidi that the captain had instructed him to shift seats. Abidi stood his ground. An argument ensued. The other passengers began to lose patience. Abidi was already envisioning a court case, and he was thinking about evidence. He knew that the air traffic controllers would be contacting the pilots: "Why aren't you moving?" And the pilots would be saying: "Some crazy fellow is creating a ruckus." All of it would be on record.

Finally the captain appeared. "I can't fly unless you move," he said. "I'll have to deboard you."

Abidi explained himself. Then he said, "Okay, I'll shift." He pulled himself by his arms to a seat in the next row.

After landing in Delhi, Abidi immediately lodged a complaint with the airport supervisor. Then he sent a letter to the chief executive of Indian Airlines informing him of the incident and warning that, if he did not receive an apology within seven days, he would sue the airline for breach of the Persons With Disabilities Act. No apology came.

Abidi realized that if he was going to waste time on a lawsuit, it would have to be for something that mattered. He certainly wasn't going to sue over aisle chairs alone. But in court he could raise other issues, such as how he always had to be carried up the steps into planes by the baggage handlers. "They're totally untrained," he told me. "One of them slips and I'm gone."

For refreshments and luggage, the airline had hydraulic lifts. Why not ambulifts for people?

The airline also offered a 50 percent price concession to blind passengers. Why not for other disabled people?

Then, of course, there was the Indian government's failure to implement the Persons With Disabilities Act. Eighteen months after the law's passage, the government still hadn't appointed the Chief Commissioner for Persons with Disabilities, the individual charged with monitoring its implementation.

Abidi filed suit against Indian Airlines, the Ministry of Civil Aviation, and the Ministry of Welfare. As a public interest litigation, it came under the jurisdiction of the Supreme Court of India, and, three months later, it was admitted. After consulting with a lawyer friend, Abidi decided to act as his own counsel.

In September 1997, when Abidi arrived for his first day of work at the NCPEDP office, he found the electricity out and all the employees sitting in the dark.

"What is going on?" he said. "You don't have a generator?"

"No."

"So what do you do when there is no power?"

The employees looked at each other in silence.

"I was so depressed," Abidi recalled. "I went back to my car and I *ran* back to the foundation."

Shortly thereafter he received a phone call out of the blue from Ashoka. "Usually awards are given to people who have already received recognition and therefore don't need them," Abidi explained. But Ashoka's support came at a point in his life when, after leaving the Rajiv Gandhi Foundation, he was feeling particularly lonely and vulnerable. "Ashoka showed me that I was part of a community of people who all had new ideas for change," he said.

The Persons With Disabilities Act contained one sentence that Abidi dubbed the "golden clause." It read: "The appropriate Governments and the local authorities shall, within the limits of their economic capacity and development, provide incentives to employers both in public and private sectors to ensure that at least five percent of their work force is composed of persons with disabilities."[10]

The golden clause not only toughened the government's commitment to hiring the disabled, it represented the first time the state had explicitly recognized that business had an obligation to employ disabled people. The challenge was to give the words meaning.

With India's size and diversity—the country has a billion people and eighteen officially recognized languages—Abidi decided to pursue a network-based strategy. "I saw that we weren't going to be setting up offices around the country," he said. (In 2002 NCPEDP had a staff of eight.) Rather, he set out systematically to forge partnerships with business leaders, government officials, and disability groups in each of India's thirty-two states and union territories. To do so, he brought on several energetic staffers, led by Rama Chari, a woman with a master's degree in economics and seven years' experience teaching children with physical and mental disabilities.

First, Abidi and his staff divided India into five geographical zones and organized conferences on disability and employment in Delhi (North), Bangalore (South), Bombay (West), Calcutta (East), and Guwahati (Northeast). Next they organized state-level seminars so participants could attack local problems more specifically. Next they connected with point bodies in key professions (law, architecture, business, education and information technology), working through their networks to spread awareness.

Finally, to sew it all together at the national level, Abidi took the initiative to turn World Disability Day—December 3—into a focal point for agenda-setting and celebration of successes. In December 1997 NCPEDP got General Motors and ActionAID to sponsor a Walk to Freedom in Delhi, which attracted thousands of disability activists, as well as prominent government officials.[11] The following year NCPEDP brought together disability groups and businesses in a National Disability Convention. And in 1999 NCPEDP launched "Disability 2000," a disability awareness campaign, inaugurating a new national awards program—the NCPEDP Helen Keller Awards—to recognize individuals and companies for their contributions to the advancement of people with disabilities. Abidi recruited famous cricketers and movie stars as "disability ambassadors," commissioned TV advertisements, and produced a documentary film, *The Invisible Minority*, which was broadcast and distributed nationally.

Along the way Abidi initiated a series of research projects to demonstrate the need for change. In conjunction with the National Association for the Blind, NCPEDP examined employment practices within India's disability sector. The organizations found that 78 percent of the executive bodies and 85 percent of regular staffers were nondisabled.[12] "It was devastating," Abidi recalled. "It sent shock waves through the sector."

Next NCPEDP examined employment practices within India's Fortune 100 companies. Again the findings came as a shock. Only 0.28 percent of private sector employees were disabled. For multinational corporations, the figure was 0.05 percent, an embarrassment. Public sector companies fared best at 0.54 percent.[13] But no firms were close to the 5 percent goal articulated in the golden clause.

"We went to town on that study," Abidi said.

Next he set out to sensitize business leaders. He established a partnership with the Confederation of Indian Industry (CII), a lobby that represents 4,000 businesses. CII's social agenda included attention to environmental and women's issues as well as HIV/AIDS, but not disability. That would have to change.

Then, noting that 20 percent of the jobs in India's fast-growing high-tech sector posed no impediments for people with most physical disabilities, Abidi joined forces with technology business leaders, who helped bring together Indian-based executives from companies such as IBM, Apple Computer, Oracle, Cisco, Microsoft, and Hewlett-Packard, to launch Equal Access, a campaign to promote job access for the disabled in the high-tech industry.

In 1998 and 1999 Abidi began to see results from NCPEDP's relentless networking and pressure tactics. The government finally appointed a Chief Commissioner for Persons with Disabilities (two and a half years after the disability act was passed).[14] Then, at a conference organized by NCPEDP, the deputy director general of the Confederation of Indian Industry announced that disability would be added to the business lobby's social agenda. Next, the new director of the University Grants Commission (UGC), Armaity Desai (who had also been a key supporter of Childline), announced that UGC, which oversees funding for higher education in India, would pursue a vigorous policy of disability inclusion.[15] Finally, the verdict from Abidi's Supreme Court case came down, and the ruling was overwhelmingly in his favor.[16] The Court issued notice to the Indian government and all the state governments and union territories, requiring them to indicate the steps they were taking to implement the Disability Act.[17] Meanwhile, Indian Airlines agreed to provide aisle chairs and access to ambulifts for all its flights, and the court ruled that the airline's 50 percent price concession had to be extended to all individuals with a significant orthopedic disability.

The case established an important precedent: The Persons With Disabilities Act was not to be ignored.

In early 2000 Abidi found a new obsession: India's census. In late 1999 he had sent a letter to the Census Commission offering NCPEDP's assistance with regard to disability and the census. A letter came back saying that the commission was "pleased to learn" about Abidi's interest, but there were no plans to include disability in the 2001 census.[18]

"Shocked and horrified," Abidi immediately dispatched a letter of protest and convened the DRG. Another letter signed by twelve prominent disability activists went out to top government officials.

Although India had conducted a census every ten years for more than a century, the country had no reliable quantitative data on its disabled population. The government's estimate was that 2 percent of the population were disabled, or about 20 million people. This was 40 million fewer than NCPEDP's estimate and 50 to 80 million fewer than the World Health Organization's. "When it comes to planning and budget allocation, numbers matter," Abidi says. "The government doesn't care about UN figures and it certainly doesn't care about NGO figures."

A few weeks later Abidi and other members of the DRG met with the census commissioner, who said that it was impossible to collect data on disability in a census. He explained that India's 1981 census had inquired about disability and had produced a poor estimate.[19] But the activists had studied data collection methods. They pointed out that the 1981 question was crudely framed—it inquired about household members who were "totally blind, crippled or dumb"—and failed to include mental disability. Moreover, there were now 4,000 disability organizations to get the word out and far better communications.

The census commissioner refused to budge, so DRG organized a local rally, then issued a call for a one-day hunger strike and a nationwide protest. Two days before the hunger strike was to be called, India's minister for home affairs, L. K. Advani, invited Abidi and several disability activists to join him in a meeting along with the census commissioner and two other government ministers: Maneka Gandhi, the minister for social justice and empowerment, and Arun Shourie, India's minister for program and implementation.

On April 22, 2000, I received an e-mail from Abidi. The subject line read: "Re: AMAZINGLY AMAZING!!!" The message began: "Disability will be included as a category in the Census 2001. I am still in a daze, truly, sincerely. . . ." He detailed how the activists had brought the minis-

NC/99-4/C   15th October, 1999

Dear Madam/Sir,

We have been reading various newspaper reports regarding the
Census to be undertaken in 2001. We believe that you are planning to
take up the issue of disability also this time. If this is so, we would
definitely like to be associated with this exercise and offer whatever
little help and expertise that we can.

We had written to the Delhi Government in this regard and they have
also suggested that we should get in touch with you on this issue.

We look forward to hearing from you.

With kind regards,

Yours sincerely,

(Javed Abidi)
Executive Director

The Registrar General
And Census Commissioner of India
2/A, Mansingh Road
New Delhi – 110 011

Telegram : "REG.GENLIND"

भ०/No. 18/1/98 - SS

भारत सरकार
GOVERNMENT OF INDIA

गृह मंत्रालय
MINISTRY OF HOME AFFAIRS/GRIH MANTRALAYA
भारत के महा रजिस्ट्रार का कार्यालय
OFFICE OF THE REGISTRAR GENERAL, INDIA
Social Studies Division
Sewa Bhavan, R.K. Puram

नई दिल्ली, दिनांक   7.12.99.
New Delhi, the

To

Sh. Javed Afridi,
Executive Director,
National Centre for Promotion
of Employment for Disabled,
25, Green Park Extension,
Yusuf Sarai,
New Delhi-110016

Sub: Disability related enquiry at the Census 2001.

Sir,

      Please refer to your letter No.NC/99-4/C dated 15th
October, 1999 on the subject cited above. We are pleased to
learn about your interest in the disability related issues. It
may however be noted that this office is not contemplating to
include the disability related item in the Schedule(s) for data
collection to be used at the Census of 2001.

                                    Yours faithfully,

                                    (M.K. Jain)
                                    Deputy Registrar General(SS)

Top: First letter to census commission
Bottom: Response from the census commission

ters to their position. A few weeks later the Census Commission officially announced that disability would be included in the census.[20] By then Abidi and his staff were busy organizing meetings in Delhi, Bombay, Calcutta, and Madras to help disability organizations across India prepare for the census.

In late 2000 Abidi seized on another opportunity to force change: He received a telephone call from an institute in Delhi that had invited the renowned physicist Stephen Hawking to India. Hawking had accepted. Unfortunately, Hawking is severely disabled with the neurological disease amyotrophic lateral sclerosis (Lou Gehrig's disease) and his hosts had no clue how he would get around. To make matters worse, Hawking had expressed a desire to visit four historic monuments—the Red Fort, Qutab Minar, Humayun's Tomb, and Jantar Mantar—none of which was accessible by wheelchair.

When Abidi heard of Hawking's requests, he told reporters that he felt like kissing the physicist's feet. "I would be absolutely grateful to Dr. Hawking," Abidi told reporters, "if he would want to go to different parts of Delhi, like Janpath, Connaught Place, the public loo, and to any of the government offices or shopping centers and hotels and embarrass the authorities."[21]

Abidi made some calls and tracked down the one vehicle in Delhi with a hydraulic lift strong enough to accommodate Hawking's heavy motorized wheelchair. Then he wrote to the Archaeological Survey of India (ASI), which manages historic sites, to request that temporary wooden ramps be installed at the monuments for Hawking's visit. He was informed that such a thing could not be done. Instead, ASI offered to make available four employees to carry Hawking and his chair up and down the steps.

Abidi promptly informed the Delhi government and the Ministry of Social Justice and Empowerment about ASI's response, and then he alerted the press. Hawking's visit was generating enormous media attention. If the physicist had to be toted around, it would be a major source of embarrassment to the Indian government.

ASI quickly succumbed to the political pressure. Within two days the wheelchair ramps were being constructed under Abidi's watchful eye. When Hawking and his wife visited Qutab Minar, they told the assembled journalists: "We wish these ramps stay even after we leave. And we hope other physically challenged people get a chance to see this architectural splendor."[22]

A few days later NCPEDP paid a surprise visit to Humayun's Tomb and discovered that ASI had already removed the ramps. Abidi immediately organized a demonstration and filed a public interest litigation in the Delhi High Court requesting a stay against removal of any other ramps. A month later ASI again bowed to the pressure, announcing that the ramps would become permanent. Moreover, ASI promised that wheelchair ramps would soon be installed at India's other monuments and World Heritage Sites, among them the Taj Mahal.[23]

Throughout 2001 and 2002, Abidi kept up the sensitization campaigns and pressure tactics, and NCPEDP continued to receive one piece of good news after another. Following a campaign of highly publicized "disability audits" at McDonald's restaurants, museums, public places, and government buildings, the Ministry of Social Justice and Empowerment appointed an "audit team" to survey all government buildings to make sure they were accessible. Then the Union Public Service Commission announced that India's civil service exam would be conducted for the first time in an accessible environment. Immediately, 3,600 disabled people applied to take the exam, which is mandatory for civil service employment.[24] Then the Hotel Association of India announced that it was issuing new disability-friendly guidelines to major hotels across the country.[25]

In late 2002 Abidi had a half dozen new plans: to look into the quality of vocational training for the disabled; to get a certain number of jobs reserved for people with disabilities in the private sector; to show companies how they could redesign work processes and make adaptations in the workplace, allowing them to hire more disabled workers without incurring significant costs.

In addition to being head of NCPEDP and convener of the DRG, Abidi had also reactivated the Indian branch of Disabled People's International (DPI-India) and been elected chair of DPI-South Asia and senior vice chair of DPI-Asia Pacific. He regularly worked until three or four o'clock in the morning. He continued to pressure the government to fulfill its legal obligations under the Persons With Disabilities Act, at one point even threatening a hunger strike.

Abidi was encouraged by the progress on a number of fronts. In the private sector, especially in the tech sector, he saw more companies making concerted efforts to recruit disabled employees. Disabled people had considerably more access to university education than just a few years earlier. And thousands of disabled people could now successfully compete for higher-grade civil service positions.

Get counted during census, disabled urged

The Times of India News Service

NEW DELHI: It was a battle, fought with grit, to ensure that the government collected separate

It is with awareness tha the NCPED ternational tion, have cc

Hawking visit focuses on the disabled

The Times of India News Service

NEW DELHI: It's just a simple l Fort, the Mantar physicist like ful-Capital in was con entre for

speaking to reporters on Thursday, "The government has been so insensitive to the issue of accessibility for the disabled even after the Persons with Disabilities Act was passed by Parliament in December 1995."

In the context of accessibility to monuments, Abidi clarifies that it isn't as though the disabled want lifts installed and ramps constructed on

Barrier-free exam centres coming

By Our Staff Reporter

NEW DELHI, APRIL 26. The Union Public Service Commission (UPSC) has sent out a circular to all 40 centres and 663 sub-centres where Civil Services preliminary examinations are proposed to be held on May 20 to make them barrier-free and disabled-friendly.

It will be the first time that these examinations would be conducted in an accessible and disabled-friendly environment. While the blind candidates have been asked to take the examination in Delhi only, the other centres have been asked to provide an extra time of 20 minutes in case any of them reports for taking examination.

While processing the applications, the Commission noticed that over 3,000 students with orthope adic dis was desl the disal this, it h dates as what fac
The t awarene Council abled Pe before tl problem giving U

All disabilities to be covered in Census 2001

By Garimella Subramaniam

NEW DELHI, OCT. 5. In a crucial development in the disabilities sector, the Commissioner of the National Population Census and his team highlighted the dis

arthritis are all movement disabled. Absence of "part of a limb" like a finger or a toe will not be considered a disability; although absence of all fingers or toes or a thumb will make a person disabled in movement. 5.) Finally, persons lacking in comprehension appropriate to their age, the mentally ill and mentally retarded, those dependent on family members to go through their daily routine will be considered mentally disabled. This would, of course, not include those unable to comprehend their studies appropriate to their age and consequently fall to qualify in examinations.

The disability of a person will be decided with reference to the date of enumeration. In case a person suffers from more than one disability, only one of the problems would be recorded. It is left to the respondent to decide which one of the disabilities he will disclose to the enumerator. Persons suffering from a temporary disability on the date of enumeration, such as immobility on account of injury will not be counted as disabled.

In view of the sensitive nature of the problem, enumerators have been advised to probe delicately so as not to offend the respondents. They have been instructed to explain the actual purpose of the question by emphasising that information on the number and type of disabilities would help the Governments in planning for the welfare of the disabled.

Stressing that the population census was different from a survey on disabilities, the Census Commissioner observed that the above definitions were kept deliberately simple and intelligible to facilitate the process of enumeration. Therefore, they may not replicate other definitions such as in the Persons With Disabilities Act 1995.

He said that over 20 lakhs enumerators were being trained in three rounds on these procedures. Audio clippings of the census campaign with a disabilities thrust and that pertaining to question 15 were played before the gathering. The Northern Region

Public buildings not user-friendly for disabled

STATESMAN NEWS SERVICE

NEW DELHI, April 11. — Preliminary findings of a two-day "disability audit" have

and yet others wheel-chair bound. Its brief was to eater public buildings and see how easy or difficult it was to access them.

According to Mr Javed Abidi whose brainchild the audit was, "the Disability Act was passed in 1995 and guidelines for disabled friendly con-

Hotels to become disabled-friendly

By Our Staff Reporter

NEW DELHI, MAY 5. The Hotel Association of India (HAI) has come out with a set of illustrative guidelines for disabled-friendly facilities to provided by hotels in the country.

Hotels have been asked to have exclusively earmarked signposted accessible parking spaces nearest to the entrar

wheelchairs. Tables should allow easy movement and approach by customers in wheelchairs. One toilet in the

Disabled protest unfriendly accessibility at restaurants

STATESMAN NEWS SERVICE

NEW DELHI, April 12. — The friendly joker of McDonald's had to confront an unhappy group today. Nearly 20 disabled people stood in silent

Basant Lok, a ramp — which is a standard feature — was demolished by the Municipal Corporation of Delhi, which claimed that it was an encroachment," said Dicky Malhotra, head, projects, McDonald's.

Newspaper reports about disability

There was still so much to be done, Abidi said. The phrase "eternal vigilance" was lodged in his mind. Nevertheless, when he reflected on the successes in the short time since 1995 when the disability bill was passed, he felt a surge of excitement. "In our wildest dreams nobody could have thought that we would have reached this stage so quickly," he said. "The disability sector is abuzz."

Six Qualities of Successful Social Entrepreneurs

It is commonly assumed that highly successful entrepreneurs are more confident and persistent than most others, including less successful entrepreneurs. This may not be true: One of the most intriguing papers I came across in my research contrasted the behavior of "highly successful" and "average" entrepreneurs and found that the most successful entrepreneurs were not necessarily more confident, persistent, or knowledgeable. The key differences had more to do with the quality of their *motivation*. The most successful entrepreneurs were the ones most determined to achieve a long-term goal that was deeply meaningful to them. Accordingly, they tended to be more systematic in the way they searched for opportunities, anticipated obstacles, monitored results, and planned ahead. They were more concerned with quality and efficiency and more committed to the people they employed and engaged with in business or as partners. Finally, they valued long-term considerations over short-term gain.[1]

Willingness to Self-Correct

Because of their motivation, highly successful entrepreneurs are highly self-correcting. This may seem a simple point, but it cannot be overstated. It is inherently difficult to reverse a train once it has left the station. It takes a combination of hard-headedness, humility, and courage to stop and say, "This isn't working" or "Our assumptions were wrong," particularly when your funding is contingent on carrying out a preauthorized plan. However, the entrepreneur's inclination to self-correct stems from the attachment to a goal rather than to a particular approach or plan. For example, when Veronica Khosa learned that the people of Mamelodi would not accept Tateni Home Care as an AIDS-only service, she wasted little time reframing the agency as a general home care service. When J. B. Schramm saw that College Summit needed to expand more systematically to achieve significant impact, he made his apologies and withdrew the program from a number of states.

Like young businesses, social change organizations usually go through many iterations as their strategies or "business models" evolve in response to problems, new opportunities and changing market conditions. If not, it is unlikely that an organization will reach a stage where it can achieve major impact. The entrepreneur's willingness to self-correct (combined with an openness to the market and a natural growth orientation) is vital to this continuous adaptive process.

Interestingly, the inclination to self-correct is a quality that seems to distinguish younger entrepreneurs from their older and better-established counterparts. It is a quality that seems to diminish with time as entrepreneurs become increasingly attached, or even chained, to their ideas. Moreover, entrepreneurs frequently lose touch with the market as their organizations grow. Increasingly, information reaches them through indirect management channels and problems come to light at later stages. At that point, it takes an extra dose of hard-headedness to stop the train and reverse it—because the correction may entail a costly and time-consuming effort to retrain thousands of people.

This was the recent experience of the Grameen Bank. In the late 1990s Muhammad Yunus learned through management channels that "internal weaknesses" in the bank's loan system were causing repayment problems and difficulties for many borrowers. It took Yunus and his managers a number of years to fully understand and diagnose the problems, develop a solution, field test that solution, and finally retrain the bank's 12,000 employees. In 2002 Yunus formally launched Grameen Bank II, an overhaul of the bank's loan program, shifting from a "one-size-fits-all" approach to a flexible banking system that is designed to be more responsive to borrowers' needs and problems.[2]

It is yet to be seen if Grameen Bank II will outperform Grameen Bank I. But it is worth noting that this sort of entrepreneurial behavior is almost unheard of in the large bureaucracies that wield power in today's world. The Nobel Prize–winning economist Joseph Stiglitz makes this point in his book *Globalization and Its Discontents*, which chronicles the failings of the International Monetary Fund (IMF), an institution that has held fast to a set of predetermined policies despite abundant evidence that those policies have fostered global economic instability and caused immense human suffering in the developing world.[3]

"How could an organization with such talented (and high paid) government bureaucrats make so many mistakes?" asks Stiglitz. "[The IMF] has been remarkably slow in learning from its mistakes—partly . . . because of the strong role of ideology and its belief in institutional infallibility, partly because its hierarchical organizational structure is used to ensure its prevailing worldviews dominate throughout the institution."[4]

Willingness to Share Credit

It has been said that there is no limit to what you can achieve if you don't care who gets the credit. For entrepreneurs, a willingness to share credit lies along the "critical path" to success, simply because the more credit they share, the more people typically will want to help them. But this quality, like willingness to self-correct, also grows out of motivation. If an entrepreneur's true intention is simply to make a change happen, then sharing credit will come naturally. However, if the true intention is to be *recognized* as having made a change happen, sharing credit may run against the grain.

Fábio Rosa belongs in the first category. Every time I referred to "his ideas," he reminded me that they weren't his. The ideas belonged to Ennio Amaral and André Voisin, and credit belonged to Ney Azevedo and his loyal colleagues Ricardo Mello and Fernando Sehn.

Similarly, in every interview with Jeroo Billimoria, Jeroo would spend half the time explaining the contributions that others had made to Childline. She would talk about Prakash Fernandes and Meghana Sawant ("They make so much happen") and Armaity Desai (the "living goddess of the social work sector in India") and Maneka Gandhi ("If she hadn't taken on Childline then we would never have had the push we got") and Anand Bordia and A. P. Singh and Asha Das, senior government officials who had helped build Childline, "and Mr. Kohli from Tata Consultancy Services and Mr. Kavarana from TELCO and Mr. Byramjee—three times when we went broke he bailed us out. . . ."

After a while, I began to understand how she had pulled everyone together.

Willingness to Break Free of Established Structures

Social entrepreneurs can cause change by redirecting existing organizations (as Drayton did at the Environmental Protection Agency and, as the reader will see, James P. Grant did at Unicef). Most of the time, however, the citizen sector is where social entrepreneurs find the greatest latitude to test and market new ideas. To be sure, there is considerable freedom in the business sector. But businesses are limited to marketing products and services for which it is possible to capture profits within a relatively short period of time. Many organizations that produce great value for society do not generate profits or take longer to break even than investors are willing to wait.

Social entrepreneurs occasionally can be found in government and academia, although the incentive structures and institutional constraints act as deterrents. The two- to four-year election cycles and the ongoing publishing demands are unwelcome obstacles for action-oriented individuals with multidecade time horizons.

This is not to imply that governments and universities do not play critical roles in social innovation. The micro-credit field could not have expanded so quickly if the idea had not been financed, studied, and disseminated by governments and universities around the world. However, social entrepreneurs who initiate their ideas while teaching in universities—Muhammad Yunus and Jeroo Billimoria, for example— usually step outside the academy to build their organizations; in doing so, they often assume considerable financial and professional risk. What they gain is the freedom to act and the distance to see beyond the orthodoxy in their fields. This is critical because all innovation entails the ability to separate from the past.

Willingness to Cross Disciplinary Boundaries

Independence from established structures not only helps social entrepreneurs wrest free of prevailing assumptions, it gives them latitude to combine resources in new ways. Indeed, one of the primary functions of the social entrepreneur is to serve as a kind of social alchemist: to create new social compounds; to gather together people's ideas, experiences, skills, and resources in configurations that society is not naturally aligned to produce.

People typically self-organize around interests, work, culture, and proximity. Universities are divided into faculties, governments into agencies, economic and social activity into industries or fields. Social entrepreneurs approach this state of order with a need to engage the world in its wholeness. As Jeroo Billimoria discovered, it makes little sense to run an emergency phone service for street children if the hospitals and police won't cooperate.

Faced with whole problems, social entrepreneurs readily cross disciplinary boundaries, pulling together people from different spheres, with different kinds of experience and expertise, who can, together, build workable solutions that are qualitatively new.

Ashoka, for example, began by applying a well-understood business concept to social pursuits. Childline brings together street kids, citizen groups, businesses, and government. The result is a network with wide reach, brand recognition, street savvy, and influence.

The "creative combining" on the part of the social entrepreneurs may be an intuitive response to the excessive fragmentation and specialization in modern industrial societies. As Renascer, Childline, and College Summit have each demonstrated, people have whole needs, and their problems cannot be solved unless many people work together intelligently. This fact may be why so many social entrepreneurs can be found today integrating functions that otherwise would remain disconnected.

Willingness to Work Quietly

Many social entrepreneurs spend decades steadily advancing their ideas, influencing people in small groups or one on one, and it is often exceedingly difficult to understand or measure their impact. Often they become recognized only after years working in relative obscurity.

Consider John Woolman, the man who persuaded Quakers to free their slaves. Woolman is best known for his famous *Journal*, which sheds little light on his role in the battle against slavery. "John Woolman's personal influence had far-reaching social and moral effects," wrote Amelia M. Gummere in a study of the early Quakers in New Jersey. However, Woolman's humility prevented him, in his writings, from making "any reference to great events in which he was an actor."[5]

After having interviewed hundreds of people for this book, I am convinced that Bill Drayton is responsible for creating a groundswell in support of social entrepreneurship. I am not referring to the financial support that Ashoka has provided to its 1,400 fellows. Most of the fellows I interviewed said that the credibility, confidence, contacts, and ideas they gained through Ashoka were more valuable than the money.

I am referring to something much harder to assess than the fellows' perceptions. Over the past twenty-five years, the process of building Ashoka's international network has produced hundreds of thousands of conversations with social entrepreneurs, activists, academics, funders, businesspeople, journalists, and others around the world. This marathon educational process—during Ashoka's early years much of it handled by Drayton personally—has encouraged many people in a number of countries to think differently about how social change happens. Through this process, Ashoka has spread a value system that recognizes and honors the extraordinary personal efforts that are necessary to solve major problems. Because of Ashoka's influence, many social funders are more likely today to think about entrepreneurial qualities when they allocate resources.

I cannot prove this assertion. It is an impression based on hundreds of interviews I have conducted over the past five years in Bangladesh, Brazil, Hungary, India, Poland, South Africa, and the United States. Indeed, the difficulty of demonstrating this kind of impact explains why social entrepreneurs receive less attention than other kinds of actors. Many social entrepreneurs wield a kind of power that is poorly understood and rarely characterized in public discourse. One can readily summon an image of a billionaire like Ted Turner declaring his intention to give away $1 billion or a charismatic leader like Martin Luther King Jr. inspiring 100,000 people at once.[6] But it is difficult to imagine the cumulative force of a person like Drayton conducting 100,000 conversations *in a row*—productive conversations, each with follow-up—over thirty years. Yet this quiet, steady, unremitting pressure is an important force for change in the world.

A person must have very pure motivation to push an idea so steadily for so long with so little fanfare. In his *Memoirs* Jean Monnet, the architect of European unification, observes that "one cannot concentrate on an objective and on oneself at the same time."[7] To Monnet, people of ambition fell into two groups: those who wanted to "do something" and those who wanted to "be someone."

"The main concern of many very remarkable people is to cut a figure and play a role," he noted. "They are useful to society, where images are very important and the affirmation of character is essential to the administration of affairs. But, in general, it is the other kind of people who get things moving—those who spend their time looking for places and opportunities to influence the course of events. The places are not always the most obvious ones, nor do the opportunities occur when many people expect them. Anyone who wants to find them has to forsake the limelight."[8]

Strong Ethical Impetus

Entrepreneurs, observed the economist Joseph A. Schumpeter, are motivated not by profit, but by the "desire to found a private dynasty, the will to conquer in a competitive battle, and the joy of creating."[9] If so, what distinguishes social entrepreneurs from business entrepreneurs?

With this question, we arrive at the bedrock of social entrepreneurship: the ethics. It is meaningless to talk about social entrepreneurs without considering the ethical quality of their motivation: the why. In the end, business and social entrepreneurs are very much the same animals. They think about problems the same way. They ask the same types of questions. The difference is not in temperament or ability, but in the nature of their visions. In a question: Does the entrepreneur dream of building the world's greatest running-shoe company or vaccinating all the world's children?

One day I sent Fábio Rosa an e-mail. "Why do you work on the kind of projects you do?" I asked. "Why don't you just want to make a lot of money?"

I waited a month for his reply.

"I guess the delay in answering your questions was due to the responsibility in sending you a good answer," he began.

> I am trying to build a little part of the world in which I would like to live. A project only makes sense to me when it proves useful to make people happier and the environment more respected, and when it represents a hope for a better future. This is the soul of my projects.
>
> Looking back, many times I have asked myself exactly the same question—since there are easier things to do. But this has been the only way I feel happy. And I also believe that persistence and coherence are virtues and I like to see that I have them.
>
> Working on the kind of projects I do means to dream with a new world in mind. My projects always renew my faith in an harmonic way of living, without misery. With our intelligence, knowledge and culture, it is not necessary to destroy the environment to build. When people work together they are powerful; there is friendship. In the end, there is peace, harmony, tranquility, optimism.
>
> If there is a deeply human motivation in all of this, it is that my projects are related to practical, doable work. We need to actuate and cause change. Even if the inspiration is romantic, it desires material results, a re-colored reality.
>
> About money—I need money. Money is very important to

accomplish my projects. But money only matters if it helps to solve people's problems and to create the world I described above. My projects help people around me to acquire wealth and in some ways this comes back to me.

It has been an intellectual and creative challenge to build models that can be used by excluded and deprived people, to create sustainable livelihoods and promote social inclusion.

Creating projects, implementing them and succeeding, witnessing one's dreams come true, is happiness. Money just makes it easier.

For all these reasons, I work the way I do. I am a slave to my dreams, thoughts and ideas. That is all.

Where does this motivation come from? When interviewing fellows about their past, Drayton has said that in most cases he finds someone, such as a parent, uncle, or grandparent, with "outstandingly strong values" who was an early influence on the fellow. Jody Jensen, who was Ashoka's representative in Hungary for five years, reported another pattern: "I heard the same story again and again. Someone had experienced an intense kind of pain that branded them in some way. They said, 'I *had* to do this. There was nothing else I could do.'"

I have found this to be true in many cases. Both Vera Cordeiro and Veronica Khosa reached a point where they could no longer bear others' suffering without acting to change it. Many of the fellows working in disability, such as Erzsébet Szekeres and Javed Abidi, have disabled children or are disabled themselves. For Ellison Pierce, the doctor who revolutionized anesthesia safety, the transformative moment was the death of his friends' daughter due to an anesthetist's error. Muhammad Yunus has often referred to Bangladesh's famine in 1974, when thousands starved to death, as the turning point in his life.

However the influences differ, a pattern remains: At some moment in their lives, social entrepreneurs get it into their heads that it is up to them to solve a particular problem. Usually something has been brewing inside for a long time, and at a particular moment in time—often triggered by an event—personal preparedness, social need, and historical opportunity converge and the person takes decisive action. The word "decision" comes from the Latin *decidere*, meaning "to cut off." From that point on, the social entrepreneurs seem to cut off other options for themselves.

Over time, their ideas become more important to them than anything else. Every decision—whom to marry, where to live, what books to read—passes through the prism of their ideas. Although it is probably impossible to fully explain why people become social entrepreneurs, it is certainly possible to identify them. And society stands to benefit by finding these people, encouraging them, and helping them to do what they need to do.

19.

Morality Must March with Capacity

James Grant, United States: The Child Survival Revolution

> The twentieth century will be chiefly remembered in future centuries not as an age of political conflicts or technical inventions, but as an age in which human society dared to think of the welfare of the whole human race as a practical objective.
>
> —Arnold Toynbee

None of the people-of-the-century lists compiled by U.S. news magazines in 1999 included the name James P. Grant. This is a telling omission given that Grant orchestrated global health changes that saved the lives of at least 25 million children.[1] From 1980 until his death in 1995, Grant, as head of Unicef, conceived and led a worldwide campaign to make simple, low-cost health solutions available to children everywhere.

Largely as a result of the "child survival revolution" that Grant launched, between 1981 and 1990 the worldwide vaccination rate for children increased from 20 to 80 percent.[2] By 1992 almost 4 million child deaths were being prevented each year from immunizable diseases and severe dehydration due to diarrhea.[3] Additionally, 3 million people who would have been crippled with polio can walk and run; millions who would have been blinded from lack of Vitamin A can see; and tens of millions of people whose brains would have been damaged due to iodine deficiency have developed normally.[4] These changes can be attributed in large measure to the vision, resourcefulness, and tenacity of James Grant.[5]

If you ask almost anyone who worked closely with Grant at Unicef to describe him, you will be regaled with tales of his "boundless energy," "limitless optimism," "complete lack of self-importance," and "absolute refusal to accept that something could not be done." Richard Reid, a

James P. Grant

colleague who worked with Grant for fifteen years, said: "Jim Grant electrified the UN. He was a genuine original, a force of nature." And Peter Adamson, who collaborated with Grant on Unicef's annual report *The State of the World's Children*, dubbed him "the Mad American" because of the sheer audacity of his vision.

In 1980 President Jimmy Carter urged the UN Secretary-General to appoint Grant as head of Unicef. In 1982 Grant read a lecture entitled "Why the Other Half Dies" written by Jon Rohde, an American pediatrician, who had developed public health programs in Bangladesh and Haiti. Each year in the developing world, Rohde wrote, 14 million children under the age of five died. And the great majority died at home from diarrhea, pneumonia, malnutrition, and immunizable diseases. Most of these deaths, he said, were preventable with cheap and simple technologies that already existed.

For malnutrition, growth monitoring—weighing the child—had proved to be an effective early detection method. With regard to vaccines, there had been major improvements in heat-stable vaccines as well as in the "cold chain" technology necessary for effective dissemination.[6] It was estimated that immunization could prevent 3.5 million child deaths per year, mostly from measles.[7]

Additionally, in the 1970s researchers had developed a simple treatment for diarrheal disease, the number-one childhood killer, responsible at the time for 5 million deaths each year.[8] Severe diarrhea, which causes a critical loss of fluids, quickly sends a child's body into shock. But researchers in Bangladesh had discovered that adding glucose to a solution of salt and water can increase the body's ability to absorb fluids and minerals by 2,500 percent. In 1978 the British medical journal *Lancet* described this finding as "potentially the most important medical advance this century."[9]

A simple oral rehydration therapy (ORT) could be prepared at home by adding eight teaspoons of sugar and one teaspoon of salt to a liter of water. Premixed packets of oral rehydration salts (ORS), which needed only to be mixed with water and drunk, cost less than a dime.[10] It was estimated that 70 percent of the child deaths from diarrheal disease could be prevented with oral rehydration therapy; in most cases, just two packets of ORS were enough to save a life.[11]

By the early 1980s, the global expansion of basic education combined with advances in communications made it possible to disseminate information around the world.[12] Most countries had a health infrastructure capable of putting ORS into the hands of mothers. Why wasn't it being done? As Peter Adamson recalled: "It was as if a cheap cure for cancer had been discovered but no one had bothered making it available."

James Grant was born to American parents in 1922 in Peking, China, where he lived until he was fifteen years old and learned to speak fluent Mandarin. As a boy bicycling to school on winter mornings, Grant often came across people who had frozen to death sleeping on the sidewalks. Later in life he would reflect that such suffering had been accepted as normal for the poor until late in the twentieth century.

Grant wasn't a doctor, but public health was very much in his blood. His grandfather had been a medical missionary and his father, John B. Grant, who headed the Department of Hygiene and Public Health at the Peking Union Medical College in the 1920s, became a world-renowned pioneer in public health. John Grant focused on providing basic, low-cost medical training in rural areas. His work influenced primary healthcare systems across the developing world and served as a model for the "barefoot doctors" initiative that Mao Zedong spread across China.[13]

At every stage in his career, James Grant displayed creativity, entrepreneurialism, and a remarkable consistency of purpose. After serving in Burma and China during World War II, he remained in China to work with the United Nation's Relief and Rehabilitation Administration. In Taiwan, he became the director of the Joint Commission on Rural Reconstruction, pushing the land reform, rural credit, education, and decentralized health programs that set the stage for Taiwan's industrial transformation.

After attending Harvard Law School, Grant became a legal advisor to the U.S. Foreign Operations Administration in Delhi, where he helped broker a temporary truce between India and Pakistan over Kashmir. In the 1960s, as a director of the United States Agency for International Development (USAID) based in Turkey, he demonstrated how the Green Revolution could be quickly scaled up. He founded the Overseas Development Council, a think tank based in Washington, D.C., which helped redirect U.S. foreign aid policy to basic needs for the poor.

All of this would add up to a remarkable career in and of itself. But in the context of Grant's work at Unicef, it reads as preparation.

After reading Rohde's paper, Grant called him up. During the summer of 1982, he visited Rohde in Haiti for two weeks, grilling him about immunization, ORT, growth monitoring, and breastfeeding—factors that pediatricians had identified as keys to child survival. When Grant returned to New York, he called a meeting and invited senior staff from Unicef and international health bodies. After Rohde presented his findings, Grant made his pitch: For the first time in history, he asserted, scientific advances and social conditions made it possible to meet the basic health needs of all the world's children. "Morality must march with capacity," he declared. Why were so many children still dying of preventable causes? The problem was not lack of human ingenuity. It was lack of vision and will— especially political will. And that, Grant insisted, was what Unicef could, and should, supply.

He then outlined his plan. He wanted Unicef to "shift gears." He wanted the organization to set itself the goal of reducing by *half* the toll of disease and disability for the world's children and to do it through a massive, focused effort to make low-cost techniques like vaccinations, ORT, and growth monitoring available to every mother and every child in every country.[14] "The audacity of this proposition is almost impossible to recapture," recalled Adamson. One official stormed out of the meeting.

At the time, Unicef operated healthcare projects in communities around the world. Some reached 50 families; some reached 5,000. The agency's budget, about $300 million, represented less than 20 cents for every child in the developing world. "Everyone had it in their minds that scale was tied to resources," Adamson recalled. "We had low-cost solutions and a huge problem. How to put them into practice on the same scale as the problem? No one had ever asked that before. People hadn't lifted their heads from their desks and seen what the UN system could really do. Grant had a completely different view of the results that could be obtained with those resources. It was so revolutionary as to make people think that the guy had lost it."

In late 1982, amid terrific grumbling, Grant launched Unicef's child survival and development revolution, unveiling a strategy that came to be known as GOBI: G for growth monitoring to detect undernutrition in small children, O for oral rehydration therapy to treat childhood diarrhea, B to encourage breastfeeding (which had declined precipitously due to working mothers and the marketing of infant formula), and I for immunization against the six basic childhood diseases: tuberculosis, polio, diphtheria, tetanus, whooping cough, and measles.[15] (They added two Fs: food supplements and family planning; and, later, a third: female education.)

To achieve these goals, Unicef would have to undergo radical changes. The organization had always conducted a certain amount of advocacy to support its projects. Grant reversed the approach. He believed Unicef should run projects to lend credibility to its advocacy. What were Unicef's competitive advantages? Prestige, moral influence, global recognition, and political neutrality. The organization was uniquely positioned to articulate a global vision for children's health and leverage commitment from every corner of the world.

To begin, Grant got the International Pediatric Association, the world's largest body of child healthcare specialists, to endorse GOBI-FFF. He won support from influential voices in the medical establishment, notably William Foege, then head of the U.S. Centers for Disease Control, who had pioneered the "surveillance and containment" strategy that was critical in eradicating smallpox in the 1970s.[16]

But Grant also encountered considerable resistance. Within Unicef, officials complained that there was nothing substantive about advocacy. Others felt that Grant's strategy would destroy Unicef's strength as a grassroots, operational institution. "It was like some huge carefully assembled market stall of ideas was overturned," recalled Adamson. "And people whose real experience was in running projects suddenly found their place in the firmament changed. A lot of noses were put out of joint by this."

Outside Unicef, Grant's staunchest critic was the director-general of the World Health Organization, Halfdan Mahler, who opposed selective "medical fixes" in favor of more comprehensive restructuring of health delivery systems.[17]

Grant's response was to assert that GOBI-FFF should be viewed as an entry strategy—a "Trojan horse"—for promoting children's rights and attacking poverty. He believed that it was essential to build political momentum for children's causes by focusing, first, on achievable goals that everyone could agree on. How could real progress come for children until the world acknowledged that 14 million child deaths each year—40,000 a day—was an outrage? He asked people to imagine 120 children-packed jumbo jets crashing each day.

In the end, Grant's most effective defense against his critics was his integrity. "Jim's idealism and commitment were so obviously genuine that in all the years, I never heard anyone question it," recalled Adamson. "For all the grand plans, Jim Grant personally was devoid of self-importance. And for all the high-profile campaigning, he never sought the spotlight for himself. For Jim, it was only and always the cause. And I believe that in the end it was this as much as anything else that won so many to his side."

Prior to Grant's arrival, Unicef enjoyed a reputation as a decentralized, "hands-on" agency whose strengths were unique in the UN system.[18] Grant exploited those strengths. He provided incentives for country offices to plan their own strategies to mobilize around GOBI-FFF. He encouraged competition, circulating a weekly telex called *Flash* to keep Unicef's country offices abreast of one another's progress. He used Unicef's major advocacy forum, *The State of the World's Children*, both to report and rank child survival achievements by country.

When it came to management, he broke with UN tradition by making assignments based not on seniority, but on ability. "Jim would always ask me in a given situation, 'Who are the movers and shakers—the entrepreneurs here?'" recalled Richard Jolly, formerly Unicef's deputy executive director for programs, who worked with Grant for fourteen years. He looked for ways to maximize his staff's potential. During management reviews, Grant rarely accepted blanket criticisms about staffers. "He would always say, 'What have we done to build the person?'" added Jolly. "Time and time again he would come back to the positive: how to build, how to encourage, how to win over."

He maintained close contact with field offices, routinely calling up country representatives just to ask how things were going. "He focused on exceptional information—where things were extremely good or bad," recalled Kul Gautam, Unicef's deputy executive director, who worked with Grant for fifteen years.

Grant bolstered Unicef's media relations unit, recruiting Harry Belafonte, Liv Ullmann, and Audrey Hepburn as "goodwill ambassadors." He looked for new ways to raise money. For example, Unicef had a greeting card business, and the job of running it had traditionally been considered a backwater appointment. Grant put one of his entrepreneurs in charge of it, and the unit was soon generating tens of millions of dollars in unrestricted revenues. (Under Grant's leadership, Unicef's budget grew from $313 million to $1 billion.)[19]

Grant also looked for support in unconventional places. "He knew that the archbishop of Bogotá had a thousand times more influence than the minister of health," noted Gautam. "But how do you get the archbishop on board? He called the Pope and asked him to send a message." He forged partnerships with hundreds of groups including the Red Cross and Red Crescent societies, Rotary International, the Catholic Church, El Azar, and the International Council of Nurses. (Since 1985 Rotary International alone has raised over $400 million toward the eradication of polio.)[20]

In 1984 Grant also figured out a way to manage the competitive tensions between Unicef and the World Health Organization. At a conference in Bellagio, Italy, organized by Dr. Jonas Salk and Robert McNamara, Unicef and the WHO agreed to create the Task Force for Child Survival and Development, pulling together Unicef, the WHO, the Rockefeller Foundation, the World Bank, and the United Nations Development Program. Grant and WHO director-general Mahler asked William Foege to oversee the task force, which became a key mechanism to resolve technical issues, strengthen commitment for the campaign, and allow UN agencies to work together without the usual red tape.[21]

Perhaps the greatest advantage enjoyed by the director of Unicef is access to heads of state. Using this access, Grant set out systematically to communicate at the top-most political levels that child survival was a winner. He kept his message simple and his pockets full. He never appeared in public without a packet of ORS in his pocket. Sitting with a prime minister, he would take it out and say: "Do you know that this costs less than a cup of tea and it can save hundreds of thousands of children's lives in your country?" "He would sit with a prime minister or king and start talking about diarrhea," explained Rolf Carriere, who has served as Unicef's country representative in Burma, Bangladesh, and Indonesia. "And many of his colleagues got uneasy with it, especially if you heard him speak five times with the same prime minister or king and each time he talked about diarrhea. They'd say, 'Oh God, there he goes again.' But he knew that you have to keep sending out the message that there's no mystery to saving child lives. He understood that you had to overcome your own inhibition of repeating yourself."

He made things personal. "Talking to a prime minister, he would say, 'Oh, you have grandchildren. Are they immunized? Does your granddaughter have a growth card?'" recalled Jon Rohde. He also made it visual. He had Unicef circulate posters with pictures of heads of state administering oral polio drops to babies. And, always, he promoted competition: "In Turkey," noted Gautam, "he would say to the head of state: 'You know Colombia is doing this. . .'."

In 1984 Grant had his first major success when he persuaded the president of Colombia, Belisario Betancur, to back a national vaccination campaign. Betancur had himself grown up in a large family in which a number of his siblings had died early in life.[22] Three national vaccination days were declared. The media promoted the campaign and 100,000 volunteers from the church, police, military, unions, public school system, Boy Scouts, and Red Cross vaccinated 800,000 children.[23]

From there, smaller campaigns spread to Burkina Faso, Senegal, and parts of India and Nigeria. For the next big push, Grant focused on Turkey, where he had served as the USAID representative years before and remained friends with Turkey's prime minister, Turgut Ozal. With Turkey's immunization rate below 20 percent, a drive was launched in September 1985 to vaccinate 5 million children. The campaign was publicized on radio and television and promoted by 200,000 school teachers, 54,000 *imams* (religious leaders), and 40,000 *muhtars* (village leaders). "From stores and corner shop refrigerators, the vaccines were moved out by car, truck, on horseback or on foot," wrote Maggie Black in *Children First: The Story of UNICEF, Past and Present*. "By the end of the final round in November, with winter weather setting in, 84 percent of the target group had been immunized."[24]

By 1985 Grant had visited thirty-nine heads of state, and the push for immunization was spreading throughout the Middle East, North Africa, India, China, and Latin America.[25] Grant traveled continuously. He kept clothes stored around the world, rarely boarding a flight with more than a carry-on bag. Richard Reid, who organized the immunization campaign in Turkey, recalled that Grant "half jogged across desert terrain," "drafted telexes in jeeps," stayed up until 3:00 A.M. "coaxing agreements out of

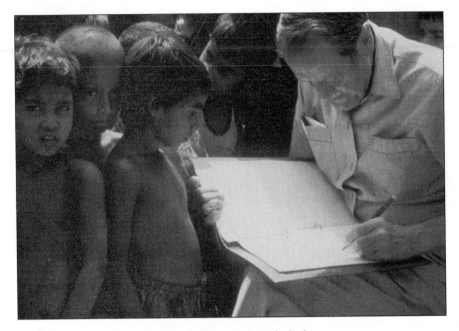

Grant with children in Bangladesh, 1990

prime ministers," then jumped out of bed at 6:00 A.M. the same morning "jabbing a pencil at a map over breakfast, laughing and insisting, 'It's doable. It's doable.'"[26]

By 1984 and 1985 average immunization rates in the developing world had jumped from 20 to 40 percent. In 1985 worldwide demand for vaccines was triple what it had been in 1983.[27] The use of ORT had increased from almost nothing to 20 percent of world families.[28]

In early 1985 President José Napoleón Duarte of El Salvador paid a visit to Javier Pérez de Cuéllar, the UN Secretary-General, in New York. At the time, the civil war in El Salvador was raging. Cuéllar had invited Grant to the meeting and after the official business was completed, Cuéllar asked Grant if he wished to make a comment.[29] As Richard Jolly recalled: "Jim said, 'Well, President Duarte, I'm very glad to be here and we've talked about the war, but are you aware that more children die each year from measles and preventable causes than all the people who have died in the war so far?'

"President Duarte says, 'No, I wasn't aware of that. But what could be done?'

"Jim says, 'Well you need to immunize all the children and it's very difficult because of the war. Many of the health clinics have closed down. They can't function. Mr. President, why don't you call for a cease-fire on a Sunday so that all the children can be immunized?

"President Duarte says, 'Mr. Grant, if I did that I would be out of office immediately.'

"Now that's where Jim's persistence and ambition comes in," Jolly said.

"Jim says, 'Of course, with respect, Mr. President, you know the politics much better than I, but are you actually sure? You know there could be a lot of support. This could show your concern with all the children."

Out of that conversation came negotiations that led to the "Days of Tranquility"—the first time that a war was halted to provide routine preventive care to children. Roughly a quarter of a million children were vaccinated that year in El Salvador.[30] The cease-fire was repeated the following year and eventually became routine. Days of Tranquility later spread to civil wars in Lebanon, Uganda, the Sudan, and the former Yugoslavia.[31]

An organization with thousands of employees can be kept doing the same thing only so long before boredom sets in. Grant often said that the easiest way to keep people motivated is to come up with a fresh idea every few years. It was much tougher to identify a simple approach that worked and stick with it. But it was important to find new ways to infuse fresh energy into ongoing campaigns. So Grant decided that Unicef and its partners needed a big goal to focus on. He didn't have to invent one. In 1977 the World Health Assembly had set a global target for universal child immunization (UCI) by 1990. A key to success, Grant saw, would be to define UCI in such a way that the goal would be both meaningful and achievable. No country had ever achieved 100 percent child immunization. However, when immunization coverage reached 80 percent, the effect was to disrupt "disease transmission patterns" sufficiently so as to increase protection for non-immunized children.[32]

Following this logic, Unicef and the WHO defined UCI as 80 percent immunization coverage for each of the six basic childhood diseases. In 1985 Grant campaigned hard to win senior-level commitment for UCI. That year the UN General Assembly, along with 74 governments and 400 citizen organizations, passed a resolution in support of UCI.[33] Meanwhile, immunization rates continued to climb in the developing world. By 1986

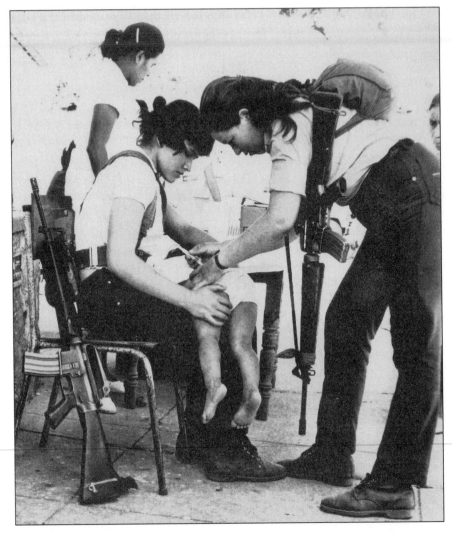

A vaccination during the Days of Tranquility, El Salvador, 1985

average rates were between 40 and 60 percent.[34] As the deadline approached, the push for UCI intensified. Unicef estimates that, during 1990 alone, 600 million "encounters" took place between children and health agencies delivering immunizations. Grant called it the "largest peacetime mobilization" the world had ever seen.

By the end of 1990—following a decade of global recession, debt crises, and austerity measures—Unicef and the WHO declared that seventy-two countries had achieved UCI, and global vaccination coverage had reached 80 percent. There was skepticism about the numbers reported by some countries. "Many officials fudged figures to please their bosses," recalled Adamson. "When India declared that it had achieved 80 percent, under 70 was probably the truth. But the point was that when this began it was about 20 percent."

Looking ahead, Grant sought to capitalize on the success of the child survival revolution—and broaden it. For years, children's advocates had been pushing to create an international convention to guarantee the rights of children. The big question was how to get the world's governments to pay attention. Grant had the idea to convene a World Summit for Children at UN headquarters in New York and invite every one of the world's heads of state. How better to place children at the top of the global agenda and pressure governments to commit to measurable goals by the year 2000?

When first proposed, the World Summit for Children was dismissed as a "pipe dream."[35] Prior to 1990, the United Nations had never sponsored such a gathering. Not only was there no precedent for it, UN rules actually forbade calling a meeting that specifically requested the attendance of heads of state. Many officials feared that the UN would be made to look foolish, particularly if only a few heads of state attended. Months before the summit date, senior Unicef officials worried that only five or six would turn up. Grant tried to relieve the stress by turning it into a betting game. "People were saying ten, fifteen, eight," recalled Jolly. "Jim won—but even he'd guessed only fifty-three."

In the end, seventy-one heads of state attended, making the World Summit for Children the largest gathering of world leaders that had ever met to discuss a single issue. More than 100 countries committed to achieving the summit's goals and 150 prepared national plans of action, which included measurable and time-bound goals related to health, education, and child protection. (The summit opened up new possibilities for activists and social entrepreneurs to directly engage governments, businesses, and multilateral organizations throughout the 1990s.) Today all but two nations—the United States and Somalia—have signed and ratified the Convention on the Rights of the Child, making it the most widely embraced rights treaty in history.

After the summit, Grant intensified his efforts to ensure that the action plans went beyond good intentions. Between 1990 and 1994 he and Unicef country representatives held over 100 meetings with heads of state to promote the goals of the Children's Summit.[36] Grant carried around a series of color-coded charts indicating where each country was on track with regard to its action plan (green), where it was falling off pace (yellow), and where it was in trouble (red). Grant made it a point never to leave a country before composing a letter reiterating any promises he had managed to extract from officials and explaining what impact each action would have on children's lives.

One of the summit's goals was to eliminate iodine deficiency disorders by 2000. In 1990, 1.6 billion people—30 percent of the world's population—were at risk of physical and mental retardation due to iodine deficiency. It was estimated that 43 million people had experienced brain damage from lack of iodine.[37] In addition to carrying around packets of ORS, Grant now traveled with a pocket salt test, which he used to raise awareness about the fact that this massive problem could be solved by adding iodine to salt at a cost of 5 cents per person per year.[38] "At a state dinner whenever Jim said, 'Please pass the salt,' all his staff took a deep breath because you knew he was going to pull out his testing fluid to see if it was iodized," recalled Jon Rohde. And if the reading was negative, he would hold it up and announce to the dignitaries: "Did you know that you gain an average of thirteen IQ points by putting iodine in salt?"[39] (During the 1990s the proportion of households in the developing world consuming iodized salt increased from 20 to 70 percent.[40])

Grant resigned from Unicef a few weeks before he died of cancer in January 1995. "Even in his final weeks of life he would still be calling me at 10:00 P.M. from his hospital bed because he had another idea and he wanted to get it out to someone who'd be able to follow up on it," recalled William Foege. "You don't need a lot of people like that to really change the world." The week before his death, Grant was still lobbying to get the U.S. government to ratify the Convention on the Rights of the Child.

The main criticism of the child survival revolution was that it was unsustainable. In recent years, about one-fifth of the world's countries have seen immunization rates fall below 80 percent. In very poor countries, rates have dropped to an average of 56 percent.[41] Four million people still die each year of diseases for which vaccines exist.[42] And ORS—the 10 cent life-saver—is still used in only 50 percent of cases where it is needed.[43] However, critics also failed to envision the degree to which the "multiplier and ripple effects" of the drive for UCI would bolster primary healthcare delivery systems in many countries.[44] Today immunization programs and

ORS drives continue to save 2 to 3 million lives each year and prevent millions from becoming disabled. In 1988, for example, there were 350,000 cases of polio in the world; in 2001, there were 480 cases.[45]

Grant's legacy goes beyond lives saved, however. Grant demonstrated the enormous untapped potential of the United Nations system. Not only did he show how Unicef could deploy its resources to massive effect, he launched a process that raised global standards for children's health. A toll of death and disability that not long ago was seen as unavoidable is today seen as unacceptable.

In 1999 the Bill & Melinda Gates Foundation spearheaded the establishment of the Global Alliance for Vaccines and Immunization (GAVI)—a consortium that includes Unicef and the WHO, as well as governments, pharmaceutical companies, and citizen groups—to reinvigorate immunization programs worldwide. GAVI, whose Vaccine Fund was initially capitalized with a $750 million grant from the Gates Foundation, is seeking to ensure that 80 percent of the children in the developing world will be receiving existing and new vaccines by the year 2005. It is an ambitious goal, but people know it can be achieved.

"Jim Grant succeeded in showing what was possible," explained Foege, who helped establish GAVI. "Once you reach 80 percent, when you fall back everyone knows you've fallen back and you're always in this position of having to justify why you fell back. If you'd never gotten there, you'd be comfortable with 70 or 60 percent. Jim Grant changed the rules. You have to ask the question: If he wasn't there what would have happened?"

20.

Blueprint Copying

Between 1990 and 2003 Ashoka spread from eight to forty-six countries and the number of Ashoka fellows increased from 200 to 1,400. As the fellows built up their organizations and broadened the scope of their work, it became clear that they stood to benefit from a range of supports. Ashoka saw that many of the services that business entrepreneurs rely on—legal assistance, management consulting, public relations, an array of financing mechanisms—were unavailable to the fellows. So, with its modest budget, Ashoka tried to respond to some of the needs by adding new "product lines," many of which were introduced by staffers whom Ashoka dubbed "intrapreneurs."

In 1988, for example, a young staffer fresh out of Brown University, Diana Wells, initiated the Fellowship Support Services in response to the fellows' requests for contact referrals, technical assistance, and media advice. In 1993 Ashoka's representative for northern India, an energetic ex-journalist named Sushmita Ghosh (who succeeded Drayton as Ashoka's president in 2001), launched *Changemakers*, a journal devoted to exploring the best strategies being pioneered by social entrepreneurs. (The journal has grown into Changemakers.net, an online information hub for social entrepreneurs.) In 1994 Drayton recruited one of Ashoka's Brazilian fellows, Valdemar de Oliveira Neto, to launch a global fellowship program with the goal of systematizing the fellows ideas and helping them to work together and benefit from one another's experience. In 1995 Ashoka created an Internet Incentive Fund to encourage fellows to get online quickly, as well as a Challenge Pot to spur collaborations among fellows.

In 1996 Ashoka recruited Anamaria Schindler, a sociologist from São Paulo, Brazil, to launch the Center for Social Entrepreneurship (CSE), a joint venture with the São Paulo office of McKinsey & Company. The CSE is designed to strengthen the profession of social entrepreneurship through consultancies, trainings, and special initiatives, including national "Business Plan Competitions" for the citizen sector. (Schindler arranged McKinsey's consultancy with Renascer.)

Of all the challenges the fellows faced, the most universal was achieving long-term financial sustainability. Almost all of the fellows were spending huge chunks of time thinking exclusively about financing—time that needed to be spent thinking about product, service, delivery, staff, marketing, and the like. Looking for new ideas, in 1996 Ashoka recruited Derek Brown, a graduate of Stanford Business School with development experience in Asia and the former Soviet Union, and dispatched him to Thailand to launch the Citizen Base Initiative (CBI). The objectives of CBI were (1) to identify fellows who had managed to build stable, decentralized bases of local support (reducing their dependence on governments and international donors), and (2) to analyze their strategies, document them, and promote them through national "Citizen Base Competitions." (Ashoka is compiling a book that will highlight 150 of these resource-mobilization strategies, many of which involve market-based income generation.)

Since 1999 Ashoka has spread the CBI to Bangladesh, Brazil, Hungary, India, Mexico, Poland, South Africa, and Venezuela. Anamaria Schindler has carried the CSE to India and Peru and initiated new Ashoka-McKinsey partnerships in Argentina, Colombia, France, Germany, Mexico, South Africa, and Venezuela. In Central Europe, Ashoka's director of International Training, Ryszard Praszkier, has launched, in Poland and India, the Bridge for Universities and Society, through which fellows train students in social entrepreneurship. In 2002 Leslie Crutchfield, a graduate of Harvard Business School who had earlier cofounded a magazine for social entrepreneurs, launched Ashoka's Accelerator for Social Entrepreneurship, an initiative designed to help fellows scale up their organizations and achieve major impact. The Accelerator matches fellows with professional firms or groups that provide services such as management consulting, communications and media advice, and legal assistance. Its initial partners include McKinsey & Company and Hill & Knowlton, both of which have a number of global offices working with Ashoka, and Latham & Watkins and the International Senior Lawyers Project, which have provided assistance to fellows based in the United States and Canada.

Many of these new "product lines" remain in relatively early stages; however, much has already been learned. For example, Schindler has tuned many of the details in Ashoka's engagement with McKinsey. "The secret to the success of the partnership is the adaptation and translation of language," she explains.

From Ashoka's vantage point, there was no doubt that a wealth of problem-solving knowledge was fast accumulating around the globe—and it was not to be found in government, academia, or big development organizations. The most promising social change strategies were in the hands of the social entrepreneurs who were dispersed, disconnected, and underfunded. As early as 1990, when Ashoka had organized its first "mosaic meeting" in Dhaka and discovered that fellows working with youths were applying similar approaches (e.g., "putting children in charge"), the organization had been exploring ways to capitalize on the collective knowledge and experience in its fellowship.

By the late 1990s Ashoka had enough "late take-off" or mature-stage fellows in different countries to begin rolling out its "mosaic" initiatives.

The idea was (1) to identify the general patterns that explained how hundreds of fellows had succeeded in their fields; (2) select from those patterns the few that, once understood, could open up major new avenues for those working in the same fields; and (3) spread those principles across the fellowship and the field's practitioners.

For Drayton, building the mosaics was at the very core of Ashoka's mission—to advance the profession of social entrepreneurship. In fact, Drayton believed that Ashoka's "greatest gift" to its fellows, and to society in general, would ultimately come from its efforts to identify and market the "pattern-setting ideas" that emerged from the fellowship. He argued that the process of "spotting the big ideas that can change how the world deals with a major challenge" and then "going out and systematically making those ideas the new reality" is the "core process" for the profession of social entrepreneurship. "It is creating *group entrepreneurship*—not just working together as individuals," he explains. "It draws upon solo entrepreneurship, but it leverages each individual entrepreneur's work and skills and allows a level of impact otherwise beyond reach."

Thus, Ashoka launched its Innovative Learning Initiative to analyze and market the strategies of 300 fellows demonstrating how society can do a far better job of helping all children and young people grow up and learn successfully. Its Environmental Innovations Initiative is engaged in an analogous process with 200 fellows changing the way society manages the "interface" between humans and the environment. And its Full Economic Citizenship Collaborative is focused on the strategic insights of

400 fellows who are changing legal and economic structures so that all people—peasant farmers, wage laborers, "microentrepreneurs"—have the opportunity to succeed economically. "Every year, the proportion of fellows in the mature stage of their life cycle is increasing," explains Drayton. "And now we have this opportunity to array these ideas that have come up around the world simultaneously and draw out of the matrix what's really exportable.

"Our goal in each initiative is to change the basic pattern in the field," he adds. "The test in each case is: Do we have universally empowering principles that would open major new advances to all practitioners? Do we *see* the jujitsu point [the point of maximum leverage]? If we have, in fact, spotted universally empowering principles, and if we can get 5 percent of the actors in key countries to take up our principles, we can tip the entire field globally."

In his book *Guns, Germs and Steel*, the scientist Jared Diamond notes that knowledge can be transmitted from one society to another by a variety of means, some of which are highly efficient and some of which are not. The least efficient way to transmit knowledge is "idea diffusion"—"when you receive little more than the basic idea and have to reinvent the details," he writes. The most efficient is "blueprint copying"—"when you copy or modify an available detailed blueprint." Ancient civilizations that enjoyed access to language "blueprints" from other cultures developed written language thousands of years faster than those that had to invent them from scratch.[1]

In recent years the power of "blueprint copying" has been demonstrated in the social arena. In India the disability movement dramatically accelerated its progress by copying the American blueprint. In Brazil the consumer protection movement also copied—and improved on—the American blueprint, with great success. During the 1990s micro-credit spread to almost every corner of the globe because its leading practitioners made concerted efforts to distribute the blueprint—the how-tos—not just the concept.[2]

Despite these examples, blueprint copying is far from the norm when it comes to addressing social problems. Millions of people in the citizen sector attend conferences, join list-serves, and subscribe to journals, but much of the "knowledge transmission" in this sector still takes the form of idea diffusion. A greater focus on blueprint copying would likely produce faster social innovation and better adaptation to new problems. Ashoka's special initiatives remain at early stages, but they point the way to a rich area for research and experimentation in the citizen sector. Of course, before blueprint copying is possible, it is necessary to create the blueprints—to identify and document models or processes that can be widely copied or adapted.

The big question is: Can blueprint copying make social innovation more systematic—more reliable or even more *scientific*? In science, of course, an experiment is considered sound only if other scientists, following the protocol, can produce similar results. An experimental outcome is not supposed to hinge on the researcher's culture, charisma, or political contacts. In the social arena, however, success is often attributed to personal qualities and practices are often assumed to be context-sensitive.

But here is where it is useful to make a distinction between leading social entrepreneurs who are driven to spread their ideas everywhere—to *redefine* their fields—and other social entrepreneurs who do not need to spread their ideas to every corner of society. Social entrepreneurs who are obsessed with spreading their ideas are obliged over time to eliminate aspects of their work that depend on their personal involvement or are designed only for particular locations or situations. If an approach is too complicated to teach, too expensive to disseminate, too politically contentious, or too context-sensitive, it must be made simpler, cheaper, less partisan, and more generally applicable. Otherwise it will not change society. It is the entrepreneur's *need* to achieve major impact that leads to the years of experimentation and adjustment that culminate in a blueprint.

The Grameen Bank's micro-credit blueprint grew out of dozens of iterations of its lending program, mostly between 1976 and 1986. If Muhammad Yunus had said to himself, "That's enough," after opening his third, or tenth, or even hundredth branch office, micro-credit may not have evolved into an approach with global visibility and application.

Let us consider a potential application of this idea: the problem of asthma in the United States. More than 15 million Americans suffer from asthma. The number of people affected by the disease has doubled since 1980, and the highest toll is among children in poor urban neighborhoods. In the Bronx, in New York City, asthma death rates are three times higher than the national average and hospitalization rates are almost five times higher.[3] Health experts do not know why the incidence of asthma has increased. However, they do know that asthma is exacerbated by air pollution, cigarette smoke, and allergies to dust mites and cockroaches.

There are many levels to this problem: It is ultimately the government's responsibility to safeguard air quality, mandate housing standards, and ensure that poor children have access to asthma medications. From the perspective of medical professionals and parents, however, the most critical piece of information about asthma is that it can almost always be better controlled at home. With proper management of the disease by parents, children's emergency room visits may be cut by 90 percent.[4] Unfortunately, the disease is not well managed. As Scott Schroeder, a pediatrician and asthma specialist based at Montefiore Medical Center in the Bronx, explained in an article in *The Atlantic Monthly*: "When kids have an asthma attack, their mothers call 911 and get an ambulance, which takes them to the emergency room. The kid is hospitalized and stabilized and given some medicine and released. A few months later the kid is back."[5]

Sound familiar? This is the same problem that Vera Cordeiro encountered at Hospital da Lagoa. Just as in Rio de Janeiro, parents in the Bronx need to learn how to take control of their children's health. In fact, asthma management is ideally suited to Renascer's posthospitalization, follow-up model.[6] In New York City a number of hospitals have initiated programs to provide such follow-up assistance to families. As we have seen, Renascer has been fine-tuning the details of this kind of engagement since 1991. What's more, it has figured out how to spread the model to fourteen hospitals in Brazil. The question is: Does Renascer possess a blueprint that can be adapted in the Bronx? Can hospitals in the Bronx be spared the trouble of reinventing all the details? How do we make the blueprint available?

In 2000, with the support of Avina and The Jenesis Group, Ashoka finally launched a North American program, electing fellows in the United States and, later, in Canada. Since then Ashoka has launched new programs in Turkey and Egypt, as the first phase of an expansion strategy into the Islamic societies of the Middle East, North Africa, and Central Asia. The organization is also preparing to expand into Western Europe and Russia and looking ahead—when political conditions become right—to supporting social entrepreneurs in China.

Ashoka has also initiated a new long-term organizational strategy to improve international planning and coordination. Dubbed the "diamond" strategy, it builds on a theory developed by the management strategist

Michael Porter.[7] The objective is to capitalize on the cross-national and cross-sectoral linkages that are beginning to accrue in parts of the world where the citizen sector has become particularly large, diverse, and sophisticated.

Applying this new strategy and making Ashoka function as a coherent whole with limited resources—in 2002 its global budget was about $15 million—has proven to be a complex management challenge. After Drayton, the job falls to Sushmita Ghosh, Ashoka's new president; Ana-maria Schindler, the head of the organization's operating committee; Derek Brown, who handles major management interventions; Michele Jolin, who is responsible for special initiatives and global collaboration programs; Lucy Perkins, who manages fellow search and support programs; and Carol Grodzins, director of international operations. (Drayton, who has launched two other organizations in recent years—Youth Venture, which supports high school students seeking to create organizations to improve their schools or communities, and Get America Working!, which promotes strategies to "structurally increase the economy's demand for labor"—remains Ashoka's chief executive officer.)

One situation that Ashoka has faced over the years is high turnover, particularly among its younger staff. Ashoka likes to hire strong-minded individuals who are at home in both the social and business sectors. These staff members, inspired by the fellows, often leave the organization after a few years to start their own organizations or businesses or to accept more lucrative opportunities. Additionally, some of Ashoka's staff members have had difficulty fitting into the organization's fast-moving, "intrapreneurial" culture, which demands a high level of self-direction and initiative. And some have experienced frustrations working under Drayton, who is still as stubborn as ever, and who expects every Ashoka staff member to bring to the job the commitment and energy—the deep caring and devotion to a mission—that is characteristic of the fellows and himself.

From a management standpoint, the overarching challenge is to put in place the communication, accountability, and training systems to realize Drayton's vision of Ashoka as an "integrated, decentralized, collegial, intrapreneurial" global structure that can continue to serve fellows and their institutions, expand to new regions, systematize the ideas in the fellowship, maintain high quality, and seize new opportunities—all at relatively low cost.

"Bill is a wonderful architect of ideas and institutions," explains Derek Brown. "He sees patterns and synergies where most of us only see pieces.

and how they can motivate human action. However, to achieve this kind of global integration, one needs very strong cultural processes that create a shared sense of identity and purpose. It's an institutionalization process that is absolutely necessary if Ashoka is to be the organization Bill and the board would like it to be after his leadership ends." To that end, Sushmita Ghosh is working to foster an open culture and management style that encourages Ashoka's staff to emulate the entrepreneurialism of its fellows.

Ghosh is also working to deepen Ashoka's partnerships with leading business entrepreneurs (from whom the organization receives most of its financing). Ashoka has received considerable new funding from the Omidyar Foundation, established by Pierre Omidyar, the founder and chairman of eBay, who believes strongly in the power of individuals to cause change. In addition to financing Ashoka's future growth, Ghosh is looking to pull together leading social entrepreneurs and business entrepreneurs to demonstrate how, together, they can construct hybrid social-business ventures: new business models that build wealth, repair the earth, and address major social problems. "We want to bring the world of social entrepreneurs and the world of business entrepreneurs together at the highest levels," she explains. "I want to position Ashoka as the global leader in this new area—helping to merge the two worlds to achieve the highest possible impact for business and for society."

Conclusion

The Emergence of the Citizen Sector

At its core, Ashoka had advanced a bold but fairly simple idea: social entrepreneurs—creative, tenacious individuals with unshakable motivation—are needed to propel the innovation that is necessary for society to tackle its most serious ills.[1]

By 2003 that idea had become well accepted in the citizen sector. New organizations had sprung up around the world with the specific mandate of financing and nurturing social entrepreneurs. In New York, for example, an organization called Echoing Green, founded in 1991 by an investor named Ed Cohen and modeled after Ashoka, has provided seed capital to 350 young social entrepreneurs, mostly in the United States.[2] In England Michael Young, a well-known social innovator, founded a School for Social Entrepreneurs in 1997 to nurture entrepreneurial talent outside the commercial sector.[3] At Oxford University, the Skoll Center for Social Entrepreneurship was recently established as a partnership between the Said Business School and the Skoll Foundation, founded by Jeffrey Skoll, the former president of eBay. The Skoll Center, which seeks to advance understanding about social entrepreneurship, will serve as an international hub for building and disseminating knowledge about social entrepreneurs' strategies and impact.

In Switzerland Klaus Schwab, founder of the World Economic Forum, and his wife, Hilde Schwab, established the Schwab Foundation for Social Entrepreneurship in 1999 to support "a global community of outstanding social entrepreneurs."

The Schwab Foundation, which is directed by Pamela Hartigan, formerly a senior official at the World Health Organization, provides international recognition, access to resources, and key networking opportunities to forty or fifty social entrepreneurs from around the world each year. In addition to bringing together social entrepreneurs for an annual summit meeting in Geneva, the foundation provides invitations to the World Economic Forum's regional meetings and its annual flagship meeting held in Davos, Switzerland—where social entrepreneurs have opportunities to meet corporate chief executives, senior government officials, foundation executives, and heads of multilateral agencies. At the World Economic Forum in January 2003, for example, Vera Cordeiro had the opportunity to discuss Renascer's work with Brazil's president, Luiz Inácio Lula da Silva, and Jeroo Billimoria spoke of her plan to create Child Helpline International with Unicef's executive director, Carol Bellamy, and Roberto Blois, deputy secretary-general of the International Telecommunication Union.

In recent years, the World Economic Forum has come under fire from social activists who charge that the exclusive gathering serves to advance global business interests but does not sufficiently address social concerns. Its inclusion of social entrepreneurs is an important early step in facilitating the kinds of cross-sectoral exchanges that can lead to improved societal responses to major problems. Indeed, these are the kinds of linkages that allow social entrepreneurs—and society—to move forward in quantum leaps.

As the role of social entrepreneurs has become better understood, so have many of the similarities between the citizen and business sectors. For example, it has become clear that both sectors "market" products and services. Both are *operational* sectors that become wonderfully inventive when the political and cultural environments are supportive.

The distinction that business does its work through a "for-profit" legal format and citizen groups usually do it through a "nonprofit" format obscures the fact that both sectors exist—and are sanctioned and regulated by the state—to create "value" for society. By contrast, the government's primary strength is not its operational ability, but its ability to represent the whole population and foster conditions to promote fairness and productive activity in the other sectors.

Another parallel is that, historically, both the business and citizen sectors emerged as a direct consequence of major social reforms. The independent business sector grew out of changes that took hold in Europe during the seventeenth century as old orders gave way to the pressures of population growth, urbanization, scientific and technological advances, improvements in transportation, accumulated wealth, and new philosophical, religious, and political thought. As major "barriers to entry" declined—crown monopolies, church edicts, feudal lords, guilds—commercial activity became feasible for large segments of the population.[4]

Over the centuries, as society gradually separated into "public" and "private" sectors, entrepreneurs distinguished themselves as key actors.[5] Societies established laws to encourage them (e.g., provisions for limited liability and joint stock ownership) and introduced or expanded services to streamline their efforts (e.g., deposit banking, check writing, institutional credit and insurance).[6] This sector building has continued to the present, with the advent of formal stock exchanges, antitrust legislation, management consulting, securities and exchange commissions, and—relatively recently—business schools, venture capital, and specialized business journalism.

The advent of free and competitive business changed the world in ways that are difficult to comprehend. According to William J. Baumol, a respected research economist and author of the book *The Free-Market Innovation Machine: Analyzing the Growth Miracle of Capitalism*, from the time of ancient Rome until the Industrial Revolution—for a millennium and a half—the growth in productivity and per-capita income in Europe (crudely estimated) was approximately *zero*.[7] By contrast, during the eighteenth century, per-capita incomes in Europe increased by 20 or 30 percent; during the nineteenth century, they rose 200 to 300 percent; and during the twentieth century, the conservative estimate is that per-capita income in free market economies increased 700 or 800 percent.[8] (These are, of course, very general, long-term growth trends that do not reflect income or wealth disparities.)

What changed was that free market competition arrived. "Because of competition, survival in business meant not only continually coming up with better inventions, but putting them to use faster than your competitor," Baumol told me. And this was something very new. In the past, many societies had been inventive, but the inventions had not led to major economic and social changes. Medieval China had invented paper, printing, gunpowder, umbrellas, compasses, and spinning wheels—but China's government prohibited or expropriated innovations, ensuring that they did not reach a wide market.[9]

By contrast, in free market economies, businesses were forced to devote resources to research and development (R&D) and marketing to ensure a steady flow of practical inventions that could be widely sold. This process both benefited from and hastened technological advance.

In the social sector, the dynamic was different. Historically, religious organizations and wealthy patrons were responsible for the delivery of social goods. However, the rapid economic growth of the past two centuries allowed governments to tax private wealth to finance public goods—canals, schools, mental institutions, rural electrification, and the like. With the rise of the welfare state in the twentieth century, the fulfill-ment of social needs came to be seen not only as the government's *respon-sibility*, but one of its primary *operational functions*. Government, however, remained insulated from the pressures and incentives that forced businesses to continually improve their products.

Often governments failed to respond to citizens' needs. Often they responded only after sustained pressure had been brought to bear by orga-nized citizens and muckrakers, particularly when it came to restraining corporate trusts and monopolies and instituting fair labor standards. Where possible, citizens took matters into their own hands by establishing community- and church-based organizations, labor unions, women's rights organizations, specialized service groups such as the Salvation Army and Alcoholics Anonymous, and so forth. However, the social entrepre-neurs of the past frequently encountered daunting economic, social, and political constraints, and they were denied the rewards, recognition, and assistance that their business counterparts enjoyed. They were often perse-cuted for their efforts.

But things have changed for the social entrepreneurs. The spread of democracy and the emergence of a vigorous citizen sector over the past thirty years has opened up extraordinary opportunities for them, and for all of society. In fact, the citizen sector is going through changes that are comparable to those that occurred in the business sector over the past three centuries.

To begin with, like business in the seventeenth and eighteenth centuries, in most countries the citizen sector has gone from being a tightly restricted sector to one that enjoys more or less open entry. Major barriers—govern-ment obstruction, lack of access to capital and education, communication costs—have dropped.[10] Consequently, millions of people have rushed into this sector, bringing new energy and ideas; among them are the social entrepreneurs in this book.

As with the private sector, the sector-building process has necessitated the establishment of new laws (e.g., provisions for tax exemption, simpli-fied registration processes, removal of legal impediments).[11] Additionally, an array of institutional supports has emerged, including specialized nonprofit consulting firms, more responsive "social financial services," and early efforts to improve performance evaluation.[12]

As with business, hundreds of universities have established courses to study the citizen sector. Nonprofit management studies, a field that didn't exist twenty years ago, has grown into a small industry.[13] Governments and international organizations, including the United Nations and the World Bank, routinely enlist the advice of citizen groups.[14] Businesses increasingly form marketing partnerships with them. In the years ahead, newspapers may introduce new sections to cover the citizen sector just as they introduced stand-alone business sections in recent decades. (The *New York Times* began running its "Business Day" section in 1978.[15])

Above all, in many societies, working in this sector has become socially acceptable, even status-worthy. Graduates from top universities in Brazil, India, Poland, South Africa, and the United States today consider pursuing careers in the citizen sector. Many think of launching their own social-purpose organizations.[16]

"When there is a critical mass of institutions, people, and ideas, they begin to feed on one another and strengthen one another," notes Drayton, who brought to my attention many of the similarities between the two sectors. "So there begins to be a culture that says, 'This is great. We're proud to be doing this. We're no longer apologetic. We admire people who do this well. We reward them.' And it's not just the actors, it's the society around them. People want to invest. They want to write about it. They do art about it. It's exactly what we're seeing at the moment in the citizen sector. The whole society is beginning to get into it.

"And twenty years from now the citizen sector will not be fully mature, but it will be almost unrecognizably more mature," he adds. "Many of the institutions that took business three hundred years to develop will be well on the way to development because of analogy, because of a much wider base of educated people and because of a faster rate of change today."

These changes represent a dramatic shift in the way the "noncommercial" or "social" business of society is structured. Around the world, this work has been dominated by centralized decision making and top-down, usually governmental, institutions. It has been managed a little like a planned economy. This makes sense from the perspective that governments are responsible for translating the will of the citizenry into public policy and public goods. But governments are often not the ideal vehicles to carry out the social R&D, just as they are not the ideal vehicles to create new businesses. As in business, advancing new ideas and creating new models to attack problems require an entrepreneur's single-minded vision and fierce determination, and lots of energy and time. It is the kind of work that flourishes to the extent that society successfully harnesses and nurtures the wide-ranging talents of millions of citizens.

The citizen sector is, in fact, beginning to resemble a *market* economy of social ideas, characterized by a rich diversity of grassroots institutions and energetic entrepreneurs crafting solutions that no one could have anticipated, let alone planned for. No government could have built or legislated Childline or the Grameen Bank; on the other hand, Childline and the Grameen Bank could not have achieved national and global impact without the financing and the legitimacy they received from governments. Powerful social initiatives emanating from the citizenry not only lead to faster adaptation, they encourage decentralized thinking and action, which strengthens democracy.

One of the essential differences between a planned and a market economy is the role of competition. In the past, citizen sector organizations have been insulated from the forces of head-to-head competition. However, as the sector continues to attract talent, competition is likely to intensify—particularly as social entrepreneurs seek to "capture" the benefits of their innovations and as funders, journalists, and citizens come to demand better performance. (More competition is also likely to produce more collaboration both within and across sectors as citizen organizations look for opportunities to improve "products," increase impact, and gain efficiency by working with one another and with business and government.) As the romance of charity yields to a healthy realism that citizen organizations should rise and fall on their merits, the result is likely to accelerate innovation. In a competitive landscape—when rewards follow the best performers—it takes only *one* innovative organization to send everyone else scrambling to upgrade their products and services lest they be left behind.

That is precisely what happened in the field of micro-credit. Fifteen years ago the micro-credit industry was made up of a handful of organizations. Today there are more than 2,500 micro-lenders and 41.6 million borrowers, and micro-credit has its own financing mechanisms, consultants, and subspecialties.[17] Just as in business, these changes came about through the aggressive marketing of a few industry leaders, principally the Grameen Bank and Accion International, which demonstrated a better way to alleviate poverty and, thus, created competitive pressures (especially among funders) that led to a rush of new entrants. (The Grameen Bank, once the dominant player, now serves less than 10 percent of the world's micro-credit clients.)

The result: In Bangladesh alone more than 500 micro-credit organizations jostle for resources and recognition.[18] Bangladeshi villagers whose only option a few years ago was to borrow from a moneylender at 20 percent interest per *month* can, in many areas, pick and choose from among three or four institutional lenders each offering competitive terms. In this environment the Grameen Bank must remain continually responsive to its clients. (Recall the bank's recent launch of Grameen Bank II.) The bank has too many competitors who have studied its systems and, in some cases, introduced better loan products.

Micro-credit lends itself to numeric assessments. In general, however, the social arena does not enjoy the easy market signals that business does. Unlike businesses, unproductive citizen organizations don't get forced into bankruptcy. If they can continue to raise funds, they can plod along ineffectually for decades.

Because it is inherently difficult to measure social value creation, funders and practitioners in the citizen sector historically have shied away from any attempt to compare the performance of organizations. As a result, notes Greg Dees, a professor of social entrepreneurship at Duke University's Fuqua School of Business, the citizen sector today suffers from a serious "capital allocation" problem. "Capital is not being allocated to the most promising enterprises so they can grow and is not being taken away from enterprises that are ineffective," he asserts. Jed Emerson, a leading researcher in the nonprofit field who teaches at Stanford University's Graduate School of Business, adds: "An organization that is not creating true social value can build itself by virtue of political connections and media coverage, with no objective measure of whether or not it is actually doing its work well."

One consequence of this problem is that the citizen sector does not experience the organizational turnover that keeps the business sector sharp. For example, of the twenty largest service-providing nonprofit organizations in the United States (excluding governmental and religious groups), twelve were established prior to 1920 and seventeen were established prior to 1960. None was established after 1980. By contrast, more than half of the thirty companies included in the Dow Jones Industrial Average in 2002 were added to the index after 1980 (displacing other companies), and more than a third were added after 1990.[19]

* * *

In the short run, the best way to improve performance in the citizen sector is to improve the "capital allocation." This is easier said than done. In the United States most funders, particularly individual donors (who are responsible for three-quarters of philanthropic giving) pay little attention to the comparative performance of citizen organizations. In part, this is because people's charitable contributions are influenced by impressions, personal relationships, and status considerations. But it is also because this sector has no simple and reliable mechanisms to compare performance.[20]

Foundations (which account for 12 percent of giving) have tended to be more discriminating. In recent years many have begun paying more attention to social entrepreneurs, creating collaborative partnerships that include long-term financing, assistance with management and strategic planning, and performance benchmarking.[21] This is an important trend.

Social entrepreneurs face their biggest financial struggles not when they are launching their ideas, but when they are scaling them up significantly. Very few funders are willing to make extremely large bets—of the order of tens of millions of dollars—on organizations that have reached a stage comparable to a business that is ready to "go public."

It's worth noting how micro-credit became one of the rare examples of a global social change. Micro-credit had all the necessary ingredients: a social entrepreneur, a powerful idea, large amounts of capital, and great marketing. During the 1980s and early 1990s, Muhammad Yunus skillfully mobilized more than $125 million in grants, loans, and loan guarantees from a consortium of governments, foundations, and international organizations, and established more than 1,000 Grameen Bank branches, capturing the imagination of the world. (The bank has not taken donor funds since 1995 and now finances its lending through depositors' savings.) If Yunus had not been able to raise so much investment, Grameen wouldn't have been able to expand so quickly, and the potential of micro-credit might still be unseen today.

In 2001 individuals, corporations, and foundations in the United States gave away $212 billion. About $81 billion went to religious groups. Foundations contributed just under $26 billion. These are not terribly large sums when considered in the context of a $10 trillion economy.[22] Given the enormity of the social problems that citizen organizations seek to address, and the vastly greater resources in the control of governments and businesses, it is worth exploring ways in which society can apply its limited philanthropic resources more catalytically to promote broad system changes at the national and global levels. One key question is: How can we help our most innovative citizen organizations "go public" the way our most innovative businesses do?

In some cases, the government can play the equivalent of the business sector's initial public offering (IPO) role—providing major financing to "roll out" the best ideas or models. But other social funders should also ask themselves how they can better work together: How can they pool their resources and expertise to channel substantial amounts of capital— IPO-level amounts—to organizations with high-impact strategies run by top-notch entrepreneurs who have demonstrated both the capacity and the determination to effect system-level change?

If there is one factor that, above all others, perpetuates the "capital allocation" problem, it is the belief that organizations can be compared reliably only if their performance can be measured and quantified. Indeed, much of today's discussion about performance evaluation revolves around the question of how to develop "metrics" that can translate social value into numbers.

Metrics can be very useful, particularly when they are developed by organizations to help manage their own work and gauge their own performance. Organizations that create performance metrics for themselves are more likely to use them than those that collect the information for funders or the government. Renascer, for example, has instituted a data-collection system to assess the "health self-sufficiency" of its families. The system is used to determine when a family can be discharged safely. College Summit keeps close track of enrollment and retention rates in order to gauge its own effectiveness. One of the ways that the Grameen Bank evaluates its banking performance is by tracking the proportion of borrowers who have acquired such things as a tin roof, beds, crockery, and a vegetable garden. And one of the ways Ashoka measures the quality of its selection process is by determining the percentage of fellows whose work, after five or ten years, has had an impact on national policy, been replicated by other groups, or shifted practices in their fields.[23]

It is not difficult to rank college access programs by enrollment rate. However, it is difficult to determine whether a college access program should receive priority over, say, a kindergarten enrichment program. An even tougher challenge is using metrics to illustrate an organization's influence on people's attitudes or expectations. How does one measure Tateni's impact on health professionals in South Africa? And, finally, how can metrics be used to lend confidence to *predictions* about the impact that an organization will have in the decades to come (which is essentially what Ashoka tries to do by examining its fellows' life histories)?

Metrics clearly have a role to play in performance assessment, but citizen groups and funders should remain cautious when embracing numerical assessments. The quest for quantifiable social returns or outcomes has become an obsession in a sector that envies the efficiency of business capital markets. Given this obsession, it is important to remember that numbers have an unfortunate tendency to supersede other kinds of knowing. The human mind is a miracle of subtlety: It can assimilate thousands of pieces of soft information—impressions, experiences, intuition—and produce wonderfully nuanced decisions. Numbers are problematic to the extent that they give the illusion of providing more truth than they actually do. They also favor what is easiest to measure, not what is most important. They can easily be used to dress up failure as success—as when a company boosts its short-term profits by slashing its R&D budget.

In the field of micro-credit, for example, where organizations have long sought to balance financial and social considerations, in recent years a number of lenders have moved away from serving very poor clients because it is more cost-effective to serve people who are less poor. No matter how much lip service is paid to the social concerns, managers in these organizations tend to pay more attention to the hard numbers, just as college admission officers pay more attention to SAT scores than the subjective information contained in student admission files.

More than creating better metrics, what seems to be called for in the citizen sector is a greater willingness and commitment to apply judgment. Rather than turning to business for guidance, here the citizen sector may find it more useful to turn to the law. Every day citizens weigh competing arguments and make life-and-death decisions that don't employ quantitative data: when they serve on juries in criminal trials. The jury system is an excellent example of a structured process that uses decision rules and analytic tools—conceptual tests such as "reasonable doubt"—and relies, ultimately, on the application of courageous judgment. The political philosopher William A. Galston has noted that when individuals with different views are "confronted with a plurality of specific interests," when issues are "qualitative, not quantitative" and it is necessary to make determinations about which considerations should be regarded as more important, or more urgent, it is possible for groups to achieve balanced decisions and "deliberative closure." "There can be right answers, widely recognized as such, even in the absence of general rules for ordering or aggregating diverse goods," he writes.[24]

For governments and institutional funders, one way to improve the capital allocation in the citizen sector would be to design decision-making processes that give people the information, incentives, analytic tools, confidence, and encouragement to apply their judgment more effectively and comfortably. In the case of individual donors, the challenge is to make information available in a simple format to facilitate thoughtful decision making. One idea is to encourage the development of citizen sector research analysts whose responsibility would be to survey organizations within different fields and publish opinions about who is doing good work and who is not.

Is this a heretical thought? Some readers will strongly oppose such a development. Making public judgments about performance in the citizen sector comes across as mean-spirited. People rarely criticize citizen organizations unless the organizations' executives are suspected of being corrupt or of betraying their public mission. Who wants to criticize people who are trying to make a difference and who are not getting rich from their efforts?

Every field has its arbiters of quality: Society enlists people to analyze and judge movies, books, restaurants, architecture, gymnasts, most valuable players, the relative merits of scientific research, the credit-worthiness of companies, and so on. Should the work of addressing urgent social needs and solving problems be treated *less* seriously than every other kind of work? Why shouldn't society also have professionals whose job is to "review" the performance of citizen organizations? They need not be simple bean counters; they could take into account many subjective factors: the quality of an organization's strategy, the degree of difficulty and depth of need for its work, the evidence of impact (quantifiable or not), the hurdles that the organization has overcome, the organization's growth potential, the energy and talent of its staff, its importance within a community, and so on.

As in other fields, citizen sector analysts (or reviewers) would rise or fall on the quality of their judgments or predictions; they would be checked by reviewers with opposing viewpoints; and they would be financed by the people and organizations that will benefit from a more efficient sector, initially public and private foundations and citizen organizations, and, down the road, individual citizens (who will be able to purchase research reports to guide their giving just as they purchase investment advice today).

If the citizen sector is to fulfill its promise in the years ahead, it will have to develop better feedback mechanisms. Funders and ordinary citizens will have to decide what work should be augmented, what work should be maintained, and what work should be discontinued. Making these decisions will feel downright *un*charitable. But a failure to do so amounts to a guarantee that society will continue to underfund its most promising ideas and its most dedicated social entrepreneurs.

Supporting Social Entrepreneurship as a Career

When I began researching this book, I had never given much thought to the "citizen sector." I had a strong sense that social entrepreneurs were important, but I had not yet come to think of social entrepreneurship as a vocation or profession that society could support systematically. To be sure, some social entrepreneurs seem hard-wired. But countless other people, perhaps less single-minded and obsessive in their focus, share the desire and possess the talent to build and support citizen organizations at all levels. "In Ashoka, we focus on the pattern-changing entrepreneurs," says Drayton. "But for every social change you need thousands of grass-roots entrepreneurs, competing, working together. It's not just the leading entrepreneurs that make it happen; it's all the other actors."

Millions of people think about starting businesses, not just to make money, but to experience the excitement of seeing their ideas take shape in the world and have the satisfaction of working for themselves. This option exists today in the citizen sector as well. Given the right financial and social incentives, more people would probably look forward to starting their own social-change vehicles, or helping others. In years to come, social entrepreneurship might become one of the career options that gets discussed at the dinner table.

Would many more people be drawn to this line of work if the path were better known? Would college graduates with huge debt loads or midcareer professionals seeking to make life changes consider this option more seriously if it were better respected and financially less of a risk? As with many career decisions, there is a threshold at which the satisfaction of pursuing an internally meaningful course of action outweighs financial or status considerations. And, as with all important questions in life, many groups—peers, teachers, parents, career counselors, mentors and the media—influence our decisions. "As an input, entrepreneurship, like any other input, can be reallocated from one task to another by a change in the relative profit prospects offered by the available alternative uses to which entrepreneurship can be put," notes economist William Baumol.[25] Of course, "profit prospects" can be construed more broadly than financial gain; they also can incorporate personal satisfaction, recognition, and the opportunity to have an impact.

Funders seeking to promote the social entrepreneurship option could establish links with high schools, colleges, grassroots groups, and journalists to develop "scouting" systems to identify and nurture potential social entrepreneurs, just as society nurtures promising athletes and musicians. They could increase the resources available to social entrepreneurs at early stages and publicize the fact, perhaps through competitions for innovative social-change "inventions" (like the Intel and Westinghouse math, science, and technology competitions).

Similarly, by incorporating examples of social entrepreneurs in school lessons and readings, students could be taught to think about how change occurs and why new ideas encounter political and cultural resistance. Students who have the inclination could be encouraged to start organizations to improve their schools or neighborhoods or to do internships with community-based groups, perhaps for class credit.

At the college and university levels, there are limitless possibilities for incorporating examples or case studies of social entrepreneurs in course work. Beyond focusing on nonprofit management techniques, the case studies could be useful for undergraduate or graduate courses in medicine, law, engineering, psychology, agriculture, social work, history, political science, economics, and so forth. Doctors and nurses could learn about people like Vera Cordeiro, James Grant, and Veronica Khosa, who have addressed health problems in creative ways; engineers or agronomists could learn from the experiences of entrepreneurs like Fábio Rosa; psychologists, psychiatrists, and social workers could study the work of innovators like Erzsébet Szekeres and Jeroo Billimoria; while public policy students could analyze the methods of social entrepreneurs who, like Javed Abidi and Bill Drayton, have been successful in the policy arena. There are enough practical solutions that haven't been documented to keep curriculum developers busy for years.

Social entrepreneurs also might be welcomed into the academy as "action researchers." Universities could link with citizen organizations (using their communities as research laboratories) just as medical schools link with teaching hospitals. Childline maintains a close working relationship with the Tata Institute of Social Sciences in Bombay and is an excellent training program for social workers.

Citizen organizations also can do more to woo college graduates by participating in job fairs and recruitment programs alongside management-consulting firms and investment banks. Teach for America, which aggressively recruits outstanding college graduates to teach for two years in low-income schools, saw its candidate pool jump from 5,000 to 14,000 applicants (for about 1,750 teaching spots) from 2001 to 2002. Seven percent of Yale University's graduating class applied for the organization's 2002 corps.[26]

The government's primary responsibility vis-à-vis the citizen sector is to safeguard the public trust that lends it legitimacy. It is the job of government to ensure that citizen organizations do not betray their public missions. However, the government also can play an affirmative role in the emergence of this sector, just as it stimulates business creation and home ownership. Governments can provide incentives for citizens who seek to establish organizations or businesses to address problems. Government agencies also should be looking systematically for ideas within the citizen sector to inform public policy, as well as for opportunities to finance successful models and form partnerships with entrepreneurial citizen organizations. College Summit is a good example of an organization that is helping public schools produce more college-bound students, thereby assisting the government in the fulfillment of its responsibilities.

Finally, the media can contribute to the development of this profession by covering it. Journalists specialize in sports, fashion, food and technology. It would make sense to have journalists who cover only the citizen sector—journalists who know when to draw attention to a promising social innovation and when to expose an organization that is making false claims or simply underperforming the market. Currently citizen organizations can count on news coverage only during the holiday season or when scandals erupt. But citizens would benefit year-round from faithful accounts of what is going on in this sector. It's not a matter of newspapers or television news shows doing more feel-good feature stories. It's a matter of the field of journalism recognizing that, across the world, many of the most creative, important, and exciting changes are emerging from this sector, yet they are going unnoticed. The changes affect everybody in society, whether in business, academia, or government, and they carry a strong personal relevance for the growing number of people who are seriously considering getting in on the action—who are searching for ideas, role models, and opportunities to participate in this sector as entrepreneurs, employees, volunteers, and investors.

When Ashoka's board member Julien Phillips graduated from Stanford University's Graduate School of Business in 1970, the idea of becoming a social entrepreneur wasn't on his radar screen. "It didn't occur to me that working in a nonprofit or starting one was even an option," he recalled. "It was either government or business.

"As I got deeper into Ashoka, my whole outlook about career options and what's important in the world changed. Furthermore, I developed such admiration for what Bill was doing and for a number of our Ashoka fellows that about ten years ago I decided that I'd made as much money as I needed to make in McKinsey and I said: 'I think *I'll* become a social entrepreneur.'"

Phillips left McKinsey and created Partners in School Innovation to help public schools in low-income communities adopt new ways of working that would enable their students to learn at higher levels.

For Phillips, becoming a social entrepreneur was an attractive second career—promising more satisfaction and challenge than the traditional version of retirement. In his book *Prime Time*, Marc Freedman observes that only one in five Americans over fifty-five is currently on the job.[27] He notes that older Americans are wealthier, healthier, and living longer, and there is ample evidence that they "hunger" for opportunities to contribute their experience and time in meaningful ways.

None of the social entrepreneurs I interviewed for this book expressed the desire to retire—ever, although a number complained about the financial pressures in their personal lives and on their families. Statements I heard repeatedly were: "I love this work." "I couldn't live without it." "I will die doing this." When I began researching this book, I assumed that the social entrepreneurs would be motivated by altruism. But social entrepreneurs are not selfless. If anything, they are self-*more* in the sense that they heed their instincts, follow their desires, and aggressively pursue their ambitions.

And the rewards are ample. Nalini Nayak made this clear to me. Nayak is a woman full of merriment who has spent decades collaborating in building a movement to protect the rights of artisanal fishworkers whose livelihoods have been threatened by mechanized fishing. Nayak, who lives in Kerala, India, has helped to incorporate women's rights and environmental perspectives into that movement. She has also established branches of the Self-Employed Women's Association (SEWA) that provide employment and other services to thousands of impoverished women.

Nayak grew up in a middle-class family and later spent years in poor fishing villages, where she learned to live without electricity and running water. When I interviewed her, I made the mistake of asking if she felt she had sacrificed much to do this work. She burst into laughter. *"Sacrificed?"* she exclaimed. "No, no, no, not at all! I have no such feeling. I have *enjoyed* my life. It's really, really full. *No, no, no,* not at all. This idea of sacrifice is not there at all. I have learned and gained *so much* in this process, I have not lost anything. Sacrifice is when you give up something, you lose something. I've gained *too* much."

Later in our conversation it came out that, a few years before, Nayak had undergone surgery for breast cancer, followed by six months of chemotherapy. "In those six months, there wasn't a day that I was alone," she offered, speaking candidly, not immodestly, but not denying herself the full pleasure of the memory. "My brother thought he must take me to a specialized chemotherapy center in Bombay, but when he came he saw all these people in a very lively, happy house. People came from in and around Trivandrum, from Bangalore and Madras. They came for as long as ten days, giving me massages, just being with me. I never asked them. I was treated like a queen. My home was like a festival for six months. I've never had an experience like this before.

"And I told SEWA that I didn't want to see a *single* SEWA woman. I knew eight hundred women would turn up. I said, 'Please, for heaven's sake. Don't do that. It would be too much. They're poor women.' The day of the surgery, these women—there must have been a few hundred—got together in the local church—the majority are Hindu women [Nayak is a Christian]—and they all took leave and prayed the whole day while I was undergoing surgery."

As value-seeking individuals, we all construct our own visions of the "good life." We are influenced by belief systems, by parents and peers, and by powerful images that bombard us daily—images of wealth, power, fame and beauty. What fascinates me most about the social entrepreneurs, at a personal level, is the way they hold to an internal vision no matter how many disruptive forces surround them. Somehow they find ways to construct meanings for themselves and hold to those meanings. On a daily basis, they manage to align their interests, abilities and beliefs, while acting to produce changes that are deeply meaningful.

In 1990, when I began doing research on the Grameen Bank for my first book, there were a few dozen micro-credit programs in the world reaching less than 2 million clients. Today, as mentioned, there are more than 2,500 reaching more than 41.6 million. Looking ahead to the next ten or fifteen years, I envision the same kind of growth in the field of social entrepreneurship—an explosion of activity. For those who seek to apply their talents to reshape a part of the world, the opportunities are endless—and they are just beginning to be seen.

Epilogue

Things which matter most must never be at the mercy of things which matter least.

—Goethe

I was halfway through this book when, on a magnificent morning in September 2001, while heading to my office, I turned south at the corner of 27th Street and Sixth Avenue, in New York and saw plumes of smoke pouring from the World Trade Center towers. In the immediate aftermath of September 11, I found myself unable to work on this book. Its optimistic tone seemed hopelessly naive.

But about six weeks later, in October, I attended a group discussion in New York that focused on the question: "Where does hope come from?" Everyone in the room had spent time walking around the city gazing at the flyers that had appeared on walls, bus stops, and phone booths days after September 11. The flyers provided physical descriptions and photographs of missing people whom friends and family hoped had not been killed in the Twin Towers. At the time, the news was dominated by Al Qaeda, anthrax, and fundamentalist mobs seething with hatred for America.

Many people in the room were angry; others spoke despairingly about the future. As I listened to the discussion, I began thinking about the images that came up most frequently: terrorists, fundamentalists, irrational mobs, backward societies. I had the same images in my mind, but they were balanced by images of people in places like Indonesia, Bangladesh, and India who were working competently, and powerfully, to bring positive change. One morning, I saw a newspaper photo of a mob in Dhaka, Bangladesh, chanting "Death to America," and I immediately thought about the 20,000 organizations that had sprung up there in the past two decades to fight poverty, improve education, and advance women's rights.

Even in authoritarian societies, the citizen sector, although still marginal and highly restricted, was gathering strength. When I reflected on this trend, it occurred to me that, despite the immediate threat, perhaps it was the fundamentalists who were on the defensive, while the progressive citizen forces and the social entrepreneurs had history on their side. Without a doubt, the past twenty years had produced far more social entrepreneurs than terrorists.

One thing was clear: The forces of violence got a lot more attention.

In this respect, little has changed in the two years since September 11. By now Americans have grown accustomed to images of wars and terrorism; many have become inured to orange-level domestic terrorism alerts. These are extraordinary times, to be sure. But even during less remarkable times, the remarkable story of the emerging citizen sector goes untold. Perhaps it is too scattered to put on a TV screen. When I turn on the news, however, the absence of this story makes the image of the world that I receive seem like a poorly doctored photograph—like a digital image of a landscape in which half of the trees—the most beautiful ones—have been edited out. And it makes me wonder: If people got to see the rest of the trees, if they were told about the potent seeds of change that are taking root around the world, would they feel more encouraged? Would they be more politically engaged? Would they think differently about their career choices? Would they be less fearful? Would they imagine a brighter future for their children?

"There is an exciting world behind this terrible world we see," Vera Cordeiro told me. "People all over the world need to see it—like they need water to drink and air to breathe."

As a journalism student, I was taught that news could be defined as "destabilizing information." If so, the social entrepreneurs are newsworthy. They are destabilizing forces: Wherever they crop up, they pose serious threats to the status quo. And they are particularly important in the post–September 11 world. If there is a perfect antithesis to the terrorist's impulse, it is the social entrepreneur's. Social entrepreneurs demonstrate the power of building things instead of destroying them. And they are addressing many of the underlying causes of today's global instability: lack of education, lack of women's rights, the destruction of the environment, poverty.

Epilogue

If I learned one thing from writing this book, it is that people who solve problems must somehow first arrive at the belief that they *can* solve problems. This belief does not emerge suddenly. The capacity to cause change grows in an individual over time as small-scale efforts lead gradually to larger ones. But the process needs a beginning—a story, an example, an early taste of success—something along the way that helps a person form the belief that it is possible to make the world a better place. Those who act on that belief spread it to others. They are highly contagious. Their stories must be told.

Notes

Chapter 1. Restless People

1. For example, a Lexis-Nexis search for the term "social entrepreneur" produced six stories in 1991 and 433 in 2001.
2. Peter F. Drucker, *Innovation and Entrepreneurship* (New York: Harper Business, 1993), 21.
3. See Joseph A. Schumpeter, *Capitalism, Socialism and Democracy* (New York: HarperCollins, 1984).
4. George Gendron, "Flashes of Genius," Interview with Peter Drucker in *Inc. Magazine*, May 15, 1996.
5. The Franciscan order attracted 5,000 members between 1209 and 1220 and was the fastest-growing religious order of its day. St. Francis also founded an order for women that became known as the Poor Clares, and a lay fraternity, the Third Order of Brothers and Sisters of Penance.
6. Sources for the growth of citizen groups: Indonesia: Walhi: Indonesian Forum for the Environment; India: Helmut K. Anheier and Lester M. Salamon, eds., *The Non-Profit Sector in the Developing World* (Manchester: Manchester University Press, 1998), 39; Bangladesh: Memorandum for Bangladesh Development Forum 2002–2003, Govt. of Bangladesh (March 13–15, 2002), 32; Slovakia: Civicus (www.civicus.org); Central Europe: Curtis Runyan, "Action on the Front Lines," *World Watch* (November/December 1999): 14; France: Civicus; Canada: Michael Hall and Keith G. Banting, "The Nonprofit Sector in Canada: An Introduction," in Keith G. Banting, ed., *The Nonprofit Sector in Canada* (Kingston, Ontario and Montreal, Quebec: McGill-Queen's University Press, 1999), 1–28. The 50-percent figure is based on a 3-percent annual growth rate since 1987; Brazil: Civicus.
7. "Number of Tax-Exempt Organizations Registered with the IRS, 1989–1998," Urban Institute, National Center for Charitable Statistics, 1998; www.nccs.urban.org.
8. The figure of 1 million organizations in Brazil is reported by Ashoka Brazil; The figure of 2 million organizations in the United States is reported in Runyan, "Action on the Front Lines," 14.

9. Runyan, "Action on the Front Lines," 14. See also Independent Sector, *Nonprofit Almanac: Dimensions of the Independent Sector 1996–1997* (San Francisco: Jossey-Bass Publishers, 1996), 15.

10. *Yearbook of International Organizations,* as cited in *The Economist,* December 11, 1999, 21.

11. John E. Seley and Julian Wolpert, *New York City's Nonprofit Sector* (New York: The New York City Nonprofits Project, May 2002), 31; www. nycnonprofits.org.

12. Lester M. Salamon and Helmut K. Anheier, *The Emerging Sector Revisited* (Baltimore: Johns Hopkins University Institute for Policy Studies Center for Civil Society Studies, 1999).

13. See James Allen Smith and Karsten Borgmann, "Foundations in Europe: The Historical Context," in Andreas Schlüter, Volker Then, and Peter Walkenhorst, eds., *Foundations in Europe: Society, Management and Law* (Gutersloh, Germany: Bertelsmann Stiftung, 2001), 2–34.

14. See, for example, the *UN Global Compact,* www.unglobalcompact.org; the *Compact on Relations Between Government and the Voluntary and Community Sector in England,* www.homeoffice.gov.uk; and the *Campus Compact,* www.compact.org; see also Shirley Sagawa and Eli Segal, *Common Good: Creating Value through Business and Social Sector Partnerships* (Boston: Harvard Business School Press, 2000).

15. See, for example, Reed Abelson, "New Philanthropists Put Donations to Work," *New York Times,* July 6, 2000; Peter Y. Hong, "Foundations Must Change to Meet Future Needs," *Los Angeles Times,* April 26, 1998; Kristi Essick, "Venture Philanthropy Brings 'Social Returns,'" *Wall Street Journal,* December 28, 2001; Michael Lewis, "Heartless Donors," *New York Times Magazine,* December 14, 1997; Karl Taro Greenfield, "A New Way of Giving," *Time,* July 24, 2000; Mario Morino, "Strategic Investments for Social Progress," *Changemakers.net* (April 2001); Nicole Etchart and Lee Davis, "Prophets for Non-profits?" *Alliance,* 7, No. 2 (June 2002), available at www.nesst.org; J. Gregory Dees, "The Meaning of Social Entrepreneurship," October 31, 1998, available from www.gsb. stanford.edu. The Independent Sector highlights several performance measurement approaches, including those used by the W. K. Kellogg Foundation, Big Brothers Big Sisters of America, Pew Charitable Trusts, and United Way; www.independentsector.org.

16. See William J. Baumol, *The Free-Market Innovation Machine* (Princeton, NJ: Princeton University Press, 2002).

17. Interview with William J. Baumol.

18. Lester M. Salamon, "The Rise of the Nonprofit Sector," *Foreign Affairs* (July/August 1994): 118.

19. See J. Gregory Dees, "Enterprising Nonprofits," *Harvard Business Review* (January-February 1998): 5–15.

20. See Gary Wills, "A Readers Guide to the Century," *New York Review of Books,* July 15, 1999, 24–28.

21. Salamon, "The Rise of the Nonprofit Sector," 117.

22. Wills, "A Readers Guide to the Century," 26.

23. Ibid.

24. See, for example, the field breakdown of social entrepreneurs in the Ashoka Fellowship (www.ashoka.org), which includes: access to learning,

adult education, agriculture, AIDS/HIV education, treatment and prevention, appropriate technology, biodiversity protection, civic participation,
communications/media, community involvement in learning, conflict resolution, consumer protection, consumerism, cooperatives, crime prevention, cultural preservation, curriculum development, dental health, development of teaching aids, disabilities, early childhood development,
economics, education, employment, environment, equality and rights,
experiential learning, fisheries, forestry, gender equity, healthcare delivery
system, higher education, housing, hunger, income generation, information technology, land management, land reform, law and legal reform, literacy, mental health, micro-enterprise, natural resource conservation, non-
formal education, nutrition, philanthropy, pollution, population, prison
reform, protection of wild animals, public policy, race relations, reproduc-
tive health, safety regulations, sanitation, solid waste and garbage, sub-
stance abuse, teacher training, transportation, violence and abuse, volun-
teerism, water management.

25. Thomas Princen and Matthias Finger, *Environmental NGOs in World
Politics*, as quoted in Curtis Runyan, "Action on the Front Lines," *World
Watch* (November/December 1999): 13.

26. Paul Hawken, Amory Lovins, and L. Hunter Lovins, *Natural Capitalism*
(Boston: Little, Brown and Company, 1999), 4.

27. See *Global Trends 2015: A Dialogue About the Future With Nongovern-
ment Experts*, a report prepared under the direction of the National
Intelligence Council for the Central Intelligence Agency, December 2000;
www.cia.gov.

28. See "The Widening Gap in Global Opportunities," in the United Nations
Development Programme (UNDP) *Human Development Report 1992*
(New York: Oxford University Press, 1992), 34–47;
http://hdr.undp.org/reports/global/1992/en. See also "Deepening Democracy in a Fragmented World," in the UNDP *Human Development Report
2002* (New York: Oxford University Press, 2002), 1–11;
http://hdr.undp.org/reports/global/2002/en. While the world's annual economic output exceeds $5,000 per person, 2.8 billion people continue to
subsist on less than $2 a day

29. Noreena Hertz, *The Silent Takeover* (New York: Free Press, 2001), 9–10.

30. Ibid., 33.

31. Ibid. See also Stephen Labaton with Jonathan D. Glater, "Staff of S.E.C.
Is Said to Dilute Rule Changes," *New York Times*, January 22, 2003, and
"Downsized Corporate Reforms," *New York Times*, Editorial, January
23, 2003.

32. Hertz, *The Silent Takeover*, 104–05.

33. Jessica T. Mathews, "Power Shift," *Foreign Affairs* (January/February
1997): 63.

Chapter 2. From Little Acorns Do Great Trees Grow

1. See www.ashoka.org; see also David Bornstein, "Changing the World on
a Shoestring," *The Atlantic Monthly* (January 1998): 34–39.

2. David Bornstein, *The Price of a Dream: The Story of the Grameen Bank*
(Chicago: University of Chicago Press, 1997).

3. See www.grameen-info.org
4. These estimates are taken from micro-credit programs that reported results to the Microcredit Summit Campaign for that year. The campaign has more than 3,500 members. See the State of the Microcredit Summit Campaign Report 2002; www.microcreditsummit.org.
5. Stephen Hadley was appointed deputy head of the National Security Council in George W. Bush's administration.
6. "Study of Local Themes Helps Schools in India Drop British Accent," *Christian Science Monitor*, May 6, 1988; "Learning the Natural Way," *The Indian Post*, September 4, 1988; "Gloria de Souza: Revolutionising Primary Education in India," *Dhaka Courier*, September 18, 1992.

Chapter 3. The Light in My Head Went On

1. William Drayton, *Profiles of the Ashoka Fellows, Ninth Fellowship Elections* (Arlington, Virginia: Ashoka, 1990), 36–39.
2. Fábio Rosa, "Utilizing the Market for Environmental Changes," *Changemakers Journal* (March 2001), www.changemakers.net.
3. Fábio Rosa and José Fernando Gomes, *Proluz I—Avaliação De Resultados* ("Proluz I—Evaluation of Results"), (Porto Alegre: Development Bank of Rio Grande do Sul, Government of Rio Grande do Sul, 1994).
4. Fernando Selles Ribeiro, "*Eletrificação Rural de Baixo Custo*" ("Low-Cost Rural Electrification"), Ph.D. diss., University of São Paulo, 1994.
5. Mac Margolis, "A Plot of Their Own," *Newsweek,* Latin American International Edition, January 21, 2002, 8–13.
6. Fábio Rosa, "My Week and Welcome to It," *Grist Magazine*, November 10, 2000, www.gristmagazine.com. See also Mac Margolis, "Not As Green as They Seem," *Newsweek*, Latin American International Edition, March 27, 2000, 10–14.
7. Margolis, "A Plot of Their Own."
8. Allan Savory, "Introduction," in André Voisin, *Grass Productivity* (Washington, D.C.: Island Press, 1988), xvii.
9. Voisin, *Grass Productivity.*
10. Paul Hawken, Amory Lovins, and L. Hunter Lovins, *Natural Capitalism*, 208.
11. Christopher Flavin, "Rich Planet, Poor Planet," in The Worldwatch Institute, *State of the World 2001* (New York: W. W. Norton, 2001), 14–15.
12. Peter F. Drucker, *Innovation and Entrepreneurship* (New York: Harper Business, 1993), 30–31.
13. David Lipschultz, "Solar Power Is Reaching Where Wires Can't," *New York Times*, September 9, 2001.
14. See www.schwabfound.org.
15. See www.thetech.org/techawards.

Chapter 4. The Fixed Determination of an Indomitable Will

1. The Florence Nightingale section is drawn from the following sources: Florence Nightingale, *Notes on Nursing* (New York: Dover Publications, 1969); Lytton Strachey, *Eminent Victorians* (New York: Modern Library,

1999); Cecil Woodham-Smith, *Florence Nightingale* (New York: McGraw-Hill, 1951); Edward Tyas Cook, *The Life of Florence Nightingale*, vols. 1 and 2 (New York: Macmillan, 1913); Michael D. Calabria and Janet A. Macrae, eds., *Suggestions for Thought, by Florence Nightingale, Selections and Commentaries* (Philadelphia: University of Pennsylvania Press, 1994); Martha Vicinus and Bea Nergaard, eds., *Ever Yours, Florence Nightingale, Selected Letters* (London: Virago Press 1989); *Encyclopaedia Britannica*, 2001 CD-ROM Edition, entry on "Florence Nightingale"; I. Bernard Cohen, "Florence Nightingale," *Scientific American*, 250 (March 1984): 128–37; and Edwin W. Kopf, "Florence Nightingale as Statistician," *Journal of the American Statistical Association*, 15, Issue 116 (December 1916): 388–404.

2. Strachey, *Eminent Victorians*, 102.
3. Ibid., 103.
4. Ibid., 105.
5. Cook, *The Life of Florence Nightingale*, vol. 1, 153.
6. The description of the scene in Scutari is summarized from Cook, *The Life of Florence Nightingale*, Vol. 1, 183–84.
7. Nightingale's administrative reforms are detailed in Strachey, *Eminent Victorians, 108–16.*
8. Cook, *The Life of Florence Nightingale*, vol. 1, 186.
9. Cohen, "Florence Nightingale," 131. The exact death rates in February and May 1855 were 42.7 and 2.2 percent respectively.
10. Strachey, *Eminent Victorians*, 116–17.
11. Ibid.
12. See Kopf, "Florence Nightingale as Statistician," 388–404; and Cohen, "Florence Nightingale," 128–37.
13. Cohen, "Florence Nightingale," 136–37.
14. The mortality rate among British troops in India was reduced from 69 to 18 per 1,000 from 1863 to 1873. Kopf, "Florence Nightingale as Statistician," 403.
15. Cohen, "Florence Nightingale," 137.
16. Strachey, *Eminent Victorians*, 105.
17. Niccolo Machiavelli, *The Prince* (New York: New American Library, 1980), 49–50.

Chapter 5. A Very Significant Force

1. Suzanne Hoeber Rudolph and Lloyd I. Rudolph, *Gandhi: The Traditional Roots of Charisma* (Chicago: University of Chicago Press 1983), 62–86.
2. Geoffrey Ashe, *Gandhi* (New York: Stein and Day, 1969), 279–302.
3. See A. L. Basham, *The Wonder That Was India* (New York: Grove Press, 1959), 53–57; D. C. Sircar, ed., *Inscriptions of Asoka*, 3d ed. (Delhi: Ministry of Information and Broadcasting, Government of India, 1975).
4. Karen Armstrong, *Buddha* (New York: Viking, 2001), xii–xiii.
5. The section on Bhave is taken from Hallam Tennyson, *India's Walking Saint: The Story of Vinoba Bhave* (New York: Doubleday & Co. 1955); Daniel P. Hoffman, *India's Social Miracle* (Happy Camp, CA: Naturegraph, 1961); Sugata Dasgupta, *A Great Society of Small Communities: The Story of India's Land Gift Movement* (Varanasi: Sarva Seva Sangh

Prakashan, 1968); and Shriman Narayan, *Vinoba: His Life and Work* (Bombay: Popular Prakashan, 1970).

6. David C. McClelland, *The Achieving Society* (New York: Free Press, 1967), 328.
7. Ibid., 238.
8. Ibid., 221–23.
9. Ibid., 234.
10. See Brian J. Cook, *Bureaucratic Politics and Regulatory Reform: The EPA and Emissions Trading* (New York: Greenwood Press, 1988).
11. Ibid., 83–101.
12. Ibid., 121–43.
13. Russell E. Train, "The Destruction of EPA," *Washington Post*, February 2, 1982.
14. Ibid.
15. Philip Shabecof, "Funds and Staff for Protecting Environment May Be Halved," *New York Times*, September 29, 1981.
16. Joanne Omang, "Internal Rifts, Huge Staff Cut Hint EPA Retreat on Programs," *Washington Post*, September 30, 1981.
17. Drayton's analysis of the long-term impact of the Reagan-Gorsuch program was given in a testimony before the Environment, Energy and Natural Resources Subcommittee of the Government Operations Committee of the U.S. House of Representatives on October 21, 1981.
18. William Drayton, "Can Half Do Twice As Much?" *The Amicus Journal* (Winter 1982): 21–24.
19. Train, "The Destruction of EPA."
20. Gregg Easterbrook, "Green Surprise?" *The Atlantic Monthly* (September 2000): 17–24.
21. Andrew C. Revkin, "178 Nations Reach A Climate Accord; U.S. Only Looks On," *New York Times*, July 24, 2001; see also Revkin, "Global Warming Impasse Is Broken," *New York Times*, November 11, 2001.
22. Vanessa Houlder, "EU Paves Way for Emissions Trading," *Financial Times*, June 26, 2003.

Chapter 6. Why Was I Never Told about This?

1. Thomas J. Peters and Robert H. Waterman Jr., *In Search of Excellence* (New York: Warner Books, 1982), 26.
2. Ibid., 225.

Chapter 7. Ten—Nine—Eight—Childline!

1. Childline Annual Report (July 1997-March 1999), 7–8.
2. Ibid.
3. Jeroo Billimoria and Jerry Pinto, "Child Rights and the Law," *National Initiative for Child Protection Resource Book* (Bombay: Childline India Foundation, 2000), 32. The act was amended in 2000 to extend benefits to all children under the age of eighteen.
4. Childline Annual Report, 8.
5. See the Convention on the Rights of the Child at www.unicef.org.

6. Childline Annual Report, 10.
7. Childline, "Hello Childline" newsletter (December 2000).
8. Billimoria and Pinto, *National Initiative for Child Protection Resource Book*, 10–17.
9. From www.childlineindia.org.in.

Chapter 8. The Role of the Social Entrepreneur

1. See G. T. Solomon and E. K. Winslow, "Toward a Descriptive Profile of the Entrepreneur," *Journal of Creative Behavior*, 22 (1988): 162–171.
2. See David C. McClelland, *The Achieving Society* (New York: Free Press, 1967), 205. Summarizing Joseph A. Schumpeter's observations about entrepreneurs, McClelland writes: "Schumpeter felt that the economy did not grow 'naturally' or inevitably, or even steadily, but rather was pushed forward in sudden leaps by the activities of key men who wanted to promote new goods and new methods of production, or to exploit a new source of materials or a new market." See also David C. McClelland, "Characteristics of Successful Entrepreneurs," *Journal of Creative Behavior*, 21 (1987): 232.
3. Anthony Giddens, ed., *Emile Durkheim: Selected Writings* (Cambridge: Cambridge University Press, 1997).
4. See Keith Bradsher, *High and Mighty: SUVs: The World's Most Dangerous Vehicles and How They Got That Way* (New York: Public Affairs, 2002), xv–xviii. Bradsher reports that a midsize SUV emits 50 percent more carbon dioxide per mile than a typical car, and a full-size SUV may emit 100 percent more. SUVs also produce up to 5.5 times as much "smog-causing" gases per mile as compared to cars. Today's large-size SUVs get about 14 miles to the gallon, comparable to a 1978 luxury sedan. SUVs have climbed from less than 2 percent of new vehicles sold in 1982 to 17 percent today. Bradsher reports that SUVs are also less safe for their own passengers than cars due to their size, weight, underbodies, suspensions, and truck-like brakes, which have longer stopping distances than cars. Their occupant death rate per million is 6 percent higher than for cars. And because they are more likely to roll over than cars, they pose a greater risk of paralysis to occupants.
5. James O'Toole, *Leading Change: The Argument for Values-Based Leadership* (New York: Ballantine Books, 1996), 248.
6. Ibid.
7. The section on Rowland Hill is drawn from the following sources: Henry Warburton Hill, *The Fight for the Penny Post* (London: Frederick Warne & Co., 1940); Roundell C. P. Wolmer, *Post Office Reform: Its Importance and Practicability* (London: Ivor Nicholson & Watson, Ltd., 1932); Samuel Graveson, ed., *Penny Postage Centenary: An Account of Rowland Hill's Great Reform of 1840 and of the Introduction of Adhesive Postage Stamps with Chapter on the Birth of the Postal Service* (London: Postal History Society, 1940); *Encyclopaedia Britannica*, 2001 CD-ROM Edition, entry on "Postal Systems"; and Peter F. Drucker, *Innovation and Entrepreneurship* (New York: Harper Business, 1993), 243–245.
8. See *Encyclopaedia Britannica*, 2001 CD-ROM Edition, entry on "Friends, Society of," "The Age of Quietism"; see also Joseph J. Ellis,

Founding Brothers (New York: Vintage, 2002), 81–88. Ellis describes how a 1790 petition by Quaker delegations from New York and Philadelphia, calling for the incipient federal government to put an end to the African slave trade, produced what was then the "fullest public exchange of views on the most deep-rooted problem facing the new American republic," 88.

9. Amelia M. Gummere, "The Early Quakers in New Jersey," in *The Quakers in the American Colonies*, ed. Rufus M. Jones (London: Macmillan, 1911), 397. "More than any other one man," writes Gummere, "Woolman aided the English speaking nations to throw off the disgrace of slavery; and although so late as 1800, there were still 12,442 slaves held in New Jersey, of these, thanks to the labours of John Woolman, almost none were held by Friends."

10. The Woolman quote is taken from Janet Whitney, *John Woolman, American Quaker* (Boston: Little, Brown and Co., 1942), 343.

11. Merry and Serge Bromberger, *Jean Monnet and the United States of Europe* (New York: Coward-McCann, 1969), 17–18. "It is surprising," the authors write, "that a young man who was not a general, an elected representative, a newspaper editor, or a high official, but merely a traveling salesman, should have made his voice heard by two governments and imposed decisions that altered the course of the war."

12. Jacques Cheminade, "F.D.R. and Jean Monnet: The Battle Against British Imperial Methods Can Be Won," *Fidelio*, 9, nos. 2–3 (Summer-Fall 2000); available at www.schillerinstitute.org.

13. Thomas J. Moore, *Lifespan: Who Lives Longer and Why* (New York: Simon & Schuster, 1993), 161–74.

14. Quoted from remarks by President George Bush Sr. on the presentation of the Congressional Gold Medal to Mary Lasker, April 21, 1989.

15. Gary Cohen and Shannon Brownlee, "Mary and Her 'Little Lambs' Launch a War," *U.S. News & World Report*, February 5, 1996.

16. Moore, *Lifespan*, 172.

17. See Jerome Groopman, "The Thirty Years' War," *The New Yorker*, June 4, 2001, 52–63.

18. Atul Gawande, "When Doctors Make Mistakes," *The New Yorker*, February 1, 1999, 40–55.

19. Ibid., 51

20. Ibid., 53.

21. From "Forty Years Behind the Mask: Safety Revisited," the 34th Rovenstine Lecture, delivered by Ellison C. Pierce to the American Society of Anesthesiologists' annual meeting, Atlanta, Georgia, in October 1995; see www.apsf.org.

22. Interview with Ellison Pierce.

Chapter 9. "What Sort of a Mother Are You?"

1. U.S. Library of Congress, Country Studies, Hungary, Chapter 3, section on "Industrial Organization"; http://lcweb2.loc.gov/frd/cs/hutoc.html (September 1989).

2. ECOSTAT Institute for Economic Analyses and Informatics, Budapest, Hungary, www.ecostat.hu.

3. Report to the Hungarian Government on the visit to Hungary carried out by the European Committee for the Prevention of Torture and Inhuman

or Degrading Treatment or Punishment (CPT), December 5–16, 1999, Council of Europe. The report was adopted by the CPT at its forty-second meeting, held July 4–7, 2000.

4. Clifford J. Levy, "Broken Homes: A Final Destination; For Mentally Ill, Death and Misery," *New York Times*, April 28, 2002.

Chapter 10. Are They Possessed, Really Possessed, by an Idea?

1. William Drayton, "Selecting Leading Public Entrepreneurs" at www. ashoka.org.
2. Historically, informal sources of micro-credit have included money-lenders, pawn shops, family loans, and traditional loan circles, such as the Su Su or Rosca.
3. The same applies in business. See "Innovation in Industry Survey," *The Economist*, February 20, 1999, 5–28. According to the article, "[A]ll big innovations need to be championed and nurtured for long periods, some-times up to 25 years," 15; "Quite often [technical breakthroughs] stem from the sheer bloody-mindedness of individual engineers who refuse to abandon a pet idea," 14.
4. Ashoka will not elect a candidate if the person is involved in partisan political leadership, has taken part in violent activities or any form of dis-crimination, or has been a member of a political party that advocates vio-lence, discrimination, or totalitarianism.

Chapter 11. If the World Is to Be Put in Order

1. UNICEF, *State of the World's Children 2000* (New York: United Nations Publications), 23–35. More than 40 million Brazilians do not have access to safe water; more than 50 million are without access to adequate sani-tation; 11 percent of children are stunted.
2. The full quotation reads: "Until one is committed, there is hesitancy, the chance to draw back, always ineffectiveness. Concerning all acts of initia-tive and creation, there is one elementary truth the ignorance of which kills countless ideas and splendid plans: that the moment one definitely commits oneself, then providence moves too. All sorts of things occur to help one that would never otherwise have occurred. A whole stream of events issues from the decision, raising in one's favor all manner of unforeseen incidents, meetings and material assistance which no man could have dreamed would have come his way. Whatever you can do or dream you can, begin it. Boldness has genius, power and magic in it. Begin it now."
3. See Global Development Network, www.gdnet.org.
4. As reported by Renascer in January 2003, based on forty-one families discharged over a ten-month period.

Chapter 12. In Search of Social Excellence

1. See Amala Reddy, "Schools With No Homework in Bangladesh," *Changemakers Journal* (November 1999); www.changemakers.net.

2. Chitrakar's organization is Environment Camps for Conservation Awareness (ECCA); see www.changemakers.net.
3. Peter Gizewski and Thomas Homer-Dixon, "Urban Growth and Violence: Will the Future Resemble the Past?" Project on Environment, Population and Security (Washington, D.C.: American Association for the Advancement of Science and the University of Toronto 1995), www.library. utoronto.ca/pcs/eps/urban/urban1.htm.
4. See www.brac.net.
5. See www.jamkhed.org.
6. See David Bornstein, "NEKI's Mission: Protect the Gypsies of Hungary," *Civnet Journal* (November-December 1998); www.civnet.org.
7. For more information about Ouédraogo's work, see also the Union Interafricaine des Droits de l'Homme, www.hri.ca/partners/uidh.
8. World Health Organization (WHO). According to WHO, there may be more than 500 million people in the world with special needs. An estimated 80 percent live in developing countries.
9. See http://scarfindia.org.
10. International Trauma Studies Program, New York University.
11. See Environmental Defense, www.environmentaldefense.org.
12. See Derek Brown, "After W.T.O: Creating Jobs for the Next Millennium," *Changemakers Journal* (February 2000), www.changemakers.net.
13. See www.sewa.org.
14. See www.asafe.org.
15. See www.transfairusa.org.
16. See Ana A. Lima, "A Lesson of Survival and Sustainability from the Brazilian Semi-Arid Lands," *Changemakers Journal* (April 2001), www.changemakers.net; see also www.apaeb.com.br.
17. See www.sfo.pl/eceat and www.icppc.sfo.pl. See also www.goldmanprize.org.
18. See Daniela Katzenstein Hart, "Combating Technological Apartheid in Brazilian Favelas," *Changemakers Journal* (May 2000), www.changemakers.net; see also Emily Mitchell, "Getting Better at Doing Good," *Time*, February 21, 2000.
19. See www.feyalegria.org.
20. Gram Vikas received the 2001 Most Innovative Development Project Award from the Global Development Network; see www.gdnet.org.
21. See www.masifundesonke.org.za.
22. See www.iavi.org.
23. Stephanie Strom, "Gates Aims Billions To Attack Illnesses Of World's Neediest," *New York Times*, July 13, 2003.
24. For example, in 1985, 85 percent of children in industrialized countries were immunized against measles. In Africa, the figure was 35 percent; in South and East Asia, the figure was 10 percent. See UNICEF, *The State of the World's Children 1986* (New York: Oxford University Press, 1985), 7.

Chapter 13. The Talent Is Out There

1. The College Board's customized mailing lists and student data include high school GPA, class ranking, and SAT scores; see www.collegeboard.com.

2. See "People 15 to 24 Years Old Enrolled in Secondary School in Previous Year by Current Enrollment Status, Age, Sex, Race, Hispanic Origin, and Family Income (for Dependent Family Members)," U.S. Census Bureau, October 1995. Based on the experience of its workshops, College Summit contends that approximately 180,000 to 200,000 of the estimated 475,000 low-income students who graduate from high school but do not enroll in college each year could succeed in college.

3. See "College Access in the Twenty-First Century: Demographics and the Demand for Financial Aid," in *Values and Practices: Confronting the Disconnects, A Report on the College Board Colloquium* (New York: College Entrance Examination Board, 2001).

4. See www.echoinggreen.org. Echoing Green provides seed funding to individuals when they are just starting organizations. Several of Ashoka's U.S.-based fellows received prior support from Echoing Green.

5. See "People 15 to 24 Years Old Enrolled in Secondary School in Previous Year by Current Enrollment Status, Age, Sex, Race, Hispanic Origin, and Family Income (for Dependent Family Members)," U.S. Census Bureau, October 1995.

6. See Jennifer Cheeseman Day and Eric C. Newburger, "The Big Payoff: Educational Attainment and Synthetic Estimates of Work-Life Earnings," Current Population Reports, U.S. Census Bureau, July 2002, 2–4.

7. Home page for Manual High School in the Denver Public Schools system: www.denver.k12.co.us/schools.

8. See www.nacac.com.

Chapter 14. New Opportunities, New Challenges

1. A grant from Avina helped support the researching of this book.

Chapter 15. Something Needed to Be Done

1. UNAIDS World Report, June 27, 2000.

2. UNAIDS, *Comfort and Hope* (Geneva: UNAIDS Best Practice Collection, June 1999), 53; see www.unaids.org.

3. Ibid., 53–63.

4. Interview with Elizabeth Floyd, director of the Gauteng Province AIDS program (February 2002); also "Terminally-Ill Patients to Benefit from Home-Based Care Programme," notice issued by Department of Health, Gauteng Provincial Department (June 11, 2002); see www.gpg.gov.za.

5. See www.unaids.org.

6. Annual Report (2000–2001) of the Gauteng Provincial Government AIDS Program.

7. Ibid.

8. Tina Rosenberg, "How To Solve The World's AIDS Crisis," *The New York Times Magazine* (January 28, 2001); see also Samantha Power, "The AIDS Rebel," *The New Yorker* (May 19, 2003).

9. Helen Epstein and Lincoln Chen, "Can AIDS Be Stopped?" *New York Review of Books* (March 14, 2002), 30. In early 2003 President Bush proposed to ask Congress to authorize $10 billion in new funding for

AIDS care, education, and research. See Rachel L. Swarns, "Africans Welcome U.S. Help on AIDS," *New York Times*, January 30, 2003.

Chapter 16. Four Practices of Innovative Organizations

1. Jerry Pinto, ed., *Listening to Children: An Overview to Childline* (Bombay: Childline India Foundation: 2001); and Childline, *Recording Children's Concerns: Documenting Childline* (Bombay: Childline India Foundation 2001).
2. See David Bornstein, "Poland's First Food Bank," *Civnet Journal* (March-April 1999), www.civnet.org.
3. Barbara Fatyga, *The Programme "Sharing the Things We Have," 1994–1997* (Warsaw: Oficyna Wydawnicza EL-PRESS, 1997), 87–88.
4. Barka received second place in the 2002 Most Innovative Development Project Award from the Global Development Network; see www.gdnet.org.
5. See www.gapabahia.org.br; see also Shannon Walbran with Harley Henriques do Nascimento, "Six Steps to Headache-Free Volunteer Management," *Changemakers Journal* (August 1999), www.changemakers.net.
6. See Ravi Agarwal, "Shifting Environmental Risk: Obliterating the Human Face," *Changemakers Journal* (October 2000), www.changemakers.net; also www.toxicslink.org.
7. See Rosabeth Moss Kanter, *The Change Masters* (New York: Touchstone, 1984), 18. Kanter writes: "The degree to which the opportunity to use power effectively is granted or withheld from individuals is one operative difference between those companies which stagnate and those which innovate."
8. See www.idec.org.br.

Chapter 17. This Country Has to Change

1. India has a population of approximately 1 billion people. The World Health Organization estimates that 7 to 10 percent of the people in the world have a disability. Abidi uses the more conservative estimate of 6 percent.
2. See Joseph P. Shapiro, *No Pity: People with Disabilities Forging a New Civil Rights Movement* (New York: Times Books, 1994).
3. Ibid., 64–70.
4. Ibid., 108–12.
5. Javed Abidi, "No Pity," *Health for the Millions* (November-December 1995): 15–19.
6. Shapiro, *No Pity*, 112–13.
7. Arundhati Ray, "Giving Visibility to the Disabled in India," *Changemakers Journal* (January 2001), www.changemakers.net.
8. Presentation by Javed Abidi at a Seminar on Employment Opportunities for People with Disabilities, Bombay, India, May 6, 1998, organized by NCPEDP in association with Confederation of Indian Industry. Proceedings published by NCPEDP, October 1998, 25.
9. Ibid.

10. See Javed Abidi, ed., *Equity*, 1, no. 1 (April 1998) (newsletter of NCPEDP); see www.ncpedp.org.
11. Ibid.
12. NCPEDP and The National Association for the Blind, Delhi, *Role of NGOs Vis-à-vis the Employment Scenario in India With Reference to People with Disabilities* (Delhi: NCPEDP, 1998), 11–33.
13. Javed Abidi, ed., "Employment Practices of the Corporate Sector ('Super 100' Companies) with Reference to People with Disabilities," *Equity*, 2, no. 1 (April 1999): 3–5.
14. Javed Abidi, "Editor's Note," *Equity*, 1, no. 3 (October 1998): 1.
15. Javed Abidi, "Schemes to Assist Universities and Colleges to Facilitate Higher Education for Disabled Persons," *Equity*, 1, no. 3 (October 1998): 3–4.
16. Supreme Court of India, Civil Appellate Jurisdiction, Writ Petition (Civil) No. 326 of 1997. Judgement issued December 17, 1998, text copy published in Javed Abidi, ed., *Equity*, 1, no. 4 (January 1999): 4–5; www.ncpedp.org.
17. Supreme Court of India, Writ Petition (Civil) No. 326 of 1997. Court order dated October 24, 1997.
18. Letter from M. K. Jain, Deputy Registrar General, Ministry of Home Affairs, Government of India, to Javed Abidi, December 12, 1999.
19. Javed Abidi, ed., "How Disability Was Included in the Census 2001—A Chronology of Events," *Equity*, 3, no. 4 (January 2001): 4–6.
20. Garimella Subramaniam, "All Disabilities to be Covered in Census 2001," *The Hindu* (Delhi), October 6, 2000.
21. "Why Disability Activist Thinks Hawking's Good News?" *The Indian Express*, December 1, 2001.
22. "Hawking Couple Want Ramps to Stay On at Monuments," *The Times of India*, January 17, 2001.
23. Lalit K. Jha, "ASI to Put Up Ramps at Monuments," *The Hindu*, February 7, 2001.
24. Rema Nagarajan, "UPSC Exam Centres to be Disabled Friendly," *The Hindustan Times*, April 26, 2001.
25. "Disabled May Find Hotels Accessible Soon," *The Hindustan Times*, May 7, 2001.

Chapter 18. Six Qualities of Successful Social Entrepreneurs

1. David C. McClelland, "Characteristics of Successful Entrepreneurs," *Journal of Creative Behavior*, 21 (1987): 219–233.
2. Muhammad Yunus, *Grameen Bank II: Designed to Open New Possibilities* (Dhaka: Grameen Bank, 2002).
3. See Joseph E. Stiglitz, *Globalization and Its Discontents* (New York: W. W. Norton, 2002).
4. Ibid., 230–31.
5. Amelia M. Gummere, "The Early Quakers in New Jersey," in *The Quakers in the American Colonies*, ed. Rufus M. Jones (London: Macmillan, 1911), 397–98.
6. It's also fascinating to reflect on the extraordinary behind-the-scenes efforts that make possible historic moments. For example, Martin Luther

King Jr. gave his "I Have a Dream" speech at the March on Washington for Jobs and Freedom on August 28, 1963. The March on Washington was the brainchild of Asa Philip Randolph, the great black labor organizer. (In fact, King initially declined to participate in the march.) The march was organized by Bayard Rustin, who maintained a low profile because he was a homosexual who had at one time belonged to the Communist Party and had been imprisoned as a conscientious objector during World War II. It was Rustin who determined the march's route, timing, and program. (When Rustin decided that King should speak last, King's followers in the Southern Christian Leadership Conference complained bitterly.) Rustin also coordinated transportation and media outreach and undertook elaborate measures to ensure that the day—humid, temperatures in the mid-80s, a quarter of million people pressed together for up to ten hours—would not be marred by violence. Rustin assigned captains for each of the 1,500 buses and 21 trains that carried demonstrators to the march and provided each with detailed instructions about what to do and where to go. He deployed a detachment of unarmed "civilian marshals," specially trained by a New York police sergeant, to serve as nonviolent peacekeepers. And he made sure ample quantities of water and cheap food were available, as well as toilet facilities and first aid. Rustin's biographer, Jervis Anderson, quotes a confidant of Rustin's, who told him: "Dr. King will go down in history as Lincoln did after the Gettysburg address. But if there had been violence that day the media would have seized upon it, and King's great speech would have been drowned out. Bayard's masterful planning of the march made King's speech both possible and meaningful." See Jervis Anderson, *Bayard Rustin: Troubles I've Seen* (Berkeley: University of California Press, 1998), 264.

7. Jean Monnet, *Memoirs* (New York: Doubleday and Co., 1978), 229–30.
8. Ibid., 519.
9. As quoted in David C. McClelland, *The Achieving Society* (New York: Free Press, 1967), 11.

Chapter 19. Morality Must March with Capacity

1. United Nations estimate. *Encyclopaedia Britannica, 1995 Yearbook,* entry for "James P. Grant."
2. Maggie Black, *Children First: The Story of UNICEF, Past and Present* (New York: Oxford University Press, 1996), 33; see also UNICEF, *The State of the World's Children 1986* (New York: Oxford University Press, 1985), 5.
3. UNICEF, *The State of the World's Children 1992* (New York: Oxford University Press, 1992), 5–11.
4. Peter Adamson, "The Mad American," in Richard Jolly, ed., *Jim Grant: UNICEF Visionary* (Florence, Italy: UNICEF, 2002), 33.
5. See Black, *Children First,* xiv–xv. Maggie Black, who has extensively documented Unicef's work, has written: "Under Grant's leadership, Unicef became an instrument for making happen things that were much larger and more significant than its size or character would ever have given grounds to expect. Some of this may be fortuitous; some is certainly due to people all over the world who made Grant's cause their cause and

laboured to fulfill his vision. . . . But much of it is due to him—to his energy, his optimism, his acuity, his unconventionality, his lack of self-importance, his capacity to transcend and to circumvent so as to keep his and others' eyes on the prize, and his refusal to accept that the undoable could not be done."

6. Ibid., 42. One of Unicef's strategies was to reduce the distances that families in developing countries had to travel for vaccines and to make services available at convenient times. UNICEF, *The State of the World's Children 1986*, 102.

7. UNICEF, *The State of the World's Children 1986*, 3. The report describes what it means for a child to die of measles: "At first . . . a child who is slightly malnourished begins to lose his or her appetite and feel the beginnings of a small fever. After a day or two, the fever is higher, appetite is gone, coughing begins, and a vivid florid rash is appearing on the skin as if from nowhere. As the days pass, the diarrhoea begins, the skin dries, and the rash spreads until the eyes also become infected and inflamed. By the second week, the rash has begun to peel, leaving open raw sores on the skin, and by now the coughing is persistent and prolonged and the diarrhoea is unremitting. No food is being taken, and water, salts, and nutrients are draining from the weakened body. Dehydrated to the point where the thirst is unbearable and racked by coughing fits which are becoming too weak to clear the lungs but too strong for the muscles of the small heart, the lights of the body begin to go out. In this way, measles killed two million children in 1985."; 6.

8. UNICEF, *The State of the World's Children 1996* (New York: Oxford University Press, 1996), 58, www.unicef.org/sowc96.

9. James P. Grant, *The State of the World's Children 1982–83* (New York: Oxford University Press, 1982), 8–9. The development of ORS was pioneered by the International Center for Diarrhoeal Disease Research, Bangladesh (ICDDR,B). See also: The Rehydration Project, www.rehydrate.org.

10. UNICEF, *The State of the World's Children 1986*, 90.

11. Nyi Nyi, "Building Foundations for the Castles in the Air," in Jolly, ed., *Jim Grant*, 69–71.

12. UNICEF, *The State of the World's Children 1996*, www.unicef.org/sowc96.

13. See the J. B. Grant International Health Society web page, Johns Hopkins School of Public Health, www.jhsph.edu.

14. The report of the meeting is taken from conversations with Jon Rohde, Peter Adamson, and Richard Jolly, and drawn from a speech by Adamson entitled "The Mad American," June 21, 1998.

15. Causes for the decline in breastfeeding are outlined in Black, *Children First*, 74–77.

16. In addition to his work on smallpox eradication, as head of the U.S. Centers for Disease Control, William Foege unraveled the mysteries of toxic shock syndrome and Reye's syndrome and published the first "safe sex" material about AIDS. At the Carter Center, he spearheaded efforts to eradicate river blindness and Guinea worm. See www.laskerfoundation.org for a brief explanation of Foege's "surveillance and containment" strategy in the smallpox eradication campaign. See also Douglas Brinkley, *The Unfinished Presidency, Jimmy Carter's Journey Beyond the White*

House (New York: Viking, 1998), which describes Foege's work at the Carter Center.

17. Black, *Children First*, 34–37.
18. Ibid., 39, 299.
19. Ibid., 299. Grant also doubled the number of countries in which Unicef worked and tripled the agency's field staff. Carol Bellamy, "A Tribute," in Jolly, ed., *Jim Grant*, 16.
20. See the Global Polio Eradication Campaign, www.polioeradication.org.
21. Correspondence with William Foege.
22. Richard Jolly, "Jim Grant: The Man Behind the Vision," in Jolly, ed., *Jim Grant*, 51.
23. Black, *Children First*, 44.
24. Ibid., 45.
25. Ibid., 36.
26. Richard Reid, "Stopping Wars for Children," in Jolly, ed., *Jim Grant*, 90.
27. UNICEF, *The State of the World's Children 1986*, 1–6.
28. Ibid., 20.
29. As recalled by Richard Jolly.
30. UNICEF, *The State of the World's Children 1986*, 10.
31. Black, *Children First*, 46.
32. UNICEF, *The State of the World's Children 1986*, 6.
33. Nyi, "Building Foundations for the Castles in the Air," 70.
34. Ibid., 81.
35. Black, *Children First*, 25.
36. Ibid., 276.
37. See www.unicef.org/programme/nutrition/focus/micronut/iodine.htm.
38. UNICEF, *State of the World's Children 1993* (New York: Oxford University Press, 1993), 34.
39. See www.unicef.org/programme/nutrition/focus/micronut/iodine.htm. According to Unicef, iodine deficiency can cause a downward shift in the bell curve (of IQ) in a population by as much as 13 IQ points.
40. Ibid.
41. "Indifference Toward Vaccinating the Poor," *New York Times*, editorial, January 21, 2002.
42. Children's Vaccine Initiative, www.who.int.
43. USAID Diarrheal Disease Control programs, www.usaid.gov/pop_health/cs/csddc.htm.
44. Black, *Children First*, 60.
45. See the Polio Eradication Campaign, www.polioeradication.org.

Chapter 20. Blueprint Copying

1. Jared Diamond, *Guns, Germs and Steel: The Fates of Human Societies* (New York: W. W. Norton, 1997), 224–25.
2. See www.grameen-info.com, Grameen Bank International Training.
3. Ellen Ruppel Shell, "Does Civilization Cause Asthma?" *The Atlantic Monthly* (May 2000): 90.
4. Ibid., 100.
5. Ibid., 92.
6. Such follow-up may also help reduce hospitalization with other illnesses.

See Lawrence K. Altman, "Follow-Up Calls Aid Heart-Failure Cases," *New York Times*, November 19, 2002.
7. See Michael Porter, *The Competitive Advantage of Nations* (New York: Free Press, 1998).

Chapter 21. Conclusion

1. See David C. McClelland, "Characteristics of Successful Entrepreneurs," *Journal of Creative Behavior*, 21 (1987): 232–33. McClelland writes: "We have had ample experience in providing money and other resources to people without the motivation or other competencies needed to use them effectively—with disastrous results that have discouraged many into thinking it's not really possible to help many underdeveloped areas. [L]et's approach the problem the other way around—starting with people rather than resources."
2. Some other organizations that target their support to social entrepreneurs include New Profit, Inc., www.newprofit.com; Acumen Fund, www.acumenfund.org; New Schools Venture Fund, www.newschool.org; and Social Venture Partners, www.svpseattle.org.
3. See www.sse.org.uk.
4. See "Society: A 'Set of Sets,'" in Fernand Braudel, *Civilization and Capitalism, 15th–18th Century, Vol. II, The Wheels of Commerce* (Berkeley: University of California Press, 1992), 458–599. For a concise (and delightful) overview of the social and political forces that produced the market system and capitalism, see also "The Economic Revolution," in Robert L. Heilbroner, *The Worldly Philosophers: The Lives, Times & Ideas of the Great Economic Thinkers* (New York: Simon & Schuster, 1961), 6–27.
5. See David C. McClelland, *The Achieving Society* (New York: Free Press, 1967), 205. See also Peter F. Drucker, "The Age of Social Transformation," *The Atlantic Monthly* (November 1994): 53–80. Drucker notes that the terms "public sector" and "private sector" emerged in the mid twentieth century.
6. Braudel, *Civilization and Capitalism, 15th–18th Century, Vol. II, The Wheels of Commerce*, 438–50. This analysis also draws on general reference from the *Encyclopaedia Britannica*, 2001 CD-ROM Edition, including sections entitled: "The Development of Banking Systems," "Commercial Transactions," "From Commercial to Industrial Capitalism," "From Mercantilism to Commercial Capitalism," and "History of the Limited Liability Company."
7. William J. Baumol, *The Free-Market Innovation Machine* (Princeton, NJ: Princeton University Press, 2002), 3.
8. Interview with William J. Baumol. See also William J. Baumol, "Towards Microeconomics of Innovation: Growth Engine Hallmark of Market Economics," *Atlantic Economic Journal*, 30, no. 1 (March 2002), 1–12.
9. Baumol, *The Free-Market Innovation Machine*, 254–57; see also David S. Landes, *The Wealth and Poverty of Nations* (New York: W. W. Norton, 1999), 45–59 and 186–212. Landes notes that Europe in the Middle Ages was also highly inventive, producing, for example, the water wheel, eyeglasses, and the clock. Landes writes that the "growing *autonomy* of

intellectual inquiry" (in Europe) combined with a "common implicitly adversarial *method*" and "*routinization* of research and its diffusion"—a process "enormously enhanced by fierce rivalry in the race for prestige and honor"—produced the breakthroughs of the Industrial Revolution; 200–209.

10. Lester M. Salamon, "The Rise of the Nonprofit Sector," *Foreign Affairs* (July-August 1994): 112–18.

11. See the International Center for Non-Profit Law, www.icnl.org.

12. See Peter F. Drucker, "The Age of Social Transformation," *The Atlantic Monthly* (November 1994): 53–80. At the time of writing, Drucker noted: "With respect to the management of the nonprofit organization we are in many ways pretty much where we were fifty or sixty years ago with respect to the management of the business enterprise: the work is only beginning."

13. See also the Campus Compact, endorsed by 860 universities and colleges, which encourages students to apprentice with local citizen groups as part of their formal education; www.compact.org.

14. In 2001, according to the Global Policy Forum, more than 2,000 NGOs had consultative status with the UN Economic and Social Council; www.globalpolicy.org. In 1990 citizen organizations were involved in 12 percent of all World Bank projects. By 1997 the figure had climbed to 47 percent; see *Civicus World* (November-December 1998), www.civicus.org.

15. The New York Times Fact Book, www.nytco.com, 32–35.

16. In the United States, an estimated 250 colleges and universities offer courses or degree programs for students interested in working in the citizen sector. See Sara Terry, "Seeking Jobs with Social Value," *The Christian Science Monitor*, August 27, 2001, 16. In 2001, 7 percent of Yale University's graduating class applied to Teach for America, www.teachforamerica.com; see also the Initiative on Social Enterprise at Harvard Business School, www.hbs.edu/dept/socialenterprise. See also Michael Hall and Keith G. Banting, "The Nonprofit Sector in Canada: An Introduction," in Keith G. Banting, ed., *The Nonprofit Sector in Canada* (Kingston, Ontario and Montreal, Quebec: McGill-Queen's University Press, 1999), 1–28. Hall and Banting write of "the spread of postmaterialist values emphasizing personal development" that have contributed to a rise in interest in this sector.

17. See the *Journal of Microfinance* (est. 1999), www.microjournal.com.

18. Credit and Development Forum, Dhaka, Bangladesh, www.cdf-bd.org.

19. For the nonprofit list, see: "NPT Top 100," *The Non Profit Times* (November 2002), www.nptimes.com. For the list of Dow composites, see: www.djindexes.com. Since 1980, eighteen companies have been added to the Dow Jones Industrial Average (which is comprised of thirty "established U.S. companies that are leaders in their industries"), and twelve have been added since 1990; however, some of these additions reflect takeovers, mergers, or readditions. What is notable about the component changes are the number of companies (close to forty) that have been displaced from the index since 1928, reflecting competitive forces and broad shifts in the U.S. economy, and the comparatively rapid rise of companies such as Hewlett-Packard, Home Depot, Intel, Microsoft, and

Wal-Mart, made possible by the systematic redeployment of investment capital from old companies to new companies and new industries. The citizen sector hasn't experienced a comparable reshuffling.

20. See the American Association of Fundraising Counsel Trust for Philanthropy, *Giving USA 2002*, www.aafrc.org; see also Katie Cunningham and Marc Ricks, " 'Competitive Necessity' or 'Specious Precision'?: Perspectives on Performance Measurement in the Nonprofit Sector," Harvard Business School Field Study (Fall 2002).

21. For an overview of organizations involved in these changes, see *Venture Philanthropy 2002: Advancing Nonprofit Performance Through High-Engagement Grantmaking* (Venture Philanthropy Partners, Inc. 2002), available at www.venturephilanthropypartners.org.

22. American Association of Fundraising Counsel Trust for Philanthropy, *Giving USA 2002*.

23. In a 2000 "Measuring Effectiveness" study, Ashoka surveyed fifty-three fellows elected in 1995. It reported that 90 percent "continued to work on the projects for which they were elected," 64 percent "reported changing national policies," 62 percent of the institutions created by the fellows were "considered leaders in their fields," 87 percent reported that "other independent groups are replicating their idea or project," and 73 percent reported that Ashoka's support had made a "significant" (43 percent) or "critical" (30 percent) impact on their work.

24. William A. Galston, *Liberal Pluralism: The Implications of Value Pluralism for Political Theory and Practice* (Cambridge, England: Cambridge University Press, 2002), 6–7.

25. Baumol, *The Free-Market Innovation Machine*, 60.

26. According to Teach for America, applicants for the 2002 program came from 395 universities. The average GPA of corps members is 3.5; see www.teachforamerica.org.

27. Marc Freedman, *Prime Time* (New York: Public Affairs, 1999), 17. Freedman calls America's healthy, aging population the country's "only increasing natural resource."

Resource Guide

For readers who are interested in becoming social entrepreneurs or getting involved with citizen organizations as employees, volunteers, funders, board members, or consultants, there are many resources available to identify opportunities—and there will certainly be more (and more systematic) assistance in the years ahead. For the time being, it takes a little ingenuity to identify an organization that is doing good work and offers the right kinds of opportunities for you. If you are a student or an experienced professional or retiree, there are many opportunities to apply your skills and intelligence at a high level working with effective organizations and top-notch entrepreneurs. You do *not* have to accept a volunteer job sorting the mail or licking stamps. However, finding the right match usually involves some old-fashioned investigation.

For people seeking financing for their ideas, the most comprehensive resource for identifying foundation grants is the New York–based Foundation Center (http://fdncenter.org), which has a library and search tools to identify potential funders from among 70,000 grantmakers. The *Chronicle of Philanthropy* also provides information about government grants, associations of regional grantmakers and funding "affinity groups." Venture Philanthropy Partners (www.venturephilanthropypartners.org) provides on its website a free guide to "high-engagement" grant makers.

There are many creative ways to finance new ideas. The best place to begin is where most businesspeople begin—working their personal networks of friends, family, colleagues, college friends, and so forth. Many businesspeople are eager to assist social organizations by serving as board members, contributing expertise or providing funding through family or corporate foundations. Many companies are looking for opportunities to associate themselves with citizen groups for marketing purposes or to boost staff motivation, and they are willing to sponsor events, donate real estate, provide pro-bono consulting services, furnish equipment, provide time off for their employees to serve as volunteers, and make available office space. In fact, family and corporate foundations may be easier to break into than large public foundations.

There is no shortage of ideas. One Ashoka fellow in Thailand actually went through the phone book calling up people with the same family name, soliciting donations for his child protection organization. He was extraordinarily successful. In her book, *One Day All Children*, Teach for America's founder Wendy Kopp explains how she initially financed her organization by sending hundreds of unsolicited letters to corporate chief executive officers. Another idea is to scan the "Who's Who" directory, or read the business press, or visit the Chamber of Commerce, and compile a list of local individuals who may have an interest in supporting your public service work. It's useful to attend conferences, trade shows, and gatherings where funders and businesspeople gather and to connect with established networks of socially responsible businesspeople, such as Business for Social Responsibility or Net Impact.

For social entrepreneurs seeking to generate revenues through business ventures, there are today a number of new organizations that specialize in helping citizen organizations do so. Two sources of information are the Washington, D.C.–based Community Wealth Ventures (www.community-wealth.com) and the Yale School of Management—Goldman Sachs Foundation Partnership on Nonprofit Ventures (www.ventures.yale.edu).

For those seeking jobs or volunteer opportunities or looking to provide funding or serve as board members, the challenge is finding the right organizational match for you. There is no one-stop shop or marketplace to identify cutting-edge citizen organizations. However, one way to identify these groups is to talk to funders who are both knowledgeable about particular fields and discriminating about whom they support. These range from smaller, well-focused organizations like Ashoka, Echoing Green, and the Schwab Foundation for Social Entrepreneurship to major funders like the Bill & Melinda Gates Foundation, the Ford Foundation, or the Pew Charitable Trusts. Many foundations have clearly defined areas of interest. Over time, their program officers become familiar with many of the key actors in fields such as women's development, community revitalization, healthcare, human rights, youth development, and the environment. Often they can provide leads to organizations doing interesting work in these areas. Many foundations also confine their grant making to specific cities or states, so they can be helpful in identifying local organizations. Foundations often publicize the names of their grant recipients on the Internet and in annual reports. The *Chronicle of Philanthropy* lists community foundations by state on its website (www.philanthropy.com). The GuideStar database (www.guidestar.org) contains a list of 850,000 citizen organizations and can be searched by zip code, type of work, revenue, and other categories. There are also a growing number of Internet-based services that help people identify jobs and volunteer opportunities in the citizen sector. A few of them are listed below.

Other potential sources of ideas are journalists and authors who write about specific fields, such as education, the environment, or disability. If I wanted to volunteer for an organization that assists people with disabilities, I would go through the book *No Pity* and make a list of some of the organizations mentioned. Then I would write to them or call them up and ask their staff for advice. Many universities offer courses on nonprofit management or social entrepreneurship. The course outlines typically include case studies on innovative local organizations and useful articles. They are often available on the Internet.

As with job hunting, the best referrals usually come through word of mouth. However, a fair amount of upfront research can be done on the Internet. Below are sites that can serve as starting points:

Resources for People Seeking Jobs and Volunteer Opportunities

The *Chronicle of Philanthropy*, www.philanthropy.com
Community Service.org, www.communityservice.org
Idealist.org, www.idealist.org
Non Profit Times, www.nptimes.com
Nonprofit Career Network, www.nonprofitcareer.com
Opportunity Nocs, www.opportunitynocs.org
Volunteer Match, www.volunteermatch.org (also Volunteer Match
    Corporate)
Wet Feet Guides, www.wetfeet.com
Yahoo!, www.yahoo.com (See categories: Community Service and Volun-
    tarism, Philanthropy, Nonprofit Resources, Grant-Making Foundations)
Youth Service America, www.ysa.org

Organizations that Identify or Support Social Entrepreneurs

Ashoka: Innovators for the Public, www.ashoka.org
Avina Foundation, www.avina.net
Changemakers Journal and Resources, www.changemakers.net (focuses on
    innovative strategies and resources for social entrepreneurs)

Draper Richards Foundation. www.draperrichards.org

Echoing Green Foundation, www.echoinggreen.org

Ewing Marion Kauffman Foundation, www.emkf.org

The Flatiron Foundation, www.flatironpartners.com/foundation.html

New Profit, Inc., www.newprofitinc.org

New Schools Venture Fund, www.newschools.org (makes investments in "education entrepreneurs")

Peninsula Community Foundation Center for Venture Philanthropy, www.pcf.org/venture_philanthropy

Robin Hood Foundation, www.robinhood.org

Schwab Foundation for Social Entrepreneurs, www.schwabfound.org

The Skoll Foundation, www.skollfoundation.org

Social Venture Partners, www.svpseattle.org

Tides Center, www.tidescenter.org (provides a fiscal home and infrastructure support for people starting social-purpose projects who have not established a nonprofit organization)

Venture Philanthropy Partners, www.venturephilanthropypartners.org

Youth Venture, www.youthventure.org

Management and Funding Resources for Citizen Organizations

BoardnetUSA, www.boardnetUSA.org

Board Source, www.boardsource.org (practical information on building nonprofit boards)

The Bridgespan Group, www.bridgespangroup.org

California Management Assistance Partnership, Nonprofit Genie, www.genie.org

Center for Excellence in Nonprofits, www.cen.org.

Community Wealth, www.communitywealth.com

Global Social Venture Competition, a partnership among the Haas School of Business at U.C. Berkeley, Columbia Business School, London Business School and the Goldman Sachs Foundation, www.socialvc.net

The Grantsmanship Center, www.tgci.com

Institute for Social Entrepreneurs, www.socialent.org

Internet Nonprofit Center, www.nonprofits.org

Dorothy A. Johnson Center for Philanthropy and Nonprofit Leadership, www.nonprofitbasics.org

Leader to Leader Institute, www.leadertoleader.org

Mission Movers, www.missionmovers.org

National Center for Social Entrepreneurs, www.socialentrepreneurs.org

Origo Social Enterprise Partners, www.origoinc.com

The Roberts Enterprise Development Fund, www.redf.org

SocialEdge, www.socialedge.org

Social Enterprise Alliance, www.se-alliance.org

Social Enterprise Magazine, www.socialenterprisemagazine.org

Techsoup, www.techsoup.org (technology assistance for nonprofits)

Yale School of Management, Goldman Sachs Foundation Partnership on
Nonprofit Ventures, www.ventures.yale.edu

Citizen Sector Networks

Civicus, www.civicus.org

Community Action Network (CAN) (England), www.can-online.org.uk

Independent Sector, www.independentsector.org

One World, www.oneworld.net

Social Entrepreneurial Organizations (England), www.seo-online.org.uk

Academic-based Resources

Canadian Center for Social Entrepreneurship, www.bus.ualberta.ca/ccse

Center for the Advancement of Social Entrepreneurship, Fuqua School of
Business, Duke University, www.fuqua.duke.edu

Columbia Business School, Social Enterprise Program, www.gsb.columbia.
edu/socialenterprise, and Research Initiative on Social Entrepreneurship,
www.riseproject.org

Harvard Business School, Initiative on Social Enterprise, www.hbs.edu/
socialenterprise

Harvard Kennedy School of Government, Hauser Center for Nonprofit
Organizations, www.ksghauser.harvard.edu

Johns Hopkins University Institute for Policy Studies, Center for Civil
Society Studies, www.jhu.edu/~ccss

Skoll Center for Social Entrepreneurship, Said Business School at Oxford
University

Stanford Business School, Center for Social Innovation, www.gsb.
stanford.edu/csi

Resources for Funders

Aspen Institute Nonprofit Sector and Philanthropy Program,
www.aspeninst.org

Center for Effective Philanthropy, www.effectivephilanthropy.com

Charity Navigator, www.charitynavigator.org

CharityVillage.Com, www.charityvillage.com (general resource for the
Canadian nonprofit sector)

Giving Global, www.givingglobal.org.

Global Giving, www.globalgiving.com.

Grantmakers for Effective Organizations, www.geofunders.org

Grantmakers Without Borders, www.internationaldonors.org

GrantSmart.Org, www.grantsmart.org
The Philanthropic Initiative, www.tpi.org
Venture Philanthropy Guide, www.VenturePhilanthropyGuide.org (venture philanthropy landscape in the United States and Canada)

Resources for Businesspeople

Aspen Institute, Initiative for Social Innovation Through Business, www.aspeninstitute.org
Business for Social Responsibility, www.bsr.org (helps companies succeed in business while adhering to ethical standards)
Global Business Network, www.gbn.org (seeks to advance innovation in business and society)
Investors Circle, a national intermediary supporting individuals and institutions investing in social responsible and sustainable businesses, www.investorscircle.net
Net Impact, www.net-impact.org (originally Students for Responsible Business; now a network with 80 chapters and 8,500 members
Social Venture Network, www.svn.org (businesspeople, investors, and social sector groups promoting socially responsible business practices)

Selected Readings

Selected Biographies

Anderson, Jervis. *Bayard Rustin: Troubles I've Seen* (Berkeley: University of California Press, 1998).

Armstrong, Karen. *Buddha* (New York: Viking Penguin, 2001).

Ashe, Geoffrey. *Gandhi* (New York: Stein and Day, 1969).

Barry, Kathleen. *Susan B. Anthony: A Biography of a Singular Feminist* (New York: Ballantine Books, 1988).

Brinkley, Douglas, and Clifford Hackett, eds. *Jean Monnet: The Path to European Unity* (London: Macmillan, 1991).

Brinkley, Douglas. *Rosa Parks* (New York: Viking, 2000).

Caro, Robert A. *The Power Broker: Robert Moses and the Fall of New York* (New York: Vintage Books, 1975).

Cohen, I. Bernard. "Florence Nightingale." *Scientific American* 250 (March 1984): 128–137.

Gardner, Howard. *Creating Minds: An Anatomy of Creativity Seen Through the Lives of Freud, Einstein, Picasso, Stravinsky, Eliot, Graham and Gandhi* (New York: Basic Books, 1994).

Goodall, Jane. *Reason for Hope* (New York: Warner Books, 1999).

Jolly, Richard, ed. *Jim Grant: Unicef Visionary* (Florence, Italy: Unicef, 2002).

Kopf, Edwin W. "Florence Nightingale as Statistician." *Journal of the American Statistical Association* 15, no. 116 (December 1916): 388–404.

Kopp, Wendy. *One Day All Children: The Unlikely Triumph of Teach for America and What I Learned Along the Way* (New York: Public Affairs, 2001).

Monnet, Jean. *Memoirs*, trans. by Richard Mayne (Garden City, N.Y.: Doubleday & Co., 1978).

Shore, Bill. *The Cathedral Within: Transforming Your Life by Giving Something Back* (New York: Random House, 1999).

Strachey, Lytton. *Eminent Victorians* (New York: Modern Library, 1999).

Selected Readings

Tennyson, Hallam. *India's Walking Saint: The Story of Vinoba Bhave* (New York: Doubleday, 1955).

Whitney, Janet. *John Woolman, American Quaker* (Boston: Little, Brown & Co., 1942).

Woolman, John. *The Journal of John Woolman* (New York: Corinth Books, 1961).

Yunus, Muhammad. *Banker to the Poor* (New York: Public Affairs, 1999).

Entrepreneurship, Leadership, and Creativity

Clifford, Donald K. Jr., and Richard E. Cavanagh. *The Winning Performance: How America's High-Growth Midsize Companies Succeed* (New York: Bantam, 1988).

Collins, Jim, and Jerry I. Porras. *Built to Last: Successful Habits of Visionary Companies* (New York: Harper Business, 2002).

Csikszentmihalyi, Mihaly. *Flow: The Psychology of Optimal Experience* (New York: Harper Perennial, 1990).

Dees, J. Gregory. "The Meaning of Social Entrepreneurship," October 31, 1998, http://faculty.fuqua.duke.edu/centers/case/files/dees-SE.pdf

Drucker, Peter F. *Innovation and Entrepreneurship* (New York: Harper Business, 1993).

Gardner, Howard, Mihaly Csikszentmihalyi and William Damon, *Good Work: When Excellence and Ethics Meet* (New York: Basic Books, 2002).

Goleman, Daniel. *Emotional Intelligence* (New York: Bantam Books, 1997).

Lessing, Doris. *Prisons We Choose to Live Inside* (New York: Perennial, 1987).

McClelland, David C. *The Achieving Society* (New York: Free Press, 1967).

O'Toole, James. *Leading Change: The Argument for Values-Based Leadership* (New York: Ballantine Books, 1996).

Social Change: Ideas, Examples, Challenges

Barber, Benjamin. *Strong Democracy: Participatory Politics for a New Age* (Berkeley: University of California Press, 1984).

Black, Maggie. *Children First: The Story of Unicef, Past and Present* (Oxford: Oxford University Press, published for Unicef, 1996).

Bonbright, David. *Leading Public Entrepreneurs* (Arlington, VA: Ashoka, 1997).

Bornstein, David. *The Price of a Dream: The Story of the Grameen Bank* (Chicago: University of Chicago Press, 1997).

Cameron, Maxwell A., Robert J. Lawson, and Brian W. Tomlin, eds. *To Walk Without Fear: The Global Movement to Ban Landmines* (Toronto: Oxford University Press, 1998).

Cusano, Chris, ed. *Leading Social Entrepreneurs, Ashoka Fellows Elected 1999 and 2000* (Arlington, VA: Ashoka, 2001).

Diamond, Jared. *Guns, Germs, and Steel: The Fates of Human Societies* (New York: W. W. Norton, 1997).

Drayton, William. "The Entrepreneur's Life Cycle" (Arlington, VA: Ashoka, 1996).

Drayton, William. "Secret Gardens," *The Atlantic Monthly* (June 2000).

Drayton, William. *Selecting Leading Public Entrepreneurs* (Arlington, VA: Ashoka, 1996).

Drayton, William with Environmental Safety's Facts Committee. *America's Toxic Protection Gap: The Collapse of Compliance with the Nation's Toxics Laws* (Washington, D.C.: Environmental Safety, 1984).

Dyson, Freeman. *Imagined Worlds* (Cambridge, Mass.: Harvard University Press, 1997).

Emerson, Jed. "The Blended Value Map: Tracking the Intersects and Opportunities of Economic, Social and Environmental Value Creation," October 2003, www.blendedvalue.org

Freedman, Marc. *Prime Time: How Baby Boomers Will Revolutionize Retirement and Transform America* (New York: Public Affairs, 1999).

Jacobs, Jane. *The Death and Life of Great American Cities* (New York: Vintage, 1992).

Jacobs, Jane. *Systems of Survival* (New York: Vintage, 1994).

Johnson, Steven. *Emergence* (New York: Simon & Schuster, 2001).

Kelly, Eamonn, Peter Leyden, and members of the Global Business Network. *What's Next?: Exploring the New Terrain for Business* (Cambridge, MA: Perseus Books 2002).

Kidder, Tracy. *The Soul of a New Machine* (New York: Avon, 1981).

Klein, Naomi. *No Logo* (New York: Picador, 2002).

Rhodes, Richard. *The Making of the Atomic Bomb* (New York: Touchstone, 1986).

Rudolph, Suzanne Hoeber, and Lloyd I. Rudolph. *Gandhi: The Traditional Roots of Charisma* (Chicago: University of Chicago Press, 1983).

Shapiro, Joseph P. *No Pity: People with Disabilities Forging a New Civil Rights Movement* (New York: Times Books, 1994).

Starr, Paul. *The Social Transformation of American Medicine* (New York: Basic Books, 1982).

Thomas, Lewis. *The Lives of a Cell* (New York: Bantam, 1974).

UNICEF. *The State of the World's Children 1982–83* (New York: Oxford University Press, 1982).

UNICEF. *The State of the World's Children 1986* (New York: Oxford University Press, published for Unicef, 1985).

Watzlawick, Paul, John H. Weakland, and Richard Fisch. *Change: Principles of Problem Formation and Problem Resolution* (New York: W. W. Norton, 1974).

Wilson, Edward O. *The Future of Life* (New York: Knopf, 2002).

Selected Readings

Wright, Robert. *Nonzero: The Logic of Human Destiny* (New York: Vintage, 2000).

Worldwatch Institute. *Vital Signs 2003* (New York: W. W. Norton, 2003).

Business, Economics, and Economic Globalization

Braudel, Fernand. *Civilization and Capitalism, 15th–18th Century, Vol. II, The Wheels of Commerce* (Berkeley: University of California Press, 1992).

De Soto, Hernando. *The Mystery of Capital: Why Capitalism Triumphs in the West and Fails Everywhere Else* (New York: Basic Books, 2003).

De Soto, Hernando. *The Other Path: The Invisible Revolution in the Third World* (New York: Perennial Library, 1990).

Finnegan, William. "The Economics of Empire," *Harper's Magazine* (May 2003): 41–54.

Hawken, Paul, Amory Lovins, and L. Hunter Lovins. *Natural Capitalism: Creating the Next Industrial Revolution* (Boston: Back Bay, 2000).

Heilbroner, Robert L. *The Worldly Philosophers: The Lives, Times & Ideas of the Great Economic Thinkers* (New York: Simon & Schuster, 1961).

Hertz, Noreena. *The Silent Takeover: Global Capitalism and the Death of Democracy* (New York: Free Press, 2001).

Landes, David S. *The Wealth and Poverty of Nations* (New York: W. W. Norton, 1999).

Stiglitz, Joseph E. *Globalization and Its Discontents* (New York: W. W. Norton, 2002).

Index

Index

Index

MacDonald, Shawn, 180
Machiavelli, Niccolò, 46
Madiath, Joe, 155
Magony, Kati, 112–14, 207
Mahler, Halfdan, 246–47, 248
Mali, 178
managed grazing in Brazil, 34–36, 37
Mann, Horace, 90
marketing, 95, 119–20
Marmor, Ted, 13
Mathews, Jessica T., 9
Mbeki, Thabo, 198
McClelland, David C., 52
McKinsey & Company, 14, 53, 141–44,
    144–45, 257
McNamara, Robert, 248
media: Abidi's disability rights work, 219; cit-
    izen sector and, 268; role in social goods
    delivery, 277; Rosa's rural electrification,
    26, 27; on threats to EPA, 57
Meljol (Coming Together) organization, 76
Mello, Fernando Collor de, 138
Mello, Ricardo de Souza, 24, 30
Mendes, Chico, 150
Menkiti, Bo, 175, 176
Mexico, 155, 178, 257
micro-credit. See also Grameen Bank: compe-
    tition in, 269; Cordeiro's Renascer work,
    145; effects of, 38; expansion, 236, 271,
    279; origins, 13–14, 120; replicability, 259,
    260; use of metrics, 273
middle class, 7
mistakes, 71, 79, 95, 120
Mogashoa, Kleinbooi, 198
Monnet, Jean, 94, 238
Moore, Thomas J., 94
mosaic meetings, 147, 258
motivation, 207–8, 233, 239–40, 251
Movimento Sem Terra (landless movement),
    33

Nacimento, Harley Henriques do, 204, 204
Nader, Ralph, 90
Narayan, Jaya Prakash, 51
National Association for College Admission
    Counseling (NACAC), 174–75
National Center for the Promotion of
    Employment for Disabled People
    (NCPEDP), 210, 221–32
National Initiative for Child Protection, 87
National Institutes of Health, 95
Nayak, Nalini, 278–79
Nemzeti és Etnikai Kisebbségi Jogvédő Iroda
    (Legal Defense Bureau for National and
    Ethnic Minorities), 149
Nepal, 147, 178
Neto, Valdemar de Oliveira, 139, 256
New York Times, 57
Nigeria, 178, 181, 182, 249
Nightingale, Florence, 12, 40–46, 93, 95
nongovernmental organizations (NGOs), 4
nonprofit sector, 4

"normalization" of people with disabilities,
    115
Northrop, Michael, 64, 178
nursing field, 40–46

Olah, Zsuzsa, 104
Oliveira, Frederico, 142, 144
Omidyar, Pierre, 263
Omidyar Foundation, 263
Onyszkiewicz, Wojciech, 200–201
Open Society Institute, 180
organic food market, 36, 37, 154, 205–6
organizational strategy: Abidi's disability
    rights work, 225–32; Ashoka, 15–17,
    146–58, 179–81, 262; Billimoria's Childline
    work, 70–72, 77–79, 80, 81, 83–88; Cor-
    deiro's Renascer work, 126, 132, 133–36,
    141–44; cross-disciplinary approaches, 82,
    236–37; de Souza's Parisar Asha work,
    18–19; flexibility, 235–36; Grant's Unicef
    work, 245–46, 248, 249, 251, 253–54;
    Khosa's Tateni work, 189–90, 192–93,
    195–96, 197; Nightingale's nursing work,
    42; patterns in, 148–50; qualities of
    successful social entrepreneurs, 233; Rosa's
    rural electrification, 36–37; Schramm's Col-
    lege Summit, 161–62, 166–69, 172–73;
    Szekeres's Alliance work, 103, 104
Összefogás Ipari Szövetkezet (Alliance
    Industrial Union), 103–16
O'Toole, James, 92
Ouédraogo, Halidou, 149
Ozal, Turgut, 249

Pakistan, 178
Paraguay, 180
Parel, Miriam, 64, 65
Parisar Asha educational program, 19
Partners in School Innovation, 278
partnerships: Abidi's disability rights work,
    225, 226; Accelerator for Social Entrepre-
    neurship, 257; Ashoka: Innovators for the
    Public, 263; Billimoria's Childline work,
    76, 83, 85; Grant's Unicef work, 248, 249;
    Khosa's Tateni work, 192, 194, 197;
    Schramm's College Summit, 175; Szekeres's
    Alliance work, 109
"Penny Post," 92–93
performance benchmarking, 5, 270–71,
    272–73, 274–75
Perkins, Lucy, 262
Persons With Disabilities (Equal
    Opportunities, Protection of Rights and
    Full Participation) Bill (1995), 220, 221,
    221–22
Peru, 180, 257
Peters, Thomas J., 62–63
Pew Charitable Trusts, 180, 304
Phillips, Julien, 14–15, 62, 179, 277–78
physical abuse, 102
Pierce, Ellison C., 96–97, 240
Pilisvörösvár Social Home, 100–102, 101,
    110, 112

Index